BRITONS AND SAXONS

The Chiltern Region 400-700

BRITONS
and
SAXONS

The Chiltern Region
400 ~ 700

K. Rutherford Davis

Phillimore

1982

Published by
PHILLIMORE & CO. LTD.

Head Office: Shopwyke Hall,
Chichester, Sussex, England

© K. Rutherford Davis, 1982

ISBN 0 85033 418 7

Printed and bound in Great Britain by
BILLING & SONS LIMITED
Guildford, London, Oxford, Worcester

CONTENTS

LIST OF PLATES

Following page 34

I   Brooches from grave 102, Dorchester III, Oxon.

II   Late Roman and early fifth-century military belt equipment
   a. Objects from the late Roman German officer's grave, Dorchester I, Oxon.
   b. The broken piece from Luton I, Beds.
   c. The Bishopstone plate, Bucks.

III   Hanging bowls and their escutcheons
   a. The large complete bowl from Sutton Hoo, Suffolk
   b. The escutcheons from Hitchin, Herts. (bowl destroyed)
   c. The escutcheon from Oving, Bucks.

IV   Saxon brooches
   a. 'Luton type' brooches from Luton I (left) and Kempston, Beds.
   b. 5-coil spiral brooch from grave 42, Dorchester III, Oxon.
   c. Scroll brooch from Luton I, Beds.
   d. A cruciform brooch from Kempston, Beds.
   e, f. Great square-headed brooches from Luton I (left) and Kempston, Beds.

V   Later Saxon brooches
   a, b, c. Large late cast saucer brooches from Ashendon (top left) and Stone (above), Bucks., and Dorchester, Oxon. (below)
   d. Late saucer brooches with the Maltese cross design from Kempston, Beds.
   e. Late composite brooch from Leighton Buzzard III, Beds.

VI   Late luxury gravegoods
   a. Gold pendant from High Wycombe, Bucks.
   b. Gold-mounted drinking horn and glass claw beakers from Taplow, Bucks.

VII   Saxon pottery
   a, b, c. Buckelurn vessels from Luton I (left), Sandy (above) and Kempston (centre left), Beds.
   d, e, f. Pots decorated in the pendent triangle panel style from Luton I (centre left), Moggerhanger (bottom left) and Kempston (below), Beds.

For permission to reproduce Plate illustrations I am much indebted to the Editor, *Archaeological Journal* (V e); Ashmolean Museum (I and IV b); British Museum (III a, IV d, V d, VI a, b): Buckinghamshire County Museum (II c, III c); Cambridge University Museum of Archaeology and Anthropology (V a); Institute of Historical Research, University of London, *V.C.H.* (V b, c); Mr. D. H. Kennett and Bedfordshire Archaeological Council (VII d, e, f); Luton Museum (II b, IV c); Oxfordshire Architectural and Historical Society (II a); Oxford University Press (VII a, b, c); Victoria and Albert Museum (III b).

LIST OF MAPS

FOREWORD

FOR FOUR HUNDRED years and more after A.D. 43 the chalk hills and gravelled valleys of the Chilterns supported a population of the Celtic British as romanised as any in the country. By the middle of the 7th century, however, the area seems thoroughly Saxon. What had happened to those who for centuries had looked to Verulamium as to their city? Had they vanished, victims of disease, invader, or simply economic collapse? Or had they long survived, albeit changed and changing, until at last they passed under Saxon control and became part of England?

This is the central problem Mr. Rutherford Davis sets out to explore and to which in this thoroughly researched and cogently argued book he gives his answer. Only Wessex and Sussex have so far been so fully treated, and in choosing an area which has been the more neglected because it did not emerge as a single well-defined Anglo-Saxon kingdom, he has done us a special service. The 5th and 6th centuries have been for too long the bad lands. There are no sure signposts, but there are some, and we are finding more and recognising others for what they are and where they point. No one will map this difficult area aright to begin with, but we have to make a start. We shall do our best to ensure that Ken Rutherford Davis has to bring out a second edition in a few years.

Meanwhile, here we have the written sources, the place-names, the archaeological evidence—all such as they are—laid out for us in full and related one to the other as far as possible. This is where the advances are being made today in the archaeology of the early middle ages, by inter-disciplinary studies combining different kinds of evidence, each with its own severe problems, but each adding to the whole picture and incomplete and incompletable without the others. This book gives the student and the general reader an idea of the kinds of evidence and how we have to try to use them. It also sets for those of us who give much time to such matters a whole series of problems and challenges. We can advance from here and Mr. Davis deserves our best thanks for making it so.

MARTIN BIDDLE

INTRODUCTION

THE WORLD OF Vortigern, Hengist, Arthur and the first English settlers has attracted men's imagination since at least the 12th century and led to many flights of fancy. So far away, it is not an easy world to understand and many of its opacities are never likely to be cleared. But it is the ancestral world from which we ultimately spring and so deserves our interest.

What broadly happened in history is obvious, for the main developments over a long period are usually plain even if the reasons and the details remain obscure for lack of evidence. We know that in 410 all southern Britain was still part of the Roman Empire, but that by the 7th century its greater part came to consist of a dozen small English kingdoms; in the space of a couple of centuries the whole character of the land and its people apparently changed, as a result of what has conveniently but perhaps rather misleadingly been called 'the Anglo-Saxon conquest'.

'How did it happen?' is always a more difficult question and often demands a complicated explanation. Almost every fact we would like to know about the Reformation and the origins of the English Civil War is available, but different interpretations of both are tenable that attach varied weight to the personalities, institutions and ideas of their time and often owe something to the onlooker's opinions. If some uncertainty is possible about the well-recorded movements of only three or four centuries ago, it is hardly surprising that much is misty about what happened largely unchronicled in most of England during the generations after it ceased to belong to the Roman Empire.

How did part of Roman Britain become England? Its cities and villas gradually fell into ruin, but what of its people and their rulers? What was the place of the earliest English before their mastery? Such questions are the heart of history and involve its inner workings, yet they cannot be satisfactorily answered from the written sources. Some recent excellent works exploring the ground deeply have dealt with these matters on a national scale. Nevertheless that scale is really too immense to be visualized, and regional variety means that a single uniform solution is not to be sought. To understand the processes at work a more restricted canvas is indispensable.

Unravelling the clues to history is rather like following a detective story, steadily nearing the solution to the known result. Clues abound, even in the Dark Ages, but they vary in kind and quality and many have perished. Sometimes even the absence of clues—the dog that did not bark in the night—is important, and that is especially true in this period.

This study of what I call 'the Chiltern region' is based on all the available evidence and tries to discover what happened there in the 300 years or so following the break in 410. Its arrangement needs a little explanation. The first two chapters bring out the problems and describe their national and local background. Then we must turn to the physical traces of the people of this period in the expectation that they will have something important to tell us. Chapter III relates what little evidence is yet available on the post-Roman native inhabitants of the region. (Post-Roman is a convenient neutral label for these people after 410, that concerns only time; the often used term 'sub-Roman' is best confined to their generally debased standard of physical life.)

Beyond that the considerable amount of varied evidence from Saxon archaeology and from place-names presents a problem, because these are disparate kinds of raw material and even brief technicalities of nearly 100 sites and long lists of place-names would be tedious and indigestible; so, while important clues appear in the text, all supporting details are relegated to appendixes where all the references can be found.

It is essentially an historical evolution we are seeking, and for that only archaeo-logical material from the Saxon side can provide the necessary chronological framework and sense of time. Unlike artifacts most place-names are intrinsically undatable, though comparisons with archaeology yield some hints on their sequence and age. Chapter IV therefore explains the nature and dating of pagan Saxon archaeology for those who wish to know what sort of material facts we rely on. Then, after glancing at heathen place-names, Chapters VI–VIII frame some historical conclusions from the evidence on the earlier part of the period.

The following chapters survey English settlement names, which generally belong to a rather later date, and look at the import of Celtic place-names. All the conclusions are woven into a summary (Chapter XI) which serves as a setting for the final chapter, on how the native British element was at length absorbed into English society. The great scholar of this period, Sir Frank Stenton, called 'the extent to which the British population survived the catastrophe of the Anglo-Saxon conquest' the central problem of the age; I hope the ideas proposed here mark an advance towards its solution.

Throughout I have called the early Germanic people here 'Saxon' instead of the customary 'Anglo-Saxon', not because it is shorter but because the Britons them-selves applied the word to all these invaders; Welsh *Saes* 'Englishman' and *saesneg* 'English' and Gaelic *sassenach* perpetuate their usage. 'English' becomes appropriate only after the widespread conquests of the late 6th century.

Any book such as this owes a great deal to one's predecessors, as the bibliography reveals, and to the help of others in the task of fact-finding. I am grateful to staff at the British Museum and the Ashmolean Museum and their colleagues at Aylesbury, Bedford, Cambridge, Hitchin, Luton, Reading and St. Albans for their aid in correspondence and facilities for examining finds; to Dr. J. N. L. Myres, Dr. I. M. Stead and Mr. D. H. Kennett for unpublished information; and to Mr. J. McN. Dodgson, Mrs. L. E. Webster and the late Dr. J. R. Morris for their advice and guidance. None of these is to blame for any errors I have committed.

Potters Bar,   K.R.D.
Hertfordshire

Notes on written sources

The main historical sources for the early Dark Ages in England are so few that they can be shortly listed. Three are in Latin. In order of date the first is by Gildas, a British monk who wrote *The loss of Britain* about 540 as a long and highly coloured condemnation of his countrymen's sins, visited by divine punishment in the form of the Saxon invasion; its historical content is small, often allusive rather than factual, and for the period before his own birth is untrustworthy on detail. Gildas had only an incidental interest in history but Bede, an English monk of Wearmouth and Jarrow who died in 735, composed a superb *Ecclesiastical history of the English people* which was derived from diligent enquiries and is an invaluable mine of information despite its limited purpose. The first part of the *Anglo-Saxon Chronicle* was written down in Old English in Wessex in Alfred's reign before 890, making use of now lost material and genealogies as well as Bede. The fourth is *The history of the Britons*, attributed in some versions to Nennius, an uncritical assemblage from varied historical sources and fables which was put together in its existing form in north Wales about 830 and contains much earlier material dating back to the 7th century, especially on the North. However uneven these accounts, they tell a coherent story which is enough to give a sound outline guide.

Chapter I

PROBLEMS AND PRELIMINARIES

THERE HAVE BEEN only two extended historical surveys[1] of English regions in the 5th and 6th centuries, the early kingdoms of Wessex and Sussex for which the *Anglo-Saxon Chronicle* preserves some literary evidence, whatever its value. No comparable study of Kent has appeared, and the dearth of similar material might suggest that no worthwhile attempt could be made to recover in any detail developments in other southern regions for which little or no written acount of this formative period survives. That, however, would be a counsel of despair, for while it is true that no annalistic framework or names of historical personages exist outside these three kingdoms they are not the only or perhaps the most reliable sources of information available; a recent interdisciplinary study of Sussex amply shows how much lies in other directions.

The first written accounts of the earliest English, in the form transmitted to us, are not contemporary with the events they relate; they are concerned with royal houses, battles and genealogies, real or concocted long afterwards,[2] and their paucity proves great selectivity, ignorance or even suppression and bias. Whether derived from remnants of tradition and saga or from entries retrospectively inserted in Easter tables in the 7th century as the result of calculations made from remembered regnal succession, these slender materials cannot often be made to bear interpretations far beyond the bare facts they overtly declare; they leave much unsaid and raise problems for which solutions must be sought elsewhere.

Where literary evidence fails or is even altogether lacking we are not entirely bereft of useful material. There exist other valuable sources that can legitimately be expected to assist, in the form of archaeology and the place-names that layer by layer have accumulated upon the map of England. Studies of physical remains and the linguistic detritus embedded in place names are equally valid approaches to the writing of total history, for they complement the written record and make good some of the immense gaps it leaves unfilled. Both artifacts and place-names speak with the authentic voice of their remote time, however enigmatically; although limited in scope, their unconscious character guarantees an objectivity that literary records cannot always claim. Each discipline contributes information that is obtainable in no other way.

The integration of archaeology with recorded history is beset with difficulty, for as Biddle[3] remarked 'Anglo-Saxon history and Anglo-Saxon archaeology, interpenetrating views of a single society, can often stand in little discernible relation one to another', and 'for both historians and archaeologists the real crux lies not so much in their lack of knowledge of another field, as in their mutual difficulty in

1

reaching a critical evaluation of each other's results'. That is not to say these problems are insuperable or that no realistic synthesis is possible; as Biddle said, 'archaeology has a positive contribution to make to Anglo-Saxon history, not simply by providing a physical and cultural setting for recorded events, but by adding substantially to our knowledge of those events and by informing us of other events and processes of which little or no written record survives'. These encouraging words apply in equal measure to place-names.

During recent decades advances in the study of Dark Age archaeology and place-names have provided means whereby we can now reasonably hope to reconstruct in outline the progress of the English immigrants and their relations with the Britons whom they found in possession, and with this fresh understanding of the setting explore one important region during the period: the Chilterns and the surrounding country that was closely associated.

Glancing references to the Chilterns as a district of late English settlement with an uncommon degree of British survival are frequently found in broad surveys of early history, without precision; the area has not been studied in depth because it has been regarded as an unimportant backwater. Seldom mentioned, apart from references to Kempston, Luton and the Icknield Way, are the adjacent areas to the north, and Hertfordshire and the Thame valley are usually ignored. Yet the Chiltern country in this early period cannot be considered in isolation because its problems involve a wider terrain; it demonstrably formed in this phase part of a single province embracing all these districts, a region which presents important questions that can be solved not by confining scrutiny to any fraction, but only by intelligibly relating its entire evidence.

This region consists of two distinct and very different areas. One, conveniently termed 'the Chiltern zone', comprises the long range of chalk hills from the Goring gap on the middle Thames to Royston, and a wide eastern belt sharing something of the same character, stretching across Hertfordshire as far as the lower Lea and its headstreams along the Essex border. The other, here called the Ouse–Thame basin, is the broad broken plain fringing the Chiltern scarp, extending from Dorchester-on-Thames to Bedford and the headwaters of the river Cam. These contiguous areas might fare quite differently but they cannot really be considered apart. Evidence has therefore been gathered from the whole of Buckinghamshire and Hertfordshire, the seven southern Hundreds of Oxfordshire and Bedfordshire south of the Ouse together with Bedford itself. Although Copley's account of early Wessex included this territory his premises are now somewhat outdated and a thorough reassessment is due.

A region so situated could hardly avoid playing an important part in the Migration and succeeding ages. It lay athwart Icknield Way, an ancient cross-country route reputed to be an early Saxon highway, and it impinged on the Ouse which was potentially another. Through it ran two great Roman roads, Watling Street and Ermine Street, that remain in use to this day, and Akeman Street which connected Verulamium with Cirencester. On the west the region touched the early Saxon settlements around Abingdon and included Dorchester, perhaps the oldest of them all and the site of the first see in Wessex, while to the north-east it marched with the early and important Germanic concentration round Cambridge. The tract was caught up in the first West Saxon attempts to expand beyond the Thames and before long was encroached on by two more early kingdoms, those of the East Saxons and Mercia. Geography dictated for it an eventful if passive roll, subject to the ambitions of powerful English neighbours.

In the first decade of the 5th century, when Britain was still Roman, this territory formed the greater part of the old Catuvellaunian canton or *civitas* dependent upon and ruled from Verulamium, the third largest and one of the most important cities of the realm and the scene of the last event in post-Roman Britain for which we have a sure date, St. Germanus' first visit to the island in 429. For almost two and a half centuries the story of the evolution of this highly romanized countryside into an integral part of the world of the English Heptarchy is virtually blank. The absence of recorded background only partly explains why discussion on the Chiltern region in the Dark Ages has been muted; it is curious that a symposium on Christianity in Britain 300–700 devoted only two passing references to Verulamium and was silent on the cult of St. Alban, well attested by Bede. Most historians glimpsing prickly problems evidently preferred not to become entangled, and in face of entrenched dogmas hesitated to express new opinions on the Chiltern area, confining themselves to allusions to the Icknield Way and remarks that thick forests discouraged early settlement to the south—a suggestion that is quite misleading and largely false.

This neglect illustrates a weakness sometimes displayed in Dark Age studies: a tendency to ignore the Romano–British foundation from which the English settlements everywhere sprang, as though Britain were a *tabula rasa* where the recent past had left not a wrack behind. Scholars have often been concerned solely with the Saxon world or concentrated primarily on the Celtic fringe, with the unfortunate result that 'the period has been reduced to the status of a kind of no-man's-land between the secure entrenchments of known Roman and unambiguous Saxon'.[4] Yet the post-Roman setting should not be lightly dismissed, and over the last generation the climate of opinion has significantly changed. As Applebaum[5] says 'in the last thirty years the views of many scholars have been moving steadily away from the assessment which had till then held the field, that Roman civilization collapsed precipitately and utterly with the removal of the imperial administration in 410, and that the following century beheld the nearly complete annihilation of of the Romano–British population in so far as it had not withdrawn to the highland zone or to Brittany'. Devotion to the English element obscured the importance of the post-Roman background. The scant attention paid to those conditions by historians and archaeologists may be partly responsible for the situation that Biddle implicitly criticizes. The Council for British Archaeology[6] recommended 30 years ago that 'every opportunity should be taken to clarify the relationship between the Anglo-Saxon settlers and the last phases of Romano–British civilization'. As Finberg[7] sagely remarked 'in the end history must be written forwards, not backwards'.

In some places this background may be unusually significant, and the Chiltern region is one where these strands are inextricably connected. It may well prove of great importance to post-Roman and early Saxon archaeology, because here some of the earliest English societies must have come into close contact with vestigial post-Roman authority and its people. This remark can be underlined by recalling that the region contains two Romano-British towns of prime importance for the beginning of this period—Verulamium and Dorchester—and a number of 5th-century Saxon settlements.

Some of the most crucial questions of this period are implicit in the precise meaning of the only event that history relates on the region between St. Germanus' visit in 429[8] and the Council held at Hertford in 672. The *Anglo-Saxon Chronicle*'s tantalizingly brief entry under 571 that Cuthwulf 'fought against the Britons at *Biedcanford* and captured four *tuns*, Limbury (near Luton), Aylesbury, Bensington and Eynsham; and in the same year he died' has given rise to much discussion,[9] principally on the identity of Cuthwulf's foes and whether the battle site should be identified with Bedford, which philologists reject. There are minor puzzles. The unexpected order in which the place-names appear, if Cuthwulf was a West Saxon leader, is curiously paralleled by the Chronicle's list of Ceawlin's conquests after Dyrham in 577: Gloucester, Cirencester, Bath—inwards towards Wessex. We notice that the four place-names are obviously of English coinage and unlike the Cotswold cities these were not Roman sites. Then it is remarkable that Bensington is mentioned but not Dorchester, only two miles away, which there is reason to believe was always a more important place.

We may suppose that the annal's language derives from a memorable fragment of some lost epic celebrating the triumphs of the West Saxon royal house, not from any straightforward or contemporary historical record; this likelihood is perhaps good assurance that Cuthwulf's enemies were indeed Britons and not fellow Saxons, as some have rather perversely proposed. Oral tradition among Saxon *scops*, as in a bardic or skaldic society, seems less liable to corruption than a written text that invites improvement or correction. The only clear inference from the annal is that the four places were not previously in Cuthwulf's hands. Neither place-names nor archaeology can tell us whether they were then independent or under British or English lordship; archaeology seldom directly reflects political conditions, but recognizes only cultural situations. If the annal gives no unequivocal indication whether land was snatched from a defeated British ruler or from Saxons outside British sway, the question must be judged in a broader context. Probably the annal's full sense was no longer clear to those who wrote it down, perhaps for the first time, in Alfred's reign.

The vital part of the annal consists of two distinct statements which if intended to be taken together as a coherent story imply that a conflict with Britons who still dominated the Bedfordshire–Buckinghamshire district resulted in the seizure of territory that had certainly contained some elements of early Saxon population, as its archaeology and place-names show. Conceivably the difficulty which lies in that apparent contradiction may simply be due to a highly condensed form, but on balance the most satisfactory explanation would obviously be one that involved the least distortion of the literal meaning of the wording, rather than one that entirely overthrew it.

Whether the two connected statements can really be reconciled therefore raises several questions: whether British forces were likely to be encountered in the district then; if so, who they were; whether the date given for the battle is even approximately right or as some have thought should be brought well forward;[10] whether Bedford is an acceptable location for *Biedcanford*; under whose lordship were the places Cuthwulf took; by what people they were then occupied; why Dorchester is omitted; and what became of any local Britons.

A later problem is the identity of the *Cilternsaetan*, a large folk of 4,000 hides whom the late 7th-century compilation known as the Tribal Hidage included in a list of peoples under Mercian lordship. The now common assumption that the term described the inhabitants of the vale below the Chiltern scarp, not the Chilterns proper, presents difficulties; it would be strange if the plain-dwellers bore no generic appellation of their own but resorted to borrowing from a feature outside their own land. There is good reason for reverting to Baldwin Brown's natural equation of the *Cilternsaetan* with the hill people.

All evidence bearing on these problems needs examining, and the insight gained in recent years can be judiciously applied to interpret and illuminate the situation. Unaided, historical sources can throw no real light on the region between 429 and 672; yet during this decisive era Roman Britain changed into England by the most profound revolution in national history, and it would be surprising if its developments left no contemporary mark in the region to witness them. To learn something of the course of the English settlement and the social relationship between the new-comers and the native inhabitants whom they either displaced or somehow absorbed we are compelled to turn to archaeology and place-names, seeking interpretations consistent with our knowledge of events on the national scale and perhaps enlarging it.

Most people would agree that, sensibly used, these sources may legitimately be employed to reach historical conclusions. Probably the biggest problem area in these fields is that of Celtic place-names, which Wainwright dismissed as of little or no value, but his rather dogmatic general objection against translating archaeological and linguistic conceptions into historical conceptions must be overcome if we believe that such phenomena do in some ascertainable way reflect the society among whom they were created. Few would deny that Renaissance painting and sculpture, for example, convey important lessons. In fact Myres' correlation of Saxon pottery with the chronological framework, Jackson's *Language and history in early Britain* on linguistic material, and Wooldridge's essay *The Anglo-Saxon settlement* relating archaeology to natural conditions show how much can be achieved in the way of a satisfactory synthesis. The contributions of the archaeologist and the linguist and the geographer's vision are not to be ignored.

The historical background

It is essential to recall the historical setting wherein English settlement was founded and developed, in which lived the society whose contemporary archaeological traces and place-names are bequeathed to us, for it forms a reliable known framework within which local features can be interpreted in the light of events on a grander scale, and a broad if mottled canvas into whose overall design they must fit consistently. The historical record is the starting point for our understanding.

In a period with few settled dates the year 410 naturally seems to mark the beginning of a new era, although its contemporary significance is easily exaggerated. While in a political sense Britain then ceased to be part of the Empire it was slow to lose its acquired cultural heritage; as hundreds of words of Latin derivation in the Welsh language now show, this legacy was tenacious even in less romanized regions. Deprived a few years earlier of many of their garrisons, the Britons found that little but the imperial link had immediately changed, and their manner of life continued for some decades until the troubles of the mid-5th century began to overwhelm them and destroy their economic basis. In 429, to judge from the description of St. Germanus' visit to Verulamium, city life was still functioning quite normally.

There was no novelty about threats to the Britons' security in 410. The pressure of tribes beyond the northern frontier was always dangerous, and by the 4th century Irish invaders were securing footholds on the coasts of Wales. About 280 the risk of Saxon raids was grave enough to call for the erection of a series of great new fortresses of novel design, the chain of Saxon shore forts from Brancaster to the Solent. These peripheral threats affected different parts of Britain and required quite distinct measures; but besides the fixed defences in the military zones a large resident mobile army could be concentrated at will to annihilate any enemy forces that penetrated these outer screens.

That comforting assessment proved unsound in 367 when not only the North but parts of lowland Britain suffered the traumatic experience of a concerted assault—the *barbarica conspiratio*—by Picts, Scots and Saxons, and the legionary forces took a crippling blow. Britain was salvaged by Theodosius, not before much destruction had been done. Among various measures taken to put the permanent defences on a sounder footing it seems that powerful client kingdoms were created in the region between the Walls, no doubt relieving the strain in that direction.

Other precautions aimed to protect the heart of the province. Some of the cities' walled defences were recast in the 4th century and equipped with solid bastions for mounting anti-siege engines; these imply trained personnel, readily available. From the latter half of the 4th century there are widespread archaeological indications,[11] in the form of distinctive belt equipment such as buckles, of some military presence, probably of both regular and auxiliary troops, among them no doubt some Germans. These units may have been replenished after 400 by local recruitment or the engagement of barbarian mercenaries. Some of these finds come from forts, others from large walled towns; perhaps smaller places and villas[12] where they occur were also occasionally provided with military detachments or a part-time militia, but some belts traced at these sites could have been worn by civilian officials or magistrates as badges of rank. At Dorchester-on-Thames a German officer of the late 4th century, and accompanying womenfolk, have come to light, and similar traces recently came from the Lankhills cemetery at Winchester; both represent soldiers, not settlers.

Neglectful of continuing dangers to Britain, in 407 Constantine III—the third island claimant to the purple that year—took away to fight his battles in Gaul the legionary field army and perhaps other regular formations. They never returned. Honorius' celebrated letter addressed in 410 to the British *civitates*—the provincial authorities—bade them assume the reins of power and legalized their defensive measures. The Roman era was over: for good or ill Britain was alone, a patchwork of semi-autonomous states ruled by senatorial councils at each of a dozen cantonal capitals, including Verulamium, and a supreme Council of advisers that now lacked a governor.

Despite signs of immediate turbulence—Gildas' mention of kings being slain soon after being anointed probably belongs here—the vacant headship was evidently soon filled; under this direction, and with adequate forces still available, the Britons repulsed their foes and entered on a spell of peace and prosperity. Hazy though our knowledge is of the political tangle, it seems that in or about 425 a ruler known to history as Vortigern[13]—a Celtic epithet meaning 'overlord'[14]—obtained a paramount position over the regional governments, with a council of notables drawn from the whole province. Their fatal decision to engage Hengist is notorious, even if its date is in dispute; as that remembered in Celtic tradition, 428, has better authority than 442 or 449 the chronology proposed by Morris[15] is followed here.

The welcome to Hengist's initially small band, contained in three ships but soon augmented, was well precedented. Shortage of manpower drove the late Empire to enlist many barbarians for its defence, individually and in companies, but there is no evidence that independent Britain continued the custom between 410 and 428: this seems unlikely as the island was sundered from the source of recruits. The British had doubtless heard of the first western settlement of *Foederati* in 418 in Aquitaine,[16] and this was presumably the formal status of Hengist's men, who were supplied with provisions.

The occasion of their hire, says Gildas, was forewarning of assault by the ancient enemies in Pictland, but Nennius' statement[17] that Vortigern's motives included fear of Roman aggression hints that Hengist's placing near the main entry port of Richborough betrays anxiety to forestall any attempt launched from Gaul to recover Britain. Vortigern's move appears to have been part of a complete strategy for defending the whole province and not merely its rich southern half against troublesome Picts and Scots. Parts of Wales occupied by the Irish were probably regained and held at this time by transplanting a tribe from the Lothians under Cunedda. The familiar inroads across Hadrian's Wall, lightly manned if at all but in effect replaced by friendly buffer states, could be repelled by adequate local forces probably still based on York, the old military capital. Since Gildas calls both Scots and Picts *transmarini* the latter evidently now approached by sea to outflank the landward defences.

Hengist's forces were evidently disposed primarily to combat Pictish attacks even if Vortigern was mindful of a possible invasion of the south coast, for Gildas assures us that thanks to Hengist's men the Britons staved off Pictish aggression. Kent however was a most unsuitable base for operations against seagoing Picts, who would be sensible to make their landfall south of the Humber with little warning. Gildas says the newcomers were stationed in the eastern part of the island, which fits their only recorded location in Thanet but does not exclude more likely districts such as East Anglia and Lincolnshire, and Nennius relates that some were sent to reinforce the north.

Like his Roman predecessors Vortigern must have appreciated the need for counter-measures well inland, since danger came from Irish raiders in the Bristol Channel as well as from the eastern shores. His main object of protection must have been the wide lowland zone where lay almost all the cities, towns and villas that enshrined the riches of romanization. The necessity for ready defences here was demonstrated in 367, a time old men would fearfully recall, when the marauders' depredations overran even Kent. The concentration of Cotswold villas with luxurious late mosaics indicates one wealthy region that an aristocratic government would be anxious to protect,[18] but the same consideration applied to the whole of what Wheeler[19] called 'the sub-Roman triangle' that included London, Verulamium, Colchester, Silchester, Winchester and a multitude of estates. Hence the late 4th-century evidence throughout the Midlands of military personnel at villas as well as towns; country magistrates would inevitably procure such bodyguards in troubled times.

Vortigern's precautions were apparently very similar, which explains why his overall strategy met with the cooperation of the *civitates* who would have to implement it. The oldest pagan cemeteries surely indicate broadly where his Saxon *foederati* were stationed: on the east in Kent, Norfolk, Lincolnshire and beyond the Humber, in the south in Surrey and the Abingdon district. London, the east coast and its navigable rivers were guarded against ship-borne pirates, and a reserve force could readily be deployed northwards by the Fosse Way, eastwards along Icknield Way or westwards to the Cotswolds. Between Cambridgeshire and the Abingdon area the Ouse-Thame basin might serve as a zone of communication; whether the Icknield Way along the Chiltern edge played a more active role or soon became a major migration route must be considered on the basis of archæological evidence.

The hypothesis that the widespread Saxon cemeteries of the earliest generation show where Hengist's men were settled prompts the question; could these bands have been built up so rapidly that they were soon able to menace and maim British society? There is no proof of earlier established mercenaries who might have turned disloyal. Vortigern's policy required an urgent build-up, and a boatload of 50 warriors every month for 15 years would produce nearly 10,000 men, twice the strength of a legion, concentrated particularly in Kent and East Anglia. It was their power for destruction in a practically unprotected countryside, rather than might of numbers, that did the damage.

Vortigern's policy was successful, but when the external danger had passed the cost of maintaining Hengist's swollen forces was resented and the Council wished to disband them. Vortigern seems to have been already challenged by political opponents, including Ambrosius, perhaps the leader of a pro-Roman party, who fought a battle at Wallop in Hampshire about 437 and may before or temporarily during Vortigern's reign have become 'emperor' of the province, for Gildas' language suggests that Ambrosius Aurelianus' father had worn the purple.

Meanwhile Vortigern's unruly allies had become ambitious and strong enough to feel the taste of power. Hengist answered a threat to end their supplies by summoning heavy reinforcements, and Vortigern seems to have been thrust into dependence on him and the cession of Kent in a fruitless attempt at appeasement.

Open warfare probably began in 442, the date when a Gallic chronicler reported with considerable exaggeration that Britain had 'come under Saxon dominion'.[20]

The revolt of the *foederati* under Hengist's leadership disrupted Vortigern's government. The *civitates* soon rejected his authority and henceforth acted on their own. An appeal for aid to Aetius in Gaul about 446 was in vain. Nevertheless British resistance, in Kent at least, was not ineffective; in the next few years three battles are reported and Hengist not only failed to take London but, if Nennius is believed, was penned up in Thanet and temporarily expelled until massive reinforcements turned the tide. If the treacherous slaughter of many British notables at a peace parley is more than legend it would account for a grave impairment of native leadership and the panic fatalism that made thousands of able-bodied Britons emigrate to Gaul from the south of England in general.[21] No account of the struggle elsewhere survives, but the density of early Saxon cemeteries in Norfolk and Cambridgeshire and evidence of a massacre at Caistor suggest that most of this region fell quite easily into Saxon hands.

Plainly chaos ensued on such a scale that the Britons could no longer restrain the mercenaries or prevent their unlimited reinforcement. For Britain had begun a new epoch comparable with that signalized in Gaul by fresh Germanic hoardes surging across the frozen Rhine on the last day of 406. The Migration movement could not be reversed, and in exposed districts such as East Anglia and Kent there is no sign that British rule was ever reasserted.

The rebels seized considerable areas beyond their initial peaceful settlements. The territory they grasped is defined by the archaeological distinction of their packed early cemeteries, that reveal intensive Saxon exploitation of almost the whole eastern littoral, the Cambridge area and land accessible from these districts. Myres[22] demonstrated that the distribution of Saxon pottery of 'the phase of uncontrolled settlement' supports Gildas' purple passages about the widespread havoc wrought at this time, when 'the fire ... destroying the neighbouring towns and lands ... reached the other side of the island and dipped its red and savage tongue in the western ocean' and buildings and men alike were felled to the ground. Whatever his exaggeration it was a calamity beyond measure and beyond redress. British control broke down widely, and the sole obstacle to Saxon destruction was whatever fragmented power could succeed in exerting itself on a local scale. These conditions inherently called for local initiative and self-reliance on both sides. The organized English kingdoms of the Heptarchy had not yet come into existence, and normal conceptions of field warfare are inappropriate. For the most part we should visualise not planned campaigns but raiding and skirmishing across an open countryside, when urban communities with the advantage of lofty town walls would be less vulnerable than isolated villas and villages.[23] Yet a corn-drying kiln inside the walls of Verulamium, in by no means its last spasm, discloses a passing phase of acute anxiety.

Although at first enfeebled and almost overcome by the shock of the Saxon revolt the Britons eventually achieved a remarkable national recovery that began in the 460s, launched from regions of south Britain that had not been trampled down. In the course of three or four decades of fluctuating fortune spirited resistance under Ambrosius Aurelianus and then Arthur culminated in a decisive British victory at Mount Badon, which must be dated close to 500 and probably occurred somewhere in the south-west. This event and the resurgence that made it possible changed the balance of power so radically that some of the disheartened invaders even left the island, as Procopius relates. The Britons evidently regained a certain amount of lost and disputed land, ejecting Saxons from tracts they had briefly occupied and perhaps suffering others to remain as tribute-payers within their new boundaries. The Saxons' disastrous set-back is clearly displayed in the distribution of their pottery.[24]

Thus the Saxon menace was stayed for two generations or more. Until the days of Ceawlin and Ethelfrith they dared no further major assault and were probably incapable of it. They needed a spell of peaceful growth and consolidation while they coalesced into embryonic kingdoms, a stage not attained until the 6th century was far advanced. The Britons, war-weary and content to rest on their laurels, made no effort to remove the free Saxons from their refuges. There is every indication that during the first half of the 6th century the stalemate was widely preserved.

Paradoxically the absence of real warfare in this period decided the final outcome. The long breathing-space allowed the Saxons to strike deep roots unhindered, rebuilding their strength and resources while the native people were divided into small kingdoms which perhaps, as in the North, quarrelled with one another. 'Tyrant' rulers had long displaced the authority of aristocratic cantonal councils. The British also seem to have been gravely afflicted by the Yellow Plague c. 550 that spread from the Mediterranean but perhaps touched their foes less severely.

From about 550 in Wessex and then Northumbria the English advance was forcibly renewed under energetic leaders, overrunning areas which were still entirely British, until by about 620 all England, save Cumbria and the south-west, was firmly in English hands. The Chronicle outlines the astonishing break-out of the West Saxons, a composite people whose largest element was drawn from Berkshire though their rulers claimed or forged a descent from an early Hampshire invader. Under Ceawlin who fought against Kent in 568, doubtless instigated the campaign of 571 north of the Chilterns, and personally conducted the conquest of the Cotswolds in 577, the West Saxons pushed beyond the Thames and acquired fresh territory. It is noteworthy that they were borderers, like the Northumbrians and the Mercians whose fortunes were later in the ascendant at the expense of both; initiative now lay with the expansionary frontier states, not the circumscribed men of Kent and East Anglia in their rear. The brief personal overlordship of Raedwald of East Anglia was exceptional.

In the scramble part of Hertfordshire fell to the portion of the East Saxons, one of whose kings in 704 disposed—with Mercian consent—of land in the district called *Haemele*, which is represented by the initial element of Hemel Hempstead. A memorial that East Saxons once secured the eastern part of the county is its inclusion in the diocese of their capital, London. Their lordship can only have been transient and they were not the principal beneficiaries of the partition of the Chiltern region, for Mercia obtained the lion's share and soon dominated Essex herself; the first notable Mercian king, Penda (r. ?632–654), controlled most of the south Midlands. By 665 the East Saxon kings owed allegiance to Wulfhere of Mercia, whose writ ran in London; his distant successor Offa in 793 granted much of south Hertfordshire to the abbey which he founded or re-founded at St. Albans, and in 796, according to Matthew Paris, died at one of his residences, Offley near Hitchin.

Only in the north and south have we historical evidence for the course of the conquest, which equally affected Mercia, and nowhere are the social conditions of the age beyond doubt; the first legal codes come from the Christian period. It is certain only that the English achieved complete dominance and were henceforth able to expand at will. There is evidence that a British population remained in more than negligible numbers, but their separate character must have begun to wither when they became trapped and assimilated in an English matrix. The clues on their status and relations need unravelling as much as those on the progress of the English settlers.

No arbitrary date can be fixed for the end of this foundation period which, interrupted by the Danish invasions, shaded imperceptibly into medieval England. If there is one other date of primary importance it is 597, when the Roman mission under St. Augustine arrived in Kent. Like the year 410, 597 had great significance for the future but its ultimate effects were somewhat delayed. By reviving learning and the art of writing it induced the birth of English historical records—chronicles and eventually charters and wills—that little more than a century later reached a magnificent peak in Bede's *Historia ecclesiastica*. From his time it is no longer really justifiable to speak of the Dark Ages, even though many aspects of life and culture are fitfully lit.

For all Bede's thoroughness he evidently discovered little about the conversion of Wessex or the south Midlands, and we know nothing of the Chiltern region except that Birinus became Wessex's first bishop in 634 with his see at Dorchester-on-Thames, which suggests the importance of the place. Cynegils and his son Cwichelm were baptized there, and it seems likely that the king resided nearby. There may have been an hiatus before Birinus was succeeded in 650 by Agilbert, who ten years later withdrew and was not replaced at Dorchester. According to Bede his departure was the result of a dispute over Wine's appointment to a new bishopric at Winchester, but Finberg[25] suggested that political changes made the Dorchester see untenable; West Saxon territory north of the Thames was seized by Penda, a stubbornly heathen king, and although Wessex briefly recovered possession some time between 654 and 661 it stayed in Mercian hands. Amidst such reversals the conversion of the Chiltern region probably made slow headway.

Yet one major 7th-century church in Buckinghamshire bears witness to the vitality of the mission: Wing, the basilican plan of which resembles that of the great church at Brixworth, though its original crypt is a great rarity. Three possible builders have been considered.[26] Birinus is the least likely for although Bede relates that he built churches Lord Fletcher pointed out 'the conditions for the establishment, or maintenance, of a large missionary community at Wing could not have been encouraging' in his time. The other candidates are Agilbert (between 650 and 660) and St. Wilfrid (between 666 and 669). The former, a Frank who later became bishop of Paris, is known to have built a crypt at Jouarre, which must favour his

claim. Fletcher prefers St. Wilfrid, and such an impressive edifice could well have
been projected by that proud and assertive cleric, but because his brief activity in
the Midlands would not allow him to carry so large a work to completion we would
have to assume that unknown contemporaries finished his task. Agilbert therefore
has the best claim but an unknown builder cannot be ruled out. Another Christian
institution of Bede's own time was the active cult of St. Alban at Verulamium, of
which he offers no explanation—perhaps significantly; the possibility of survival
from Romano-British times must be considered.

These obscurities have a bearing on archaeology. As mysterious as the Conversion
itself is its uncertain effect on burial customs and the timing of changes that were
not solely due to the coming of Christianity. Heathenism was already on the wane.
The common people of Mercia, though not their nobles, appear to have abandoned
its funerary habits before any missionaries arrived.[27] Although Christians were
forbidden the superstitious practice of burying objects with the dead the effectiveness of prohibition must have depended on the arrival of missionaries, the devoutness
of the people and the vigilance of priests who were at first so scarce that teams
working from minster centres had immense areas to cover. The terminal date of
pagan burial custom is often disconcertingly unsure, and in exceptional cases grave
offerings continued into the late 7th and rarely even into the early 8th century.

Usually the Church banned the use of old pagan cemeteries and established new
Christian graveyards—originally with only a preaching cross to sanctify them—since
this way the abolition of old habits was more easily enforced, but the combination
of a new site with residual heathen practices sometimes produced a recognizable
type of late semi-pagan cemetery which is found in the Chiltern region, as elsewhere.
By that time the foundations of England had been securely laid and its destiny
settled as a society with almost unadulterated English cultural traditions.

Chapter II

THE LOCAL BACKGROUND
BEFORE AND AFTER THE DARK AGES

IN ANY STUDY of human behaviour the physical setting needs to be investigated; the influences of nature cannot be disregarded, nor the inheritance of man's previous handiwork, for both have been potent factors.

The physical background

The Chiltern range runs right across the region from south-west to north-east, and attains a maximum elevation of 857 feet, about 600 feet above its base platform, but descends somewhat towards Royston. The northern scarp is steep in many places, the dip-slope highly serrated by valleys with small streams. North of the Chilterns lies a broken plain with detached hills rising to about 500 feet. Encircling both are two major rivers, to the south the Thames, to the north the Ouse, and their tributaries. On the east the Lea is joined at Hertford and Ware by small feeders, the Mimram, Beane, Ash, Rib and Stort, while the broad Ouse valley receives the Ivel and the Lovat or Ouzel. The Thame and the Ray drain the western part of the northern basin.

The vast erosion that sculptured this relief created the pattern of solid geology. The Chiltern range is composed of massive Chalk capped by stretches of clay-with-flints and drifts; at a lower level the chalk extends eastwards across most of Hertfordshire where it is usually covered with boulder clay, often rather chalky, but in the extreme south-east London Clay forms a plateau at about 400 feet. The complicated structure of the northern basin consists of several different rocks in belts of irregular width, most of them forming heavy soils, that run parallel to the escarpment. The southernmost, usually narrow, is the Upper Greensand; next is the Gault clay, often two to three miles wide; then in Bedfordshire comes the Lower Greensand, varying in width from a mere trace to two miles, which in the Thame valley is replaced by patches of Portland beds. Further north occur a narrow band of Cornbrash and Kimmeridge and Oxford clays. At the Bedfordshire end of the vale the solid rocks are overlain by boulder clay drifts.

In broad detail the significance of unusually hospitable areas is apt to be lost. Many valleys such as the Lea streams and the Vale of St. Albans offered level floors of rich alluvial soil. Wooldridge[1] emphasized the prime importance to early cultivators of loamy or intermediate soils, neither too light nor too stiff, and pointed out that the junction of the Chalk massif with other rocks to north and south is often a valuable spring-line. Water is seldom far below the surface of the chalk, unless the water-table is reduced by pumping. Conditions in the scarp-foot are especially favourable and where a bench of Upper Greensand occurs here it offers easily worked soils. The Icknield Way traverses this narrow well-watered chalk-marl

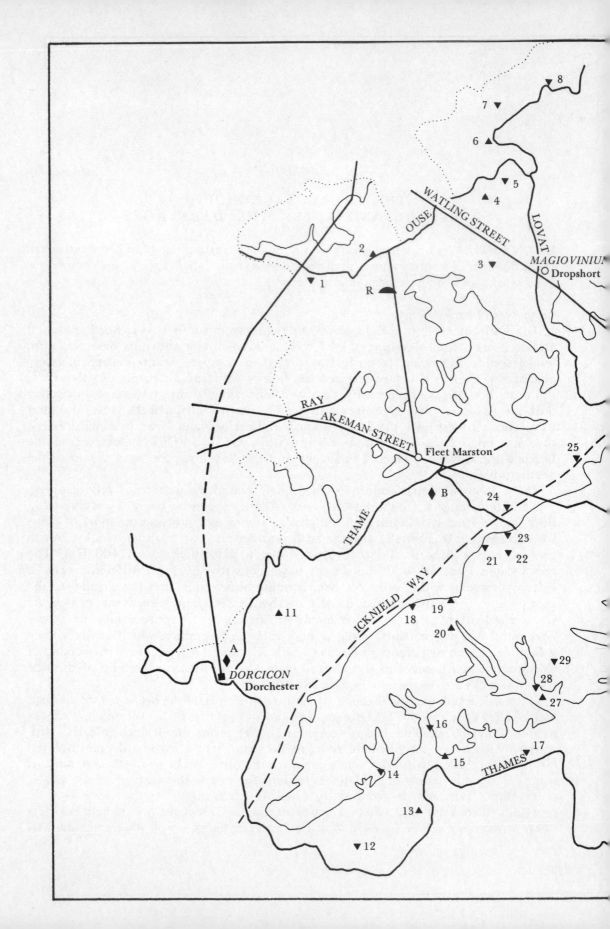

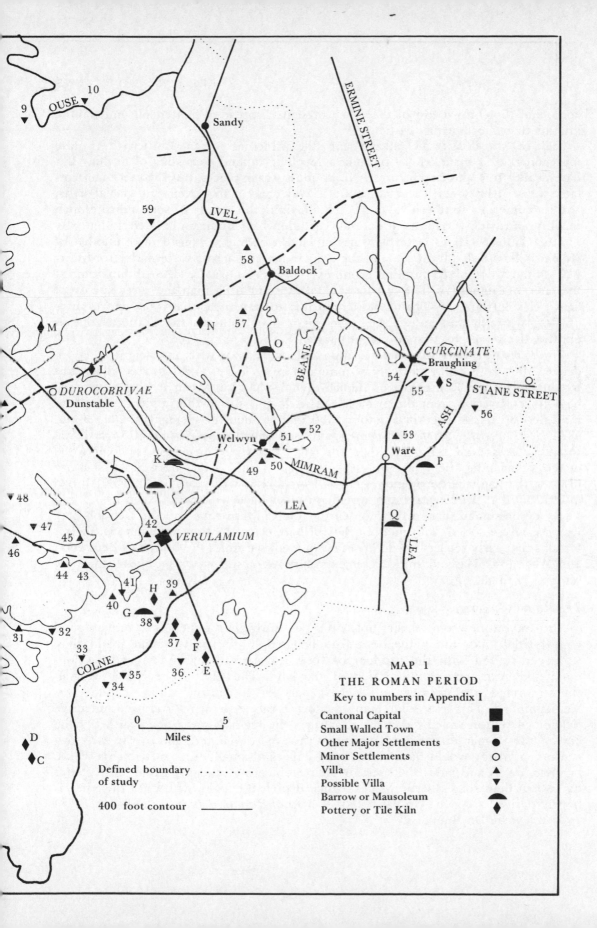

9

OUSE 10

IVEL

59

58

Sandy

ERMINE STREET

Baldock

M

N 57

O

BEANE

CURCINATE
Braughting

54

55

S

STANE STREET

56

53

ASH

L

○ *DUROCOBRIVAE*
Dunstable

Welwyn

51 52

49 50

MIMRAM

Ware

P

K

J

LEA

Q

LEA

48

47

45

46

42

VERULAMIUM

44 43

41

H 39

40

G

38

31 32

33

COLNE

37

F

E

35

36

34

0   5
Miles

D

C

Defined boundary . . . .
of study

400 foot contour —————

MAP 1
THE ROMAN PERIOD
Key to numbers in Appendix I

Cantonal Capital   ■
Small Walled Town   ■
Other Major Settlements   ●
Minor Settlements   ○
Villa   ▲
Possible Villa   ▼
Barrow or Mausoleum   ◗
Pottery or Tile Kiln   ◆

zone, and the Oxford end of the valley presents a spread of lighter soils much more inviting than those further east.[2]

Talk of 'the deserts of Chiltern' and 'the wilderness of the Chilterns'[3] is quite misleading. It is mistaken to imagine a repelling upland consisting of nothing but bare chalky turf and beech forest. No doubt it was in places, but the range contains large areas of brick-earth and patches of clayey chalk marl, gravels and glacial drifts, and its numerous southern valleys a rich alluvium; the variety of soils indicates high fertility and wide variations in natural vegetation.[4] As Branigan insisted 'potentially . . . the Chiltern valleys were rich farming land' of which a considerable number of Roman villas took advantage, and the zone extending across eastern Hertfordshire, well suited to a mixed farming economy, bore an unusually dense population at the time of Domesday. The district was far more inviting than the vast expanse of heavy clay in the Ouse–Thame basin, and it is not surprising that it became a centre of Belgic wealth and power. Any assessment that dismisses the Chiltern zone as unattractive to early settlers is patently false.

The extent of early woodland is impossible to recover with any degree of confidence. Most soils will eventually acquire a more or less continuous tree cover, but by the end of the Roman period human agencies had long been at work reclaiming land for cultivation from the primeval waste. Map 7 shows the surviving woodland indicated by names recorded before 1350 that contain the elements *wudu*, *weald*, *holt*, *hyrst*, *fyrhth*, *graefe* and *hangra*; and *leah* which denoted natural or artificial clearings. A special symbol is used for *feld*, suggesting open country, where the medieval meaning 'field' is not suspected. The result is far short of satisfactory because the haphazard evidence is drawn from a very wide span, but it gives a broad indication that 1,500 years ago woodland must have been very extensive. It can safely be presumed that in the 5th century the Chiltern tops and the London Clay were heavily wooded, and much of the northern clay vale; they were among the last terrains that early settlers would break in. In medieval times the forests of Bernwood and Whaddon Chase in mid-Buckinghamshire were still extensive, but little now remains of them.

The Roman Legacy

The Saxon newcomers did not enter an altogether unpeopled, undeveloped countryside. Like the native-born who lingered in the post-Roman world they were confronted with the product of four centuries of highly civilized development and even longer exploitation of the land. The Chiltern region in Roman times formed the greater and richest part of a canton whose capital was Verulamium.[5] This city like many smaller local settlements followed intensive Belgic occupation which did much to harness the region's potential wealth. By the end of the Roman era its human ecology was well developed, and in the early 5th century a visitor would have seen towns large and small, rural settlements, villas, hamlets, farms and industrial sites, or their mouldering remains, all linked together by an excellent road system. Map 1, which depicts the main features of this kind, is largely derived from the Ordnance Survey *Map of Roman Britain* (4th edition 1978) and surveys by Dr. Branigan.[6]

Whereas individual buildings such as villas might perish with their context and even towns wither into ruin, the sturdy Roman roads must have formed a visible and enduring framework, largely surviving to this day. The map marks only roads whose existence and course are incontrovertible and omits several that the Viatores[7] claimed to discover but for which the flimsy evidence is rather unconvincing; minor roads were of insubstantial construction and liable to easy decay. There must, however, have been a fine network of tracks serving the many villas in the Chiltern valleys.

Apart from the city of Verulamium, large by the international standards of its day, the region contained few real towns. In the east Braughing, successor to a Belgic centre, and in the west walled Dorchester were both much smaller. Welwyn and Baldock, both also Belgic in origin, and Sandy ranked as major unprotected settlements. Roadside communities existed at Dunstable (*Durocobrivae*) and Dropshort (*Magiovinium*) on Watling Street, at Fleet Marston on Akeman Street and near Bishop's Stortford on Stane Street. Other towns of the Catuvellaunian *civitas* that lay outside the region's limits—Alchester, Towcester, Godmanchester, perhaps Water Newton—were quite small, and the regular posting stations along the trunk roads minuscule. Verulamium enjoyed undisputed supremacy.

Villas may be regarded as the most typical feature of Roman Britain, if not the most important. They display the quintessence of civilized Roman life and an ample assessment of their place in that society is now available.[8] Their social milieu is inseparable from the towns around which they tend to be grouped, and it is not surprising that a large proportion of the hundred or so villas that must once have graced the Verulamium territory lay within easy reach of the city.

The discovery of villas is a matter of chance and more are likely to turn up in the course of fieldwork and development. In this region only the Roman sites of the western Chilterns, where building has concentrated on the narrow valley bottoms and adjacent slopes, have been systematically studied; the majority of villas here appear to have been of middling status, neither private palaces nor mere farms. An equal number of sites with evidence of substantial buildings cannot be classified by superficial traces, but their distribution is so similar as to suggest many will also prove on investigation to rank as villas.

Curiously few villas are known throughout east Hertfordshire and in south Oxfordshire. Although this may point to local social and economic differences they are not altogether absent; their apparent scarcity may be due to the lack of development and archaeological inactivity in remoter districts not threatened by building. More can be expected to come to light in the vicinity of towns such as Braughing and Baldock, where the Youngsbury and Great Wymondley villas seemed unlikely to stand alone before one at Mentley near the former and a probable site near Bulls Green, Datchworth, were recently discovered.[9]

The villa distribution in the region is quite uneven; noticeably few are situated in the northern half and these mostly close to the Ouse. Between the Ouse and the Chilterns villas are practically unknown. This scarcity is too marked to be explained by the accidents of discovery and points strongly to the relative undesirability of the heavy clay there.

Villas and probable sites cluster thickly in the Chiltern zone, especially in and around the high country west of Verulamium. These fall into three groups: along the Icknield Way scarp-foot, along the bank of the Thames, and within the massif itself, particularly in the southern valleys reaching deep into the hills. Villas extend sparsely to the north-east. The concentration of so many close to Verulamium is no doubt to some extent a facet of social amenity, but it would be an exaggeration to suggest that all their owners were numbered among the ruling aristocracy. Another powerful reason for the distribution can be deduced; villa builders were not backward agriculturalists, and a fair number of these sites began life as Belgic or Roman farmsteads. The villa grouping well underlines the previous remarks about the potential value of much land in the Chiltern zone and contradicts the legendary but misconceived 'deserts of Chiltern'. Although villas exemplify only one aspect of the economy their concentration round the city and its abnormal size show that it was the centre of a numerous and thriving population in Roman times.

Comparatively little is known about other Roman rural settlements in the region because sites outside modern development are seldom found by accident, and timber buildings in the native tradition leave slight traces and yield a poorer assemblage of objects than town houses and villas. Few are large enough to be called villages and most, like one in the fields between Swangle's Farm and Fanhams Hall near Ware, are small and remote from later occupied sites. One of fair size, however, was recently excavated at The Cow Roast near Berkhamsted. Several kilns are known but their workers' dwellings are missing, although a cemetery was discovered next to the potters' kilns at Stone, Bucks. Previously unsuspected Roman rural sites appear so often on air photographs, however, as to give the impression that they must have been surprisingly numerous and probably sheltered a considerable population, which would agree with the current view that 'the population of Roman Britain was far higher than we have hitherto supposed'[10] and greatly exceeded Collingwood's outside estimate[11] of one million made nearly 50 years ago and even Wheeler's[12] of one and a half million. Frere's more recent computation[13] arrived at 'almost two million', a figure little different from that of the population of England at the time of the Norman Conquest.

The Domesday situation

Before turning to the Dark Age evidence it is worth looking ahead to its outcome, the local conditions in the 11th century, because just as the earlier foundations of the Migration era cannot be ignored, so we are conscious that the ripened pattern of settlement disclosed in Domesday, 20 generations after the world of Hengist and Arthur, grew by the natural course of development from the potential of the land itself; any artificial barriers to expansion had long gone. There is no reason to believe that intervening changes in agricultural technology and practice invalidate comparisons between the pattern of 1086 and the evidence of the pagan age. Soils were a constant factor at all times.

No doubt great changes including the growth of real towns meanwhile occurred, and many place-names indicating late settlement and expansion bear witness to steady development. Domesday depicts an advanced stage in this evolution, a phase

MAP 2

DOMESDAY POPULATION DENSITY

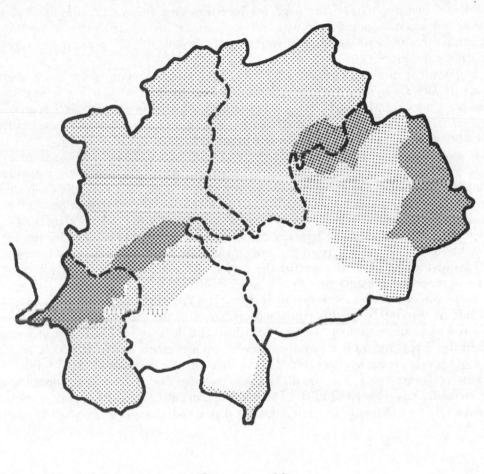

0   10

MILES

Over 10 persons recorded per square mile

5 - 9 persons recorded per square mile

Less than 5 persons recorded per square mile

Internal County Boundaries within the Region

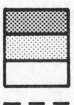

in the exploitation of the countryside which in its inequalities reveals varied natural influences at work. The Domesday census portrays the simple response of early medieval agriculture to intrinsic factors that early technology could not easily modify; woods might be burned or slowly cut down piecemeal, but in a society still far from overpopulation the urge to drain marshes was as lacking as the means. Where the agrarian population of 1086 was abnormally dense or sparse the influence of fundamental factors such as different soils or the original presence of forest and marsh can be discerned.

In 1086 the population density varied considerably. A convenient series of county maps in *The Domesday geography of south-east England*[14] shows the position and relative size of individual settlements and the average density of occupation in natural subdivisions (Map 2). Particularly striking are a few areas of unusually high density with over 10 recorded persons per square mile. A district with 13 per square mile extends round Hitchin and Ashwell, straddling the Hertfordshire-Bedfordshire border. Adjoining is a similar broad belt abutting the Essex border from Royston to Stanstead Abbots. The third is a long strip immediately north of the Chiltern scarp from Dorchester to Aylesbury, with marked intensity of population below the scarp line.[15] Clearly these three were zones where conditions were intrinsically most favourable to early agriculture and whenever possible sought after by immigrants; they demonstrate the reality of the geological considerations mentioned earlier.

Throughout most of the rest of the region the density ranged fairly evenly from 5 to 9 recorded persons per square mile, pointing to a long period of expansion while secondary settlements spread into the less desirable lands. Two tracts however formed an exception to this equalized distribution. In the Chilterns proper, except round Tring, and in south-east Hertfordshire the density was well below average, as might be expected in a district containing many steep slopes difficult to plough and ridges covered by clay-with-flints, and on the London Clay plateau where extensive forest tracts remained. The low average for the Chiltern district, which superficially suggests an almost unpeopled terrain, disguises the fact that there were considerable settlements in the Chiltern valleys and along streams such as the Colne and Ver.

Chapter III

A HANDFUL OF POST-ROMAN SITES

ONLY THREE post-Roman sites in the region are so far known. The emphatic words here are 'so far', as these have been revealed in recent years and more will undoubtedly be discovered as a result of improved archaeological techniques and growing awareness that sub-Roman occupation in England must have left some identifiable traces. This awareness is a fairly recent development, too late to recover what must have been destroyed undetected in earlier excavations such as those at Verulamium nearly 50 years ago when not a single 5th-century feature was recognized and even fallen painted ceilings were missed; more recent work on a much smaller scale shows that much was previously overlooked.

The uppermost levels of Roman sites have suffered from erosion, pillage and tilling. These partly account for the scarcity of recognizable post-Roman material, but the real reason for the paucity of such finds is the reduced cultural state of southern England in the 5th-century, which is emphasized in Chapter VI, and the consequent lack of well-typed finds like pottery on which archaeologists heavily depend.

Verulamium, near St. Albans, Hertfordshire (OS 1 in. 7th edn. Sheet 160, TL 13 07)

Excavations under Professor Sheppard Frere[1] in the early 1960s showed that civic building activity went on into or beyond the middle of the 5th century— 'impressive evidence for the continuing functioning of town life well into the fifth century'. He summarized:

'Building XIV 3 was a small house or shop not built until about 370, and thereafter undergoing alterations which take it into the fifth century.

Building XXVII 2 gave even clearer evidence. It was a large and prosperous courtyard house . . . first constructed after 370. In a second phase, perhaps about 390, some rooms had been enlarged and supplied with big expensive mosaics. . . . These were the homes of wealthy men . . . it was to the occupants of such houses that Honorius' rescript was directed. This phase lasted long enough for one of the mosaics to be clumsily patched. . . . in a third phase, one of these luxurious rooms was sacrified to house a corn-drying oven. We may infer that (perhaps *c.* 410–420) barbarian or peasant disturbances were making the countryside unsafe, and the harvest was hurried within the protection of the town-walls and there treated. The corn-drying furnace had a long life, for its stoke-hole had been reconstructed . . . Finally the house itself was demolished, and its site occupied by a large hall or barn . . . How long this building lasted could not be established; but

21

when finally it in turn had perished, its site was crossed by a pipe-line trench still containing the iron collars for jointing the wooden water-main. . . . It would not be wild guesswork to assign this pipe-line to a date around 450; it might indeed be later. The importance of this sequence is that it shows that even at such a late date the urban traditions of the past—clean water, aqueducts, public fountains—were still alive, and so was the craftsmanship which could construct or maintain them. Thus well into the middle of the fifth century Verulamium survived'.

From the late 4th- or early 5th-century filling of the Theatre came a bronze buckle shaped like a pair of confronted dolphins—a piece of the military belt equipment mentioned in the next chapter—and some 'Romano–Saxon' ware.

About the middle of the 10th century abbot Wulsin of St. Albans built St. Michael's church on the site of the basilica. Squatter occupation among the ruins of the city continued down to the 11th century.

Latimer Roman Villa, Buckinghamshire (OS 1 in. 7th edn. Sheet 159, SU 998986)

Steady dilapidation of the villa began in the mid 4th century and the main building was gradually abandoned. Four subsequent phases of occupation were marked by substantial new timber structures—one of cruck construction—both within and outside the old courtyard. The first of these phases was dated to the late 4th century and the last placed 'very late in the fifth century if not later'. All seem to be connected with farming; the villa economy changed to emphasis on cattle and pigs, with much deer-hunting. There was some locally made pottery. Dr. Branigan[2] remarked 'we should not expect Latimer to be in any way atypical of the Chiltern villa sites in the fifth century'.

Dorchester-on-Thames, Oxfordshire[3] (OS 7th edn. Sheet 158, SU 57 94)

The earthern ramparts were replaced by stone walls about 270, and the small town seems to have been flourishing at the end of the Roman period. One of its late cemeteries was at Queensford Mill, outside to the north-east, where nearly 200 Christian inhumations were identified and 78 excavated, within a rectangular enclosure, already much quarried away, that may have contained over 700 graves. The ditches and plough-soil had worn sherds of late Roman pottery. The burials were carefully spaced in rows, all with heads to the west, and 35 per cent of those examined had coffin nails or fittings but there were no gravegoods. A late or immediately post-Roman date was presumed and appeared to be borne out by a radiocarbon dating of A.D. 420 ± 100. The number of burials surely indicates that its use must have been prolonged well into the 5th century. Another possible early Christian cemetery, revealed by air photographs, lies at Overy on the east bank of the river Thame.

Late Roman burials of Germanic personnel outside the town have long been known, and more recently an early Saxon cemetery at Berinsfield two miles to the north; these are mentioned in Chapter VII and summarized in Appendix II.

Excavations in 1962 in the south-west of the town revealed timber-framed buildings, and a post-Honorian building cut by unmortared stone footings suggesting a timbered upper structure. Similar buildings stood nearby. Some of these 'might well be considered as the simple housing provided for the military force in garrison'. Not far away was a Saxon hut of possibly the early or mid 6th century, still apparently observing a Roman street line; above it was a large rectangular wooden building perhaps contemporary with sherds of 9th or 10th century wares around it. Close by a wall had disturbed a hoard largely of coins of Honorius and Arcadius. South of the town numerous sunken dwellings appear in air photographs.

Frere remarked that Dorchester is 'one of a small group where the coinage of the Theodosian period, instead of dwindling to 1 or 2% of the total, actually rises considerably. This . . . must mean that official payments, or at least provision of small change, were maintained here to a much greater extent than elsewhere. We can hardly avoid associating this with the [Germanic] mercenaries . . .' and said 'we have a town taken over by Saxon settlers or soldiers, and occupation is continuous from Roman times; there are a few pieces of Anglo-Frisian pottery to show early or mid-fifth century occupation . . .'.

Excavations in 1972 amplified this picture. In the north-west area of the town the site of a house that decayed in the 4th century was converted to industrial use and equipped with kilns and furnaces; there followed three phases of Saxon occupation lasting from the 5th to the 9th century. First came sunken huts aligned on Roman streets, then tiny timber-framed houses like those found in a post-Roman phase at Wroxeter, and finally houses built of dry stone and mud, roughly dated by a penny of Burgred of about 865 under the latest wall. A similar succession was found in the south of the town.

These discoveries confirmed that occupation continued throughout the Saxon period till about 900, when Dorchester was superseded in importance by Oxford, first mentioned in the Burghal Hidage of 912. Dorchester's decline may have been due to the decay of the Roman road from Silchester to Alcester and the growth of a new route from Southampton to the Midlands via Oxford. The town was the see of Birinus and two successors between about 634 and about 660, but was not again a bishopric for 200 years.

(*Note:* The cemetery with 39 orientated inhumations at Beacon Hill, Lewknor, Oxon. (SU 722972) is now known to be of Middle Saxon date: radiocarbon tests put two burials in the 9th century.[4] This site therefore does not appear in the maps.)

Chapter IV

EARLY SAXON ARCHAEOLOGY AND ITS DATING

EARLY SAXON ARCHAEOLOGY is still largely concerned with burials and the objects found with them, though today numerous dwellings are known. The Ordnance Survey *Map of Britain in the Dark Ages* makes a ready but rather crude guide, since it omits loose finds and shows no chronological distinctions between sites. In a long period, however, it is vital to distinguish between what is early and what is late. For that important differentiation we must turn to the gravegoods contained, helped by critiques such as Dr. Myres' invaluable study of Saxon pottery which paid particular attention to dating. Another observation about this map is essential; over most of England it amounts to a sketch of evidence for the pagan Saxons and does not profess to cover traces of contemporary non-English people. We must therefore be alert to the implications of negative evidence.

An inventory of all Saxon burial sites known in 1960 was given by Mrs. Meaney[1] who included a few that do not appear on the Dark Ages map. *Medieval Archaeology* and county journals report a few recent discoveries, and some previously overlooked finds have been brought to notice. A summary of all the regional sites is given in Appendix II which includes finds not definitely associated with burials, and an important early *burh*.

The vast majority of the cemeteries in the region are small, only 10 being known to exceed 20 burials, although the full extent of most was probably not explored. Moreover half the sites contained not more than three graves, in many cases a single one. Many sites discovered before the days of scientific excavation were very badly recorded. Worse, in several cases finds have survived incompletely or not at all; from what must have been a very large and important cemetery at Warmark not one object remains. Only a handful of sites have received adequate modern study. A short critical survey of the Bedfordshire ones was given by Dr. Morris in 1962,[2] but nothing comparable exists for the other counties; Head's sketch of Buckinghamshire[3] had little historical perspective.

Because discovery is almost entirely a matter of chance, usually in building and gravel extraction, finds do not necessarily reflect the true distribution of occupation. The question whether this has significantly distorted our impressions is discussed later.

The dating of Saxon finds

Various weapons, ornaments and domestic articles were interred with the heathen Saxons; many cannot be at all closely dated, others can typologically be placed in a rough but serviceable sequence of changing fashions. The dating of the oldest

24

objects[4] rests partly on evidence from the late imperial Roman context on the continent, and historical events there, partly on comparisons and contrasts between finds in England and abroad.

The earliest distinctions turn on the beginning of the Germanic migration to England, for types found only on the continent or in a Romano-British setting must be earlier and those common to both England and the continent must be later. There is no reason to believe that any permanent settlement of Saxon *communities* antedated Vortigern's invitation to Hengist; the few Germanic burials in this country that occur in a Roman context are clearly those of men in military formations and their womenfolk. Dr. Myres' view[5] that the origins of mass Saxon settlement go back to the 4th century can hardly be sustained when the alleged early date of certain types of pottery found in England, on which his argument depends, is not corroborated by any finds of Germanic metalwork of that period, which are notably missing here, and it conflicts with Brown's demonstration that the earliest Saxon cemeteries began after the collapse of the Roman pottery trade.[6] The second quarter of the 5th century is still the earliest appropriate time for the deposition of Saxon objects, except those that occur in a definite Roman milieu, though a few pieces brought over by the first immigrants were probably made up to a generation earlier in Germany.

Similarly, objects associated with the uncontrolled Saxon settlement after Hengist's outbreak cannot have been used here before about 450. Another dividing line can be drawn about 500 when the main stream of migration came to an end; some types found only in Britain are presumably later.

The arrival of Salin's zoomorphic Style I can be put about 500 and about 600 the influence of Kentish hegemony and continental trade can be seen in the spread of designs of Kentish origin and imports of such luxuries as Mediterranean metalwork, as occasional Byzantine and Frankish coins with burials confirm. Finally, towards the very end of the period of pagan burial customs certain innovations attributable to Christian influence are detectable.

In all cases greater accuracy than a generation in dating cannot be claimed; new fashions did not displace old ones immediately, and an article buried with its owner may have belonged to him for a lifetime or a few months.

"Military" accoutrements of the late 4th and early 5th century

Nearly twenty years ago certain kinds of bronzework that occur in southern Britain and more frequently in northern Gaul and the Rhineland behind the Roman frontier were first surveyed by Mrs. Hawkes and Dr. Dunning.[7] These articles— buckles with confronted animal heads, strap-ends, disc attachments and narrow tubular-sided bars—were standard fittings of the uniform belt (*cingulum*) of the late Roman army. The *cingula* of officers and higher civil officials, who at this time ranked as officers, were also adorned by decorated belt-plates. The styles of ornament employed, 'classical in origin but barbarian in feeling', reflect the taste of the largely Germanic troops and auxiliaries who were engaged to defend the continental frontier zones.

The British finds, mainly buckles, come principally from Roman contexts: forts, walled towns, rural settlements and villas. Over a dozen buckles, however, are from Saxon graves. From buckles of types IIIA and IV, which are common on the continent and here are found mainly on the eastern side of England, developed the almost entirely insular types I and II, which have a wider distribution over southern England.

Since belt plates of type II were worn on the continent in the middle decades of the 4th century, and two there were buried about 350, the date of introduction of this type into Britain may be not much later. Most if not all the over 30 known buckles of this kind found in Britain were evidently made here, 'probably over a longish period', but by the late 4th century some were already broken or very worn. Much of this gear seems to indicate the widespread distribution of garrisons and auxiliaries during the late 4th century, but there has been some discussion as to how much of it could have belonged to civilian officials. Mrs. Hawkes has since pointed out that gravegoods associated with some type II belts mean that their wearers must 'surely have been pagan barbarians, probably Germans, and thus soldiers rather than civilians', and she concluded 'there remains a case for saying that, while some of our [type II] belt fittings may have been worn by civil officials, many, perhaps the majority, had been worn by the military'. In either case these objects are relics of official authority.

These judgments may not apply to the buckles of type I—over 40 are recorded— which dating evidence suggests 'were being manufactured during the last three decades of the fourth century, and being worn out by the early fifth'. Although some of these probably belonged to military personnel, many of the belts to which they were attached were so narrow that they 'seem more appropriate to non-official civilian dress'; and belts were favoured by German women. In fact all nine Saxon graves containing type I buckles were those of women, a few of them definitely connected with late Roman or early post-Roman military forces.

Three local finds of this material occur in a Roman setting. A soldier's burial at Dorchester I was accompanied by a type IIIA buckle, strap-ends, disc attachments and bars, and his Germanic origin can be assumed from the presence in an adjacent woman's grave of a decidedly Teutonic proto-cruciform brooch, as well as a worn type IB buckle. These burials are hardly any later and perhaps even slightly earlier than 400, for though continental analogies would permit a date a decade or two later the Germanic imports here and at Dorchester II would agree with deposition before 400. At Verulamium a type IIA buckle came from the refuse dumped in the theatre in the late 4th or early 5th century.

From Saxon sites in the region come a fragment of a IIA buckle in a 6th-century woman's grave at Luton I, a IB buckle from Walton by Aylesbury, a strap-end from a late 5th-century hut at Stevenage, and an early 5th-century belt-plate from an undated but probably late 6th-century burial at Bishopstone II, Bucks. None of these could be possessions interred with a Germanic mercenary, and the late deposition of two indicates either early loot or souvenirs handed down to the descendants of Saxon auxiliaries or *foederati*.

Weapons

Spears are of little use for dating as many types were in simultaneous use.[8] Almost the only weapons that can be pinned down are the seax knife (scramasax) which seldom occurs before the 7th century, and can usually be attributed to that time,[9] and the francisca or throwing axe which is normally late 6th or 7th century but does occur earlier. Shield-bosses with silver rivets seem to be no earlier than the late 6th century and high conical ones indicate a 7th-century date.[10] Swords are very rare in the region where none of definitely early date is known.

Cruciform brooches

The elements of typology and a division into five broadly successive and increasingly elaborate groups were worked out 50 years ago by Aberg,[11] but his dating framework needs revision because he felt unable to breach Bede's time for the first presence of Saxons in England, so that his 'c. 450' now becomes 'c. 425'. His classification of the later groups was developed by Leeds[12] and has since been expanded.[13] Groups I and II occur both in England and in Germany where later ones are absent.

A prototype ancestral to Group I, from the late Roman soldier's grave at Dorchester I, was probably buried about the last decade of the 4th century. Not all groups are represented in the region. Groups I and II occur only at Kempston and lie firmly in the 5th century. There are no florid brooches of Anglian type, only a modestly decorated example of group IV, probably from Toddington I, and a plain group V one from Kempston, both quite late in the series.

'Luton type' brooches

Continental parallels show that the very rare 'Luton type', primitive small brooches with a reeded headplate bearing minute prongs on top, must belong to the first quarter of the 5th century; these objects were probably brought over by the earliest Saxon settlers, the foederati under British rule. In this region they occur at Dorchester III, Kempston and Luton I.

Equal-arm brooches

Perhaps from the 'Luton type' developed brooches with matching head and footplate of equal size, in fashion about 450, as found at Kempston.

Saucer brooches

The vast majority of 105 saucer brooches from 20 sites in the region are late forms. There is no accepted classification but a bewildering variety of designs and sub-types was reduced to order by Morris[14] and cross-connexion datings established. The cast brooches are generally the older, and those with an applied ornamented disc and rim hardly occur in England before 500, but solid brooches persist to the end.

The earliest motifs are the chip-carved 5-coil running spiral which is typical of the 5th century and lasted into the 6th century and in multiplied forms continued well into that period, and the quadruple recurved scrolls which developed into the floriated cross and similar patterns. Marked changes in fashion begin to be common

when zoomorphic ornament is introduced about the mid 6th century, in its last
quarter becoming transformed into medley shapes, some skilfully and finely
executed, but soon tending to incoherence. One by-product is the 'legs' and 'spider's
legs' family. Towards the end of the 6th century garnets and relief simulating them
are found, aping Kentish fashions. About this time there originated among craftsmen
of the applied school, probably in Cambridgeshire, the complicated Maltese cross
of 'Kempston' design and the related 'six faces'. Probably the last of the series in the
region are giant cast brooches up to 8 cm. in diameter which bear geometrical and
basketwork motifs and represent the 'Saxon' equivalent of the great square-heads;
several found in the western part of the Ouse–Thame basin are probably of about
600 or even slightly later. Thereafter saucer brooches went out of fashion.

Great square-headed brooches

This family was introduced into England about or soon after 500, but most
belong to the mid or later 6th century. Their classification was established by
Leeds.[15] The 'Luton' group found there and at Toddington, and the 'Barrington'
group with an example from Kempston, are late in the series and placed towards the
close of the 6th century; the 'East Midland' specimen from Kempston is later still,
probably early 7th century. A 'Southern' group one comes from Dorchester III.

Glassware

The whole field was examined by Harden[16] who supplied a dating framework.
The vessels can be divided into survivals from the Roman period and those made
between then and the 7th century, many of them imports. The first category is
represented only by a mould-blown beaker from Newport Pagnell, and local
examples of the second are not numerous. Cone beakers of types attributed to the
5th or early 6th century come from Dinton and Kempston. Newport Pagnell produced a claw beaker of a degenerate type, probably late 6th century, and the rich
Taplow burial had no less than four of about 600. The 7th-century palm cups from
Kempston and Wheathampstead are a well-known type with continental examples.

Pottery

Myres' comprehensive work on pagan Saxon pottery[17] clarified a mass of
varieties and confusing detail. Recognition of types is not simple because over a long
period many vessels share a family likeness in shape or method of decoration;
elementary forms of ornament—line and dot, chevrons, neckbands and stamping—
are naturally conservative. It is however possible to follow changing styles, and the
more bizarre and mannered ones stand out clearly.

Carinated bowls and the frequent use of finger-mark dimples, both common on
the continent, are recognized as characteristic of the late 4th and early 5th
centuries; also in the latter may be placed plain biconical and hollow-necked urns. In
the later 5th century well-marked types distinguished by barbaric splendour become
apparent: the long-boss style, often feathered, and the fully evolved Buckelurn
groups with their increasing tendency to profuse stamping. Groups I–IV are considered to belong to the latter half of the 5th century, group V to the early 6th

century. The greater part of the 6th century seems to have produced rather indeterminate varieties and few local vessels can certainly be attributed to the first two-thirds. The last decades of the 6th century are, however, characterized over much of England by the stamped pendent triangle panel style, usually with generous stamping.[18] This fashion is so pronounced that its influence can be detected even in poorly executed vessels like those from Kingsey and Ippollitts. In the 7th century extravagances disappear and the commonest shapes are gourd-like or have long necks, usually undecorated.

Hanging bowls and their escutcheons[19]

Though the source and purpose of these remarkable prized objects—the only known large-scale insular bronzework of the period—are disputed it is agreed that they were not made by Saxon craftsmen, as the exclusively Celtic ornamental motifs show, but were the products of some Celtic milieu. Many may have been acquired by pillage and some appear in Viking graves in Norway. The origin of their type and technique is late Roman but the design of bowls and escutcheons, often enamelled, seems to have undergone long development. No doubt some late ones were made in Ireland, but Françoise Henry's claim that all were made by Irish craftsmen is not generally accepted; it is not unlikely that the skill spread thither from Celtic Britain, considering their common Christianity and the intercourse proved by the Latin and early Welsh loanwords in Irish. Some bowls were probably made in areas that were not taken over by Saxon rulers until the latter part of the 6th century, and it is conceivable that British smiths there continued to produce them for English lords.

Attempts to classify the bowls in a typological sequence have not been entirely satisfying, and Elizabeth Fowler concluded that parallel development made absolute dating impossible. Examples such as those from Sutton Hoo (one, superbly decorated, was patched with silver) and Winchester can however be recognized as probably of 6th- or perhaps early 7th-century manufacture. Indeed most hanging bowls discovered in Saxon graves seem to have been deposited about the latter time. Though the Hitchin bowl was destroyed its surviving escutcheons and similar discs from Dunstable and Oving can be identified as belonging to the 'developed trumpet pattern' which is thought to be late in the evolution; the occurrence of yellow enamel as well as red on the Hitchin discs favours a 7th-century date.

Cowrie shells

In 1931, 13 known burials with these shells ranged from the late 6th to the 7th century.[20] They probably found their way to Britain as a result of Frankish trading contacts.

Rich early 7th-century burials

The barrow grave of about 600 at Taplow, with garnet-set gold buckle, gilt-mounted drinking horns, claw beakers, gold-woven cloth and an imported Coptic bowl, by far the most richly furnished grave in the region, reflects the splendour of the famous ship burial at Sutton Hoo with which it is broadly contemporary. A gold pendant from High Wycombe of the same time or a little later shows the widespread

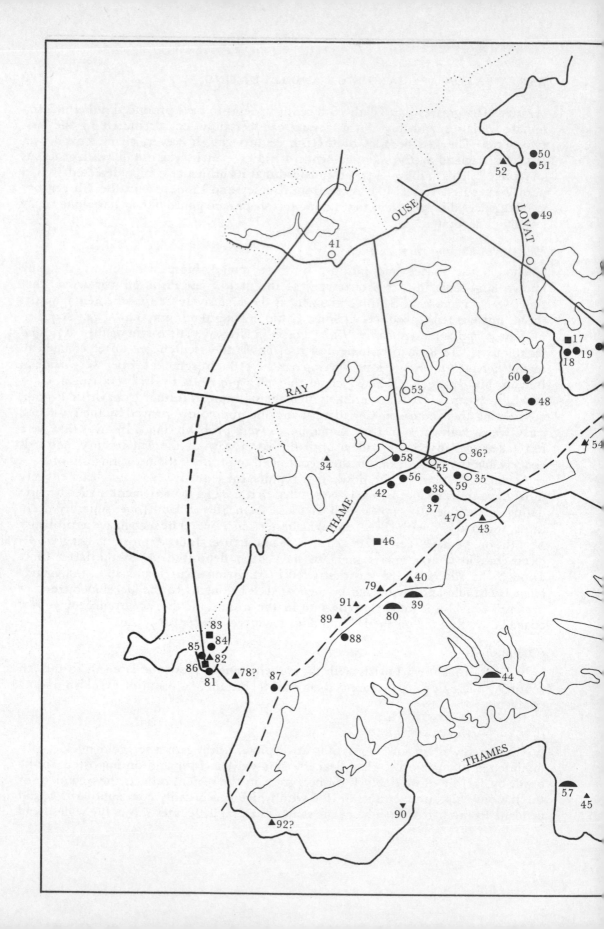

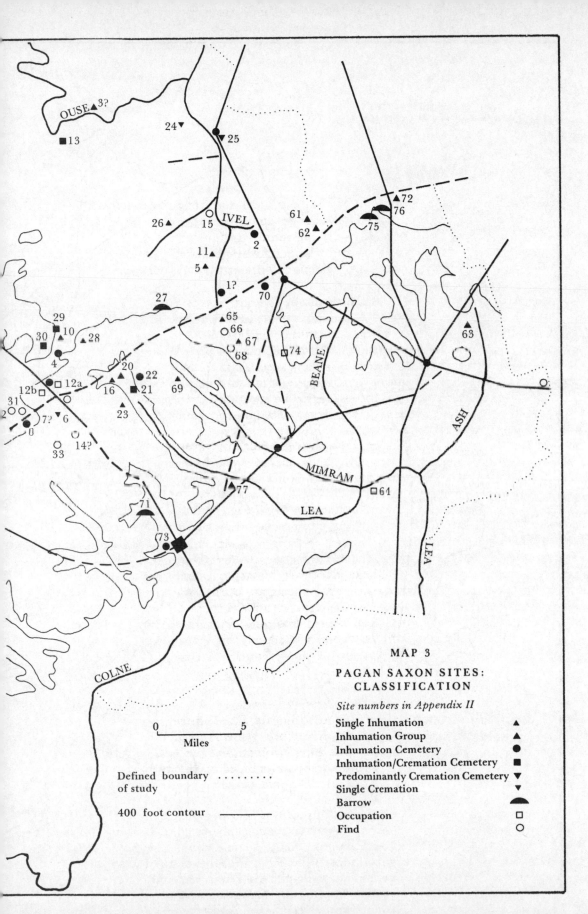

OUSE ▲ 3?

■ 13

24 ▼

▼ 25

▲ 72
76

26 ▲   ○ 15   IVEL   61 ▲   75
                                62 ▲

            11 ▲   ● 2
            5 ▲
                    ● 1?   ● 70
27

            ▲ 65
29   ○ 66   ▲ 63
30 ▲ 10   ▲ 67
    ■   ▲ 28   ○ 68   □ 74

4
                ▲ 20 ● 22
12b ■ □ 12a ▲ 16 ■ 21 ▲ 69   BEANE
31   ○
2 ○   ASH
▲   ● 0 7? ▼ 6 ▲ 23
        ○ 33 ○ 14?

                            ● MIMRAM
                    ▲ 77   □ 61
        71   LEA
        ◗
    ● (73) ◆   LEA

                                COLNE

MAP 3

**PAGAN SAXON SITES:
CLASSIFICATION**

Site numbers in Appendix II

Single Inhumation	▲
Inhumation Group	▲▲
Inhumation Cemetery	●
Inhumation/Cremation Cemetery	■
Predominantly Cremation Cemetery	▼
Single Cremation	▼
Barrow	◗
Occupation	□
Find	○

0 ———————— 5
Miles

Defined boundary · · · · · · · ·
of study

400 foot contour ——————

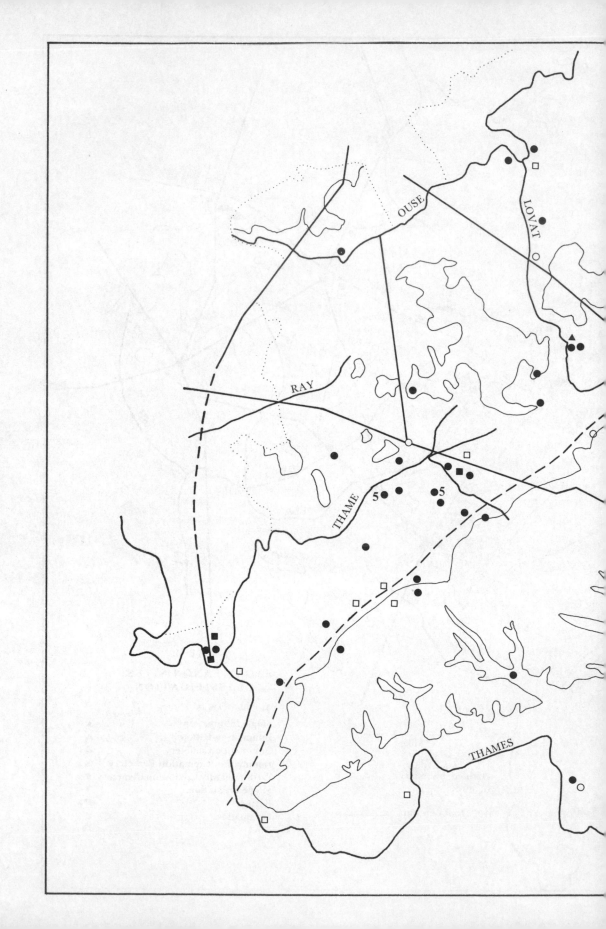

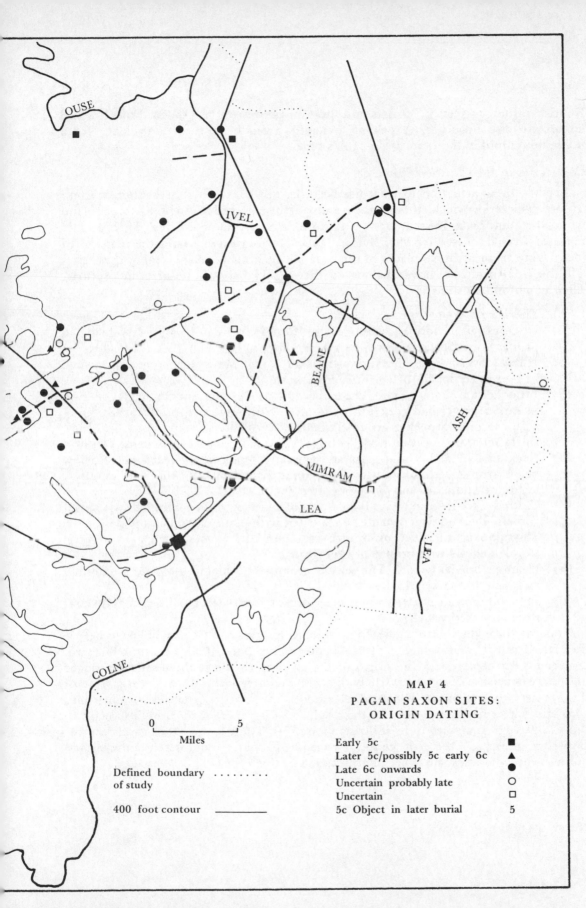

OUSE

IVEL

BEANE

ASH

MIMRAM

LEA

LEA

COLNE

MAP 4

PAGAN SAXON SITES:
ORIGIN DATING

0   5

Miles

Early 5c	■
Later 5c/possibly 5c early 6c	▲
Late 6c onwards	●
Uncertain probably late	○
Uncertain	□
5c Object in later burial	5

Defined boundary . . . .
of study

400 foot contour ————————

Kentish influence seen in garnets and their imitations on late saucer brooches and composite disc brooches. A golden 'pyramid' from Dorchester is evidence for a noble household in the vicinity about this time.

Cemeteries of the Christian Saxon period

Leeds[21] drew attention to what has been described as 'a highly distinctive group of late cemeteries which, though they are widely scattered in Anglo-Saxon England from Northumbria to Wessex, are very uniform in their characteristics'. Their generic features were discussed by Mrs. Hyslop[22] and Mrs. Hawkes,[23] with the reasons for identifying them as burial-places of the post-Conversion age. At several of these sites 'all the best-furnished graves belong to the second half of the seventh century'. Their common features are:

(a) There is no cremation.
(b) Orientation is normal, with graves often in regular rows, a few being in primary or secondary barrows with ring ditches.
(c) A few graves possessed luxury articles but a high percentage were unfurnished or poorly equipped, often with only a knife.
(d) Brooches are absent or rare. The cruciforms, saucers and square-heads common in earlier graves had gone out of fashion. With few exceptions, mostly survivals, the only brooches are small annular ones and rich composite brooches, the latter scarce outside Kent; neither type occurs before the seventh century.
(e) Necklaces of amber and glass are generally replaced by festoons of a few beads strung with silver wire rings. Gold and silver beads appear, amethyst beads are common, and pendants often occur.
(f) Clothes were fastened with linked pins of silver or gold, sometimes with inset garnets. Buckles were usually small, often with plain rectangular plates.
(g) Threadboxes of silver or bronze are found in women's graves, and little wooden chests with bronze or iron fittings.
(h) Weapons are fairly rare. The seax is prominent, shield-bosses are usually tall and include the sugarloaf variety.
(i) The commonest pottery wares are globular forms with tall necks and squat wide-mouthed vessels.

None of these distinctive cemeteries contains any grave that can be dated before the 7th century, and some, such as Chamberlain's Barn II at Leighton Buzzard, replaced older cemeteries. The origin of the changes visible in them must be sought in Kent, whence the Conversion widely disseminated new fashions, as the sculpture of the age also goes to show. Theobald's Penitential prescribed penances for Christians who still performed pagan rites for the dead, and a letter from St. Boniface seems to show that such practices were still rife about 750. There is no other candidate for Christian graves of the 7th century—except of course completely unfurnished burials—and conversely no other interpretation of this type.

PLATES

I. Brooches from grave 102, Dorchester III, Oxon. (later sixth century).

II Late Roman and early fifth-century military belt equipment

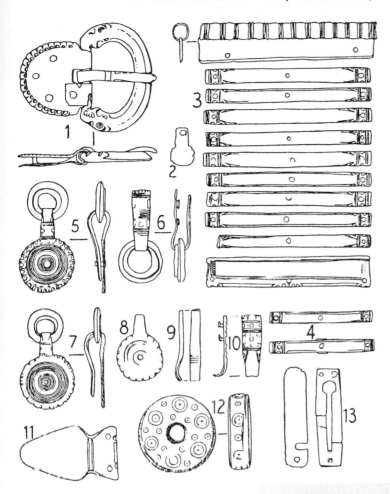

IIb. The broken piece from Luton I, Beds.

IIa. Objects from the late Roman German officer's grave, Dorchester I, Oxon.

IIc. The Bishopstone plate, Bucks.

IIIa. The large complete bowl from Sutton Hoo, Suffolk.

IIIb. The escutcheons from Hitchin, Herts. (bowl destroyed).

IIIc. The escutcheon from Oving, Bucks.

IV Saxon brooches

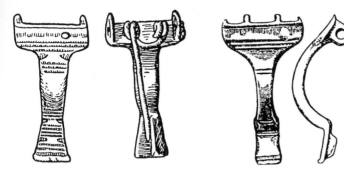

IVa. 'Luton type' brooches from Luton I (left) and Kempston, Beds.

IVd. A cruciform brooch from Kempston, Beds.

IVb. (above) 5-coil spiral brooch from grave 42, Dorchester III, Oxon.

IVc. (above right) Scroll brooch from Luton I, Beds.

IVe, f. Great square-headed brooches from Luton I (left) and Kempston, Beds.

Va, b, c. Large late cast saucer brooches from Ashendon (top left) and Stone (above), Bucks., and Dorchester (below), Oxon.

Vd. (bottom left) late saucer brooches with the Maltese cross design from Kempston, Beds.

Ve. (bottom right) Late composite brooch from Leighton Buzzard III, Beds.

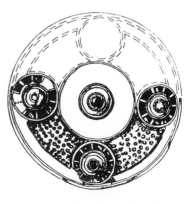

VI Late luxury gravegoods

VIa.   Gold pendant from High Wycombe, Bucks.

VIb(i).   Gold-mounted drinking horn from Taplow, Bucks.

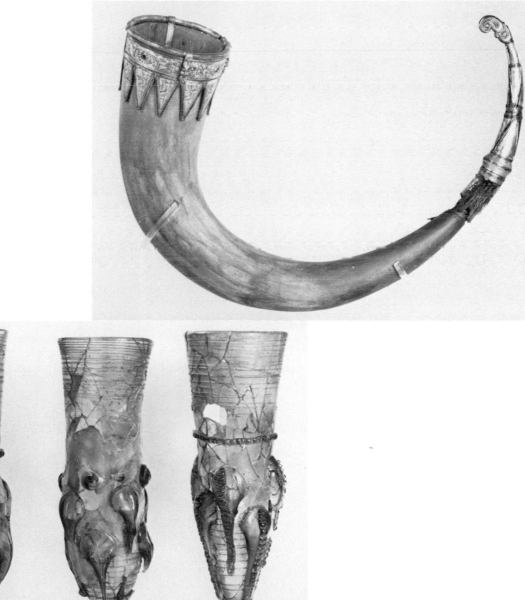

VIb(ii).   Glass claw beakers from Taplow, Bucks.

VIIa, b, c.   Buckelurn vessels from Luton I (top left), Sandy (above) and Kempston (left), Beds.

VIId, e, f.   Pots decorated in the pendent triangle panel style from Luton I (below left), Moggerhanger (bottom left), and four from Kempston (below), Beds.

Chapter V

HEATHEN PLACE-NAMES

MANY PLACE-NAMES alluding to heathen worship and practices must be broadly coeval with the physical remains of the pagan period; they could have been given only while heathen customs were current or still recollected. Possible names of this character with varying degrees of credibility and a few others denoting superstition, are listed in Appendix III.

The most unequivocal names in this category contain the Saxon words *hearg* 'heathen temple or grove' and *wig* or *weoh* 'idol, heathen shrine'. *Hearg* occurs in Harrowden 'temple hill' (*dun*), south of Bedford, and *weoh* at Weedon 'idol hill' north of Aylesbury. It is unlikely that the lost name *Welei* and Wain Wood near Hitchin contain *weoh*.[1] Perhaps of pagan import are two names from *heafod* 'head'[2] —Manshead Hundred in Bedfordshire and *Hertesheved* (now Bushey)—that may indicate places where human beings or animals were wont to be sacrificed.

Weoh probably also occurs in the name of Wing, where stands the fine 7th-century church mentioned in Chapter I. Early forms[3] show the name was originally that of a group of people whose designation ended in *-ingas*, one of those whom we meet in Chapter IX, but the first element is disputed. Many years ago Wallenberg suggested it was *weoh* but Ekwall thought this could not explain some forms and proposed personal names which could have produced them. He agreed, however, that the oldest spellings are conflicting and that at least one must be corrupt, which leaves the solution open. Curiously, modern place-name scholars have ignored the presence of the greatest early church in the region, the sign of a 7th-century mission centre. The possible form *weoh-ingas* 'the people who worship at the heathen temple' could account for the deliberate siting of an important church on a spot hallowed by pagans. The coincidence of a 7th-century minster and a place-name that may contain *weoh* is too striking to dismiss as fortuitous. Moreover it is possible that if *weoh* is present here it actually refers to the church, a usage known in Germany.[4] In that case it would illustrate the transference of a current heathen mode of reference to a new Christian feature: 'the people with a church'.

Wenslow Hundred in Bedfordshire is a reminder of the pagan deity Woden, but Grimsdyke—an Iron Age earthwork, unlike the well known Wansdyke—which may contain his alternative name is recorded too late to have real evidential value and could have been given after the heathen period. Early forms do not support the derivation of Thundridge from the god Thunor.[5]. Thunderfield, Grimes Brook and Grymescroft, all in Cheshunt, are probably names of medieval origin. It is highly unlikely that the war god's name Tiw enters into Tewin; no instance of a divine name coupled with *-ingas* is known.

35

Many names suggesting ancient burial places must refer to Saxon sites, but Barley is more likely .to mark some prehistoric burial. The most convincing of these is The Node (Codicote), most probably from *ād* 'funeral pyre'. There are several instances of *byrgels* or *byrgen* 'burial place, tumulus'. A barrow at Burn Hill (Stone) produced Iron Age or Saxon skeletons, Kinsbourne (Harpenden) means 'Cyne's grave', and Oxfordshire has four examples: Berins Hill (Ipsden) where burials were found, tenth century mentions of *haethenanbyrgels* in Pyrton and Crowmarsh that seem to preserve a memory of graves more recent than prehistoric, and Cowberry Lane (Watlington) from *cu* 'cow' and *byrgels* which hints at sacrifice. Bernwood perhaps contains *byrgen* but a Celtic source is possible.

It is rarely possible to be sure whether other elements concern pagan burial. *Beorg* means 'hill' or 'barrow' and in the latter case is not confined to Saxon antiquities. *Hlaw* (-low in modern spellings) with the same senses commonly came to signify 'hill', especially in the North, but as the root meaning is 'covering' it is likely that many hills became called by the names of barrows on them; so many -low names probably indicate barrows, particularly when the element is combined with an early type of Saxon personal name. In Derbyshire at least 30 of 70 -lows are attached to a tumulus.[6] Taplow with a rich barrow burial is a definite local case, and Bledlow may allude to the Cop barrow on the hillside above. In half a dozen cases in the region *hlaw* is linked with a personal name and the Hundred name Wenslow joins it with Woden. Goldenlow (Dunstable) refers to hidden treasure found in Henry III's reign, perhaps in a Saxon barrow. Cumberlow (Rushden) is a singular instance mentioning a Briton.

The heathen names make a rather weak impression. *Hearg*, *weoh* and the only certain god name Wenslow are in the north of the region, but there is no site on the upper Ouse. Most of the burial names occur close to Roman roads and the Icknield Way, but there is little infringement of the Chiltern zone except for *ād* at Codicote and at the western margin.

At the level of superstition that need not belong to the pagan period are Bastow (Anstey) and *Berdestaplesholme* (Stanstead) which may refer to a fertility cult centred on a 'bearded' post, perhaps a kind of maypole.

Chapter VI

THE BRITISH POST-ROMAN SETTING

IN A TRACT of about 2,000 square miles, three post-Roman sites and an assortment of 90 pagan burial grounds and occupation sites together with a number of heathen names provide an adequate foundation for a broad interpretation of the first two centuries after 410. We need not linger on the post-Roman sites except to remark that active occupation continuing far into the 5th century at Verulamium and a typical Chiltern villa is now no more surprising than the presence of late 4th-century Germanic soldiers at Dorchester-on-Thames, to which we shall return.

Sometimes it is wise to start an enquiry by ignoring the individual trees and concentrating on the wood instead, however illogical that seems at first. It is essential to get a bird's-eye view by setting the beginnings of English settlement in its proper place, its context. Putting the oldest Saxon sites under a microscope would tell us nothing about the contemporary conditions in which they lived. A sense of proportion comes from seeing the picture of the 5th and 6th centuries as a whole, and in that world the Saxons had a very small part indeed.

Here we need merely note that only five local Saxon sites could represent *civil* occupation before about 450. It seems sensible to consider this handful together with other Saxon sites in a separate chapter detailing the evolution of early English settlement; at this stage the problem of interpretation requires a different approach.

A glance at Map 4, which discloses that most of the region is bare of Saxon sites that began in the 5th or early 6th century, leads to the observation that the Chiltern region was clearly not an area of primary Saxon settlement such as Kent or East Anglia, which expanded from a considerable 5th-century population. The map conveys the immediate impression that this was pre-eminently a zone of secondary settlement, however old some few of its Saxon centres were. Important though that earliest stratum is we must understand its background in order to assess it.

When did pagan burial customs end?

The distribution map also reveals a most striking feature: the extremely uneven occurrence of known local archaeological sites of the pagan era. Indeed the significance of the overall distribution needs to be grasped, because its marked irregularity is fundamental to interpreting the entire picture. The differences obviously reflect a strong variation in the time of settlement. If so, we must ask what is the upper limit of the period that the pagan sites as a whole portray? The answer can only be a broad judgment, for cessation of the heathen custom of burying gravegoods was neither a rapid nor uniform process and depended upon local and fortuitous circumstances. Mrs. Hyslop[1] recalled that the Church found it necessary to castigate the survival of superstitious practices in the 8th century. Obviously the conversion of the Chiltern region can have made little headway before 650, and until Archbishop Theodore's reorganization the Church was probably in no fit state for the thorough-going proselytization of England. At least another generation would be necessary to achieve much impact on the majority of the rural inhabitants of this rather neglected part of the country, remote from the bishop's stool at Winchester after the see of Dorchester lapsed in 660.

One notable monument to the Church's activity in this area in the 7th century still stands little altered at Wing, a place-name discussed in the previous chapter. Although Mrs. Hyslop[2] saw 'nothing to indicate why Wing should have been chosen as a site for this exceptional building' a motive is implicit in the possible derivation of the place-name from *weohingas* 'the people who worship at the pagan temple', a heathen community persisting in their old cults when the grip of paganism was weakening. To any fervent missionary like St. Wilfrid, who while in exile almost single-handed converted the stubbornly heathen South Saxons, a pagan shrine at Wing would cry out for special attention. If so, in accordance with Pope Gregory's advice to Mellitus,[3] the church would be placed where the heathen temple once stood, both to obliterate its influence and to transfer the people's awe to the true God; the same doubtless happened at Harrow on the Hill, a *hearg* name. Wing must have been a minster church serving a wide area, and perhaps some other ancient local minsters such as Braughing, Welwyn and Hitchin were founded about this time or soon afterwards; the holding of Theodore's first Council at Hertford in 672[4] probably indicates an unrecorded establishment of this kind.

Residual paganism was likely to persist for some time. The partial success of the Conversion can be seen in the distinctive type of cemetery typified by Chamberlain's Barn II at Leighton Buzzard, where a heathen burial ground was abandoned for a new site with Christian hall-marks—almost universal orientation of graves, heads to the west, and regular spacing in rows—but with still unsuppressed deposition of gravegoods in a good proportion of burials. Cemeteries of this type, noted in Chapter IV, cannot be placed before the late 7th century, and some objects in them may, like a hoard of sceattas of the second quarter of the 8th century in a grave at Garton, Yorks., have been interred even later.[5]

There are signs, however, that some communities accepted the change to Christian custom smoothly and without evasion. Many village churchyards were established round a preaching cross long before any building was erected. The occasional discovery of late and usually unfurnished burials immediately outside them, as at Wing itself, is more likely to indicate a new Christian graveyard which eventually became partly forgotten before it was enclosed than part of an old pagan cemetery consecrated to Christian use by a compromise. It is likely that many instances of this sort have never been reported because they were undatable.

We cannot overlook that late 7th-century pagan traces are quite rare in this region, and if the place-name Wing does indicate the persistence of an active heathen cult after about 650 it also betrays an uncommon survival, because such a name would distinguish an unusual community. Pagan religion was dying without missionary efforts and its rites must already have ceased in many places, although the age-old habit of depositing gravegoods was likely to outlive formal religious observances. A reasonable terminal date for the deposition of articles in most districts of the Chiltern region would be about 650, since a fair number of local early 7th-century burials are known but the custom had evidently been widely abandoned well before the end of that century. The pagan remains and the few emphatically heathen names define the fullest extent of the territory settled by the English before the custom altogether ceased; conversely we can deduce that considerable areas where pagan traces are completely absent had not yet been occupied by English people. Furthermore, this conclusion should provide a useful yardstick for place-name material where no direct dating method is available, for any English place-name element or type of construction that often occurs outside the range of pagan remains must have been current beyond their terminal date, even if some of its formations were earlier.

The negative areas

In this light the archaeological distribution can be examined. There are a few burials along the Thames, including the rich barrow at Taplow, but nearly all the pagan remains lie in the northern basin where a number of concentrations are noticeable: a string of sites along the western part of the Icknield Way and near Aylesbury, most of them quite small and certainly late; another group including some sizable cemeteries in the Leighton Buzzard–Luton district; and a string from Hitchin down the Ivel valley to Moggerhanger, not connecting with a large and ancient cemetery at Kempston.

Apart from these obvious clusters there are isolated small cemeteries and minor sites in the interstices between definite groups, others sprinkled sparsely in or round the margins of districts that are either altogether empty of pagan sites or distinguished by their scarcity.

Three of these districts stand out prominently. North-west Buckinghamshire beyond Ashendon and Newport Pagnell exhibits only a solitary pair of brooches from near Buckingham; the only heathen place-name here is Winslow. Equally remarkable and far more extensive are the Chiltern range and eastern Hertfordshire which together form the Chiltern zone. As if to emphasize the contrast between the Chilterns and the valley runs a chain of minor sites along the Icknield Way, with only a single trace implying pagan encroachment within the massif, a 7th-century inhumation at High Wycombe that no doubt signifies intrusion from the direction of the Thames. The upland contains no heathen place-names. East of the Chilterns are a cemetery outside the walls of Verulamium and a small site at Wheathampstead, both of the 7th century, and at Redbourn the barrows perhaps of the same time that were opened in 1178.

The third district, south of the Icknield Way and east of Hitchin and Wheathampstead, is an almost complete archaeological void rimmed by insignificant sites, the only cemeteries anywhere near being small ones at Letchworth and Ashwell. The only intrusions into this area are an inhumation group at Furneux Pelham on the Essex border and a hut at Stevenage, early but probably short-lived.[6] The restricted occurrence of pagan remains is matched by the heathen names, which fringe a large barren area. The Node in Codicote and Kinsbourne in Harpenden commemorate pagan rites, and *Hertesheved*, an earlier name of Bushey, suggests a sacrificial cult on the Middlesex border. There is no clear trace of heathen worship in this quarter, as it is very doubtful whether *Welei* and Wain Wood indicate a pagan sanctuary in Ippollitts.

Future discoveries are unlikely to require any serious modification of these negative districts. Making allowance for the casual nature of archaeological finds in the course of farming or building, and the inevitability of some fresh sites that may add a little emphasis here or adjust the confines of the pagan area there, the contrasts are too pronounced to entertain the prospect of major revision. The pattern is too strong for that.

There is no escaping the conclusion that by about 650 the tide of Saxon settlement had not yet flowed appreciably into these negative districts. Moreover this argument can be taken back further, for behind this picture a still older one can be detected; we are really looking at the penultimate stage of a much earlier situation that was already dissolving. Since the vast majority of pagan sites are not earlier than the late 6th century, and many in marginal districts are no older than the 7th, the Saxons evidently reached these outposts not very long before the use of gravegoods ended. To emphasize how extremely limited the range of Saxon settlement was before the late 6th century, there are no earlier sites along the fertile Icknield Way between Luton and Dorchester. If the design we discern about 650 is no more than the ghost of an earlier one, the explanation for extensive areas then still archaeologically blank plainly lies in circumstances that long before dictated a pattern that influenced the course of English settlement for generations ahead.

Inevitably two questions arise. Why was the advance of English settlement so widely retarded, and what was the significance of the apparently blank and undeveloped areas that so long remained wholly unoccupied by the Saxons?

The Chiltern zone

The crux of these problems surely lies in the Chiltern zone. It is perfectly clear that there was hardly any Saxon settlement in the tract south of the Icknield Way in pagan times, and then to a minor extent on the fringes, mainly in comparatively late locations near the Way. The sole early exceptions are Luton and Stevenage, for which a suitable explanation can be found. Apart from the latter Sir Frank Stenton's observation over 50 years ago that 'no site between the middle Thames and the upper Lea has yielded objects which can definitely be referred to the late fifth or the early sixth century'[7] remains substantially valid and is upheld by Myres' work on Saxon pottery. To account for this remarkable situation Smith[8] suggested that in Hertfordshire at least 'a heavily wooded terrain unsuitable for their occupation probably discouraged encroachment by the East Saxons or the Angles', and Head[9] advanced a similar reason for late English entry into the Chilterns.

That explanation is manifestly inadequate, refuted as unsound by the facts of geology related in Chapter II, as by the pattern of Iron Age and Roman settlement. Throughout much of the Chiltern zone are soils highly suitable for cultivation, that as many villas show were extensively exploited in Roman times, and once broken in were not likely to have been abandoned or overlooked; the alluvial valleys and drift-covered uplands on well-drained chalk were vastly more attractive to early settlers than the repellent, endless heavy clay lands to the north which favoured a luxuriant forest growth. We recall that by the time of the Norman Conquest the population density in the whole northern half of Hertfordshire was well above average; in fact development had progressed so far that the entire district was approaching saturation point. It is no accident that here lie many deserted and shrunken villages, the result of complete clearance of the waste and the exhaustion of soil fertility.[10] The origins of heavy exploitation in a district much favoured by early cultivators must be carried back several centuries before 1086.

Such inviting territory, the rich Vale of St. Albans and the Chiltern valleys, would certainly not discourage Saxon pioneers. All offered a far better welcome than the stiff clays, and no opportunity of taking them would be neglected by men who certainly had the necessary equipment. We might have expected at least a determined nibbling at the large Chiltern zone much earlier than the 7th century and occasional successful attempts to penetrate deeply and colonize the most desirable localities, but evidently no effective inroads were made.

One particularly telling departure from the indications of geology is the absence of early Saxon occupation west of Luton on the belt of unusually attractive soils along the Icknield Way, where sites are on an almost insignificant scale and bear a markedly late complexion; none is certainly older than the late 6th century. This unconformity with the physical background is most striking because of the chain of Roman villas along the Icknield spring-line, to which there is no early Saxon counterpart. As the Icknield belt was again well populated by Norman times the significance of an unnatural omission cannot be ignored: the reach of early Saxon movement was inhibited from exploiting this favourable zone.

The missing factor

Geographical factors cannot explain pagan Saxon avoidance of the Chiltern zone, which contrasts strongly with their intensive occupation of adjacent regions, Cambridgeshire and the upper Thames. Yet the dictum that nature abhors a vacuum is perfectly applicable to human affairs; if this fertile expanse—all within a day's forced march of important early Germanic centres—was not settled by early Saxons, the conclusion is unavoidable that they failed to take possession for some compelling practical reason. The highly circumscribed extent of 5th- and early 6th-century Saxon occupation in the region demands a responsible factor operating then but no longer existing in the 7th century when the pattern was crumbling into decay.

The problem is strictly insoluble on the basis of Saxon archaeology and heathen names. The scene they evoke is seriously incomplete: some vital element which they cannot convey is missing, a clue without which the design is unintelligible. We must heed Wheeler's warning that 'the recognition of resistant but (in the archaeological sense) largely negative cultures is as essential to his [the archaeologist's] task as is the diagnosis of tangible evidence'.[11] For a meaningful ensemble it is necessary to add cognizance of another kind of evidence.

Throughout the region certain place-names (see Chapter X) betray the former presence of British people. The unusual frequency of British names here has often been noticed; *Chiltern* itself and most of the river names are Celtic. Several of these names contain elements of the native vocabulary which eventually passed into English speech and so became perpetuated in place-names, and one remarkable instance—early forms of the river name Beane—proves the existence of a living Celtic language in central Hertfordshire two centuries or more after Britain ceased to be Roman. A few other names denote English reference to the indigenous people. All these names serve as an apt reminder that early Dark Age archaeology is extraordinarily one-sided, offering the barest trace of non-English people to counterpoise the vast quantity of Saxon material—an imbalance explained later—and faintly correct a disparity which the general history of the period assures us is illusory.

The archaeological blankness of the Chiltern zone was until the late 6th century shared by most of the Ouse-Thame basin, where Myres[12] commented on the extreme dearth of early material. Professor Jackson[13] fully appreciated the implied conditions here in his remark 'the story of the battle of Bedcanford in 571 seems to point to the survival of British inhabitants as late as the third quarter of the sixth century, strong enough to have prevented much settlement in central and northern Buckinghamshire'. That judgment is equally valid for the Chiltern zone, almost untouched by Saxon settlement till the 7th century.

A British province

Only one explanation fully accounts for the situation. Saxon presence was long effectively barred from virtually the entire region by the resistance of a British redoubt able to repel external assault, prevent infiltration and regulate a few small permitted Saxon communities of the *foederati* whom we met in Chapter I; in the known context of 5th-century history these are not an embarrassing and discordant exception to the dominance of the British society they served. Nothing less can explain the massive evidence of archaeology, and the immunity of the Chiltern zone suggests where the centre of resistance lay.

From this gloss on Jackson's appraisal two further vital steps are required to reach a complete solution. First is realization that the British strength evident throughout the region betokens an organized state. The maintenance of successful defence over a long period implies nothing less than some kind of state apparatus, for an impromptu array of farmers and woodsmen without permanent leadership and planned resources would be quite incapable of sustained resistance lasting several generations. Recalling British conditions in the post-Roman world we must see a political as well as a social entity in the region.

Second, this realm must be identified with the people and continuing authority of the *civitas* of Verulamium, a city that was still functioning normally when St. Germanus visited it in 429. Knowing that this important cantonal capital possessed the official institutions and organization which the situation demands, we need look no further for the instrument of local British power. This conclusion accords with Myres' opinion[14] that the cities of southern Britain were strong enough to control their own affairs in the 5th century and bears out Morris' lesson on the integrity of British society beyond the age of Arthur.

A confused recollection of this little Dark Age state seems to have lingered in medieval Welsh tradition. Morris[15] noticed amidst an old Welsh list of 'the principal territories of Britain' one described as *Argoed* [16] *Calchvynydd rhwng Trenn ag Afon Tain*—'the land of the chalk (or limestone) hills between Trent and Thames', which is much more likely to mean the Chiltern country than the Midland oolite belt, especially as it appears next to the Silchester region. The name of one of its rulers, Cadrawd or Cadrod, seems to be preserved among 'the Men of the North' of Welsh heroic story, where it perhaps strayed because of the attraction of their fame.

Nor does Verulamium stand as a solitary instance of a British provincial capital living into the Dark Ages. Archaeology provides a powerful case for Silchester, around which lie the boundary earthworks of the *territorium*, attributed to the late 5th or 6th century.[17] Into a well in the city was thrown an Irishman's memorial stone inscribed in Ogham characters, which is 'hardly earlier and perhaps later than the sixth century'.[18] The impressive endurance of this city, dangerously exposed to the early Saxon colony on the upper Thames, neatly complements the survival of Verulamium.

The role of Verulamium

In 429 Verulamium was thriving, and archaeology confirms that Roman civilization and civic life survived there well into the 5th century. Further traces are so far unrecognized or unrecognizable, due to the physical poverty of sub-Roman culture which is explained a little later on; this applies to every Roman city. The city's strong walls conferred immunity from Saxon raids, but little Dorchester, though walled too, was at risk from its Germanic contingent, and no other local town had even ramparts. Only Verulamium was reasonably secure, and archaeology indicates that it never fell to assault.[19] Whatever happened elsewhere, there is no reason to suspect that it was supplanted by chieftains living in Iron Age style in hillforts. It is to Verulamium that we should look for the capital of this region in the post-Roman period.

Changes there would be, apart from a grave decline in material culture. During this time the provincial councils of Britain were replaced by men who usurped power, princelings in whose families that would naturally tend to descend. Gildas unsparingly rebuked the ubiquitous *tyranni* who had supplanted the patrician rulers in each province he mentioned. The incidental record of 'a man of tribunician power' in 429[20] and not many years later of Elafius who was first citizen in his realm—*regionis illius primus*—mark rapid stages in this process. Now we hear only of men like Vortigern and Ambrosius Aurelianus whose father had 'worn the purple' in imitation of imperial custom. Only in districts known to have retained their British character into historic times are such dynasties recorded, but as both rulers whom Germanus met plainly belonged to the south-east their rise seems to have been universal, affecting regions not overcome by the English till much later. This was no surprising phenomenon, for among councils composed largely of hereditary landowner-nobles, some perhaps with military experience, active leaders would emerge in the stresses of war; conditions called for commanders, not committees. There can be little doubt that the council regime at Verulamium was sooner or later followed by some *tyrannus* of Cadrawd's family who, whatever his pretensions to authority, ruled his province like a Chinese warlord.

The evolution of opinion

Fifty years ago the forthright conclusion that early Saxons failed to occupy the Chiltern region because British rule denied access was unthinkable. It is the outcome not so much of new evidence as of a gradual development of outlook. Historians were slow to acknowledge the uncompromising meaning of the evidence and in the absence of any direct witness apart from the 571 annal, which some chose to disbelieve, they hesitated to ascribe it to the endurance of British power. That judgment was inhibited by regarding the Chilterns as an unimportant backwater and underestimating the tenacity of the post-Roman world; it sprang from the predominant Germanist view that Roman Britain and Saxon England were utterly different and quite unconnected compartments, divided by a well-nigh unbridgeable breach.

That impression was drawn from Gildas, Bede and the Chronicle, and the unalloyed character of Old English society and language that seemed to prove the complete extinction of any older culture—except in the Danelaw, when there was not a shred of post-Roman evidence, and place-name studies were in their infancy. Even so it was a rather partial interpretation because it attached little importance to contrary indications in early law codes that mentioned 'Welshmen'. Since then available written sources have been extended and exhaustively dissected, and great advances made in archaeology[21] and place-names; all these compel a major revision of old simplistic views. Just as Cuvier's 'natural catastrophe' hypothesis was supplanted by the Darwin–Wallace theory of evolution, earlier historical notions of abrupt social displacement are no longer tenable. We too must think in terms of change within continuity.

The growth of awareness on the Chiltern region is instructive. In 1925 Sir Frank Stenton, writing the introduction to the English Place-Name Society's volume on Buckinghamshire,[22] expressed a most cautious view: 'no settled, peaceable, British life is likely to have survived in this region until the year 571. But it is not in itself improbable that the district to the north of the Chilterns may still have been debateable land, in which a sparse British population maintained a precarious existence, harried, perhaps, from time to time by the Saxons from beyond the Thames, but allowed to remain in occupation of its territory until the Saxons needed new land for settlement'. Although this passage expressly concerned the Ouse basin he added it was probable that 'the British inhabitants of a country which, like the Chilterns, did not invite early settlement might long remain unmolested there'.

That rather lame explanation wrongly dismissed the Chilterns as uninviting. One must remember, however, that fifty years ago many scholars were daunted by Leeds' uncontradicted claim that Saxon folk poured freely along the Icknield Way into the upper Thames region. Nevertheless Stenton's diagnosis was quite unconvincing because it simply could not account for the facts. If the Britons only continued to occupy their land on sufferance the bounds of tribal settlement would have become blurred in the course of the four generations before 571 as more powerful neighbours seized any good agricultural land they could, leaving undeniable traces of their coming in distinctive gravegoods; but nothing of the kind happened until late in the pagan period and even then it scarcely touched the Chiltern zone. If the Britons were so feeble as to be denied a 'settled, peaceable life' it is inconceivable how they could muster enough strength or organization to maintain their position so long. Nor did the proferred explanation take cognizance of the changed British fortunes that resulted in and from their victory at Badon.

Later writers were less restrained, and a decade later Hodgkin's *History of the Anglo-Saxons* and Collingwood and Myres' *Roman Britain and the English settlements* showed better understanding. Opinion had advanced enough for Dr. Hodgkin[23] to talk of 'a large pocket of Britons sheltering in the woods of the Chiltern hills', conclude that 'on the strength of the annal for 571 we can believe that the forest lands to the north and west of London remained the refuge of more or less independent Britons until that date' and hazard that 'the Britons defeated by Cuthwulf were presumably the remnants of those who had long sheltered in the forest lands of the eastern Midlands, allied perhaps with other British forces from the London–Verulamium enclave'.

Stenton's own maturer judgments in *Anglo-Saxon England*[24] stressed the severe setback suffered by the Saxons about 500 and admitted 'the evidence for a migration of Germanic peoples from Britain in the first half of the sixth century raises something more than the mere possibility that the battle of 571 meant, not the conquest of lands which had always been British, but the recovery of territory won in the first energy of the Saxon invasion and lost after the defeat at Mons Badonicus. ... on this view ... (the annal) ceases to imply that the British occupation of the plain beneath the Chilterns was unbroken for a century and a half after the severance of Britain from the Empire'. The postulated post-Badon Saxon loss of the Ouse basin still offered no satisfactory solution, for like the 'Icknield highway' theory it tacitly assumed that there was previously nothing to hinder Saxon settlement. The recognition of British power at a late date was however an important advance, though without awareness that a local British regime must have been responsible. Copley[25] conceded virtual British control of the area between Luton and Dorchester but also failed to realize that this implied something more stable than 'British bands in their upland fastnesses', and although he visualized a British community surviving round Verulamium he did not suspect that the institutions of the city and its canton were the key.

With the admission of British strength recent scholars concur,[26] and Frere[27] carrying this logic to its conclusion bluntly averred 'the Chilterns did form a British reserve until the renewal of Saxon conquest in this area in 571'. The denouement of the problem that once vexed historians is implicit in his verdict on Verulamium: 'If life there survived until the German tide was halted late in the fifth century by the British recovery signalised for us by the battle of Mt. Badon there was nothing to prevent it continuing peacefully until the Saxon victories of 571'—a far cry from the halting diagnosis of 1925, since it envisaged the lengthy survival of a post-Roman regime.

'571' clearly marks some critical event in the region. We are tempted to assume that a resoundingly defeated British state then came to an end and was promptly absorbed into an English realm, but judgments on the annal's full significance, the fate of the native people, and whether the precise date given by the Chronicle is correct should be reserved until the whole evidence from both the English and British sides has been considered.

The hypothesis of a small British dominion, which is consistent with an abundance of detailed evidence yet to be seen, provides a convincing answer to the sceptics who once assumed there could be no effective British authority at this date in the southern Midlands. This local regime must have formed an integral part of the wide British society that survived far into the 6th century. Although of this principality there is no trace other than the 571 annal in early historical sources, and of its people and culture as yet scarcely any physical remains to show, something of its character and relations with early Saxons can be deduced.

The silences of history and archaeology

A Dark Age British realm enduring in the Chiltern region presents a double paradox, historical and archaeological. With the exception of the oblique and sibylline 571 annal and the Welsh memory of *Calchvynydd* nothing is recorded of it, not far though it was from several early English kingdoms. Extant sources are however highly selective and for that reason beguiling. The Chronicle's early devotion to Kent, Sussex and the Solent area can easily encourage us to forget that similar but unrecorded struggles happened elsewhere. These were not the only theatres, as Nennius' mention of Octha[28] in the north and speculation that some of Arthur's battles took place there remind us. Unsung, the East Riding suffered the same fate as Kent, and there were other Germanic settlements of like origin round which the conflicts of the time could revolve. The Saxon hosts in East Anglia were as strong as Hengist's men in Kent, to judge from numerous early cemeteries, but we hear nothing of them. If the Saxons were baulked on the Chiltern front, they seldom boasted of defeats and until the 7th century they were illiterate, unlike the Britons. Early West Saxon traditions embodied in the Chronicle had no reason to be concerned with outside events in this quarter, and the Kentish and South Saxon annals of their neighbours are really an irrelevance to be grateful for.

If the Chronicle's outlook often amounts to West Saxon bias or lack of interest, Gildas' other side of the story can also be most deceptive. It is apparent that he was writing of the world he knew and not well informed of the past, nor interested in it for its own sake. He shows no acquaintance beyond the parts of Britain he mentions, Wales, the south-west and their marches. Of British states that existed elsewhere he has no word: he refers to neither Elmet nor other northern British realms which survived for nearly a century afterwards, and ignores the regions whose capitals were once Winchester, Silchester and Verulamium, which did not then form part of the Saxon domains. His silence does not prove that these territories retained no organized British states.

Although only meagre traces of the local British inhabitants of this age have yet been discovered there is unfortunately nothing peculiar about the Chiltern region in this respect. In the 5th century Britain slid rapidly into a sub-Roman phase where the tangible apparatus of Roman civilization—building in stone and brick, coins, mass-produced pottery, domestic utensils of durable materials and fine metalwork—ceased to exist, and reversion to more primitive conditions entailed recourse to barter. Instead what Wheeler[29] aptly called a 'negative culture' made use of perishable wood, bone, leather and cloth, which in our climate have not normally survived to attract the archaeologist's notice. It is impossible to believe the Britons no longer made or used iron tools, but as a Scottish antiquary remarked a century ago 'old iron is shovelled into oblivion without a moment's hesitation'.[30] Unless accompanied by artifacts of known typology shapelessly corroded pieces of metal are unrecognized and disregarded.

In the Celtic world inscribed memorials were confined to stony regions. For prehistoric periods the archaeologist depends heavily upon tombs and the pottery and weapons laid with the dead, but this sort of evidence fails him in the post-Roman era as Christians abandoned gravegoods. A chalice buried with a medieval priest is a mark of sanctity, not superstition. Apart from partly furnished cemeteries of the Chamberlain's Barn II overlap type Christian burials of the Dark Ages, like those of medieval date, are universally lacking in gravegoods; except for their west-east alignment they are unrecognizable and quite undatable. It is hardly surprising that museum showcases are almost bare of artifacts from a British milieu to set beside the wealth of material from pagan graves; if the Saxon settlers had been Christians we would know little about them. In the present state of knowledge British society has left virtually no identifiable structures or artifacts to vouch for its existence outside the south-west. Elsewhere little serious attempt has been made to seek objects made or used by post-Roman Britons, and as the Latimer site shows more could be done to redress the balance. Regrettably, the uppermost levels of Roman sites that might supply the want have been severely affected by ploughing, spoliation and inadequate excavation. Nevertheless with the technical resources now at the archaeologist's command we should not despair of eventually learning considerably more about the physical remains of the British side, and a strong plea should be entered for the careful examination of Dark Age levels at places like Verulamium—most of its 200 acres are still undisturbed—that might yield this evidence.

Latimer and recent work at Verulamium were a welcome local beginning in this direction. In the south-west of England and further north, mainly near the western seaboard, numbers of Celtic sites belonging to this age are now known, following the recognition in the 1930s of imported Gaulish and Mediterranean pottery,[31] recently identified in London.[32] We can confidently expect the list of pottery-verified British sites to grow, and it would be no surprise if these exotic wares turned up at Verulamium.

It cannot be too strongly emphasized that by its very nature any British community in south-east or central England that became absorbed into the dominant social stream would leave no historical traces in English or Celtic tradition. It had no political heirs to perpetuate its memory and left no distinct class to carry on its cultural heritage. Its society was fragmented and destined soon to be assimilated.

Early law codes reveal a transitional stage that distinguished dispersed grades of incorporated natives whose blood compensation payments—*wergilds*—were below their English counterparts', not a setting in which the deeds of British leaders were likely to be long recalled or committed to writing. The losing side left no one to honour it, except in Cymru.

Almost everywhere there is a marked contrast between post-Roman archaeology and the historical evidence we possess. We know of powerful British kingdoms whose rulers—the *Gwyr y Gogledd*, 'the men of the north' celebrated in early Welsh poetry and the pages of Nennius' *Historia Brittonum*—were mighty enough to raise armies that held the Northumbrians at bay for generations. One famous poem, the *Gododdin*, is all that is left to commemorate a kingdom whose capital was Edinburgh until its capture in 638. Yet about the British in southern Scotland at that time archaeology until recently counted little but religious sites including long cist cemeteries and a handful of chieftains' tombs.[33]

This example is a salutary reminder that although the Midlands and the south were not fortunate enough to preserve even a shadowy recollection of their post-Roman phase, the apparent absence of non-Saxon traces is no warrant to suppose it never existed. Wheeler's dictum about negative cultures should not be forgotten. The Chiltern region is not the only one where Dark Age British archaeology is represented by a blank space on the map; another was the Pennines where the British Church survived in places until the mid 7th century. Surely neither was empty of the people at whom the ubiquitous transmission of pre-English place-names hints.

Until the late 6th and early 7th centuries the western two-thirds of England was still in British hands, and its fate was not decided until the aggressive wars of Ceawlin, Ethelfrith and Edwin overwhelmed regions from the Thames to the West Riding. Before being submerged by the English tide all these territories must have shared the sub-Roman character we can detect in the Celtic lands of the far west that remained free from anglicization till the conquest of Cornwall and Wales. Until overcome by Cuthwulf the Chiltern region belonged to that world.

The Chiltern region and the British revival

The conclusion that formidable British power protected its Chiltern homeland helps to explain the Britons' revival that culminated in victory at Badon. How they rebuilt their damaged fortunes is a mystery, but the language of Gildas and Nennius points to two generations of see-saw struggle in which they eventually got the upper hand. We can speculate that various regions probably played a part by independent military action or by supporting the national leaders, Ambrosius Aurelianus and Arthur. Obviously some important provinces remained relatively unimpaired and retained their organization fairly intact throughout the period of strife, for without such nuclei the Britons could not have offered prolonged resistance and achieved final success.

The brunt of the defence against Saxon marauders must have fallen to the most romanized parts of Britain that lay within striking distance of the primary Saxon areas in Kent, East Anglia and the east Midlands. Among exposed regions important parts were probably played by the cantons based on Silchester and Winchester[34] —notwithstanding the early Wessex annals in the Chronicle—and no doubt by London so long as it survived. They may have been supported by the rich villa country of the Cotswolds.

To all these states and more the possibility of unchecked invasion from East Anglia and the Wash meant a grave peril. One obstacle alone stood in the way of this threat; the Verulamium canton was inevitably in the front line and its resistance was of vital importance to the whole of southern Britain. If it collapsed the strategic outlook for the rest would be bleak.

That the Chiltern realm did not succumb until long after the 5th-century wars the 571 annal and the emphatically negative evidence of archaeology prove. Its endurance goes far to explain why the campaigns ultimately went in the Britons' favour, and why as Myres[35] observed the decay of British authority in the Midlands was evidently not shared by the southern cities. In itself the British victory was not surprising, since with them long lay the advantage of greatly superior manpower,[36] but to make that tell the organization of the provincial states was essential. Undoubtedly we should recognize in the Chiltern region one of the leading British territories in those wars, a bastion of British strength that made possible their general resurgence towards the end; without the survival of the Verulamium regime their recovery and victory would not be credible.

The East Anglian dykes

Regained British mastery at Badon tilted the balance of power and caused wide repercussions, such as an exodus of despairing Saxons from Britain to the continent related by Procopius. The new situation is perhaps commemorated by some of the East Anglian dykes which may well belong to this context. This series of linear earthworks straddles the Icknield Way, the westernmost near Royston, but two that appear to be entirely pre-Roman can be ignored. All possess a ditch on the western side of the bank, that is they face south-west and betoken a threat from that quarter. They are substantial works: the Devil's Ditch on Newmarket Heath is 7½ miles long and at one point its rampart still stands 60 feet above the ditch bottom.

The making or improvement of these enormous defences implies grave insecurity but there has been no unanimity about their precise date and circumstances. Excavation has shown they are at least partly of post Roman construction and it is agreed they cannot be later than the 7th century.[37] Some have connected them with frontier struggles between Mercia and East Anglia but history is against this theory.[38] Lethbridge's idea that they were built to pen up Saxon raiders with the aid of cavalry in the last decades of Roman rule[39] is more ingenious than satisfactory.

If the dykes antedate the rise of Mercia the most tenable candidate for the role of aggressor is the British state based on Verulamium, towards which the defences appear to point. Certainly a thrust from the Chiltern Britons, flushed with victory about the time of Badon, has a better claim than a hypothetical *drang nach osten* by the discrete Middle Angles, who were unable to resist digestion by Mercia. Phillips[40] considered the dykes 'may be the relic of a post-Mons Badonicus sixth century phase in which Anglo-Saxons in temporary retreat secured themselves in East Anglia against British pressure', and if so it is difficult to see who but the Chiltern Britons could have been responsible for the threat. Blair[41] conjectured the builders were refugees who had been compelled to leave the upper Thames.

It is conceivable that in the season of Badon the alarmed eastern neighbours of the Chiltern region, joined perhaps by displaced Saxon settlers, decided to demarcate and fortify their boundary against British expansion or assault. The dykes suggest stages in retreat rather than advance, for the westernmost, Heydon Ditch, seems intended to cover some Saxon villages near Cambridge, while the Fleam[42] Ditch lies behind them, hinting that an attempt to hold the first line failed and that the defenders were forced to fall back on a second. In that case the even mightier Devil's Ditch might indicate a final and successfully held frontier.

On this interpretation the East Anglian dykes would not only massively illustrate Blair's reminder that 'British opposition to the Anglo-Saxon invasions was conducted with greater skill and effectiveness than has often been supposed', but also show that at its greatest extent the lordship of the Chiltern region was once wider and more powerful than Cuthwulf's campaign suggests.

Chapter VII

ARCHAEOLOGY AND THE EARLIEST
SAXON SETTLEMENTS

THE ORIGINS OF local Saxon settlement must be sought in the plain that stretches from the upper Thames to the Ivel, where a few sites offer sure evidence of 5th-century foundation and for others a relatively early date can be suspected. But these were not the first Germanic people to live in the region.

An intimate Saxon relationship with Britain goes back at least to late Roman times when the presence of some Germans among mercenary reinforcements is strongly suggested by finds of the types of military equipment decorated in late imperial style—buckles and the like mentioned in Chapter IV. One of these buckles found among rubbish thrown in the Verulamium theatre in the late 4th or early 5th century does not prove the presence of imperial troops, because Roman contingents marching along Watling Street must often have visited the city, but it perhaps belonged to a territorial detachment. Amidst the same rubbish was a sherd of 'Romano-Saxon' ware—of normal Romano-British shape ornamented in barbarian fashion—that may have been made specially for the taste of the Germanic soldiers who were numerous in the late Roman army.

The classic site for a definite association is Dorchester-on-Thames where it was first recognized that Germanic auxiliaries and their families were established within a small Roman town under late imperial rule. Fortunately, though the male burial of Dorchester I denotes no more than a Roman officer who happened to be a German, the female graves of Dorchester I and II assure us that his contingent, probably a specially recruited body of mercenaries, was accompanied by women-folk of his own race. The new site at Berinsfield (Dorchester III), yielding a very early 5th-century 'Luton type' brooch, seems to show a similar function of this kind of generation or more later.

Other sites that produced early 5th-century material, but not in a Roman context, lie in Bedfordshire. Kempston, Sandy and Luton I are all sites with cremation, an early rite[1] that is pronounced at Sandy and probably predominated in the first phases of the other two. The oldest of the Kempston finds have a very early look, and others are not much later. Some of these relics—a very rare 'Luton type' brooch as early as about 425, a window urn, other pottery, perhaps a saucer brooch with five running spirals—fit a date before Hengist's historic revolt about 442, and fragments of military accoutrements, no doubt locally derived, are decisive of period and character. At a time when British authority was still in unchallenged control these can only mean the official settlement of a community of Germanic *foederati* and their families, introduced by Vortigern and deliberately stationed for defensive

51

purposes. The cemetery begins too early to represent an unlicensed land-taking following Hengist's outbreak when British rulers were too weak or too occupied to prevent it, and one or two of the earliest pots may betray native influence.

If we had any doubt of the right explanation Kempston's situation would help to resolve it. It is by no means an ideal place to settle, but it adjoins a paved ford that carried a Roman road[2] across the Ouse, and 'the earliest settlements are found in places advantageous to the defence of Roman Britain, rather than on the easiest agricultural land'.[3] The riverside position superficially resembles Dorchester's but was not a strategic one as the location was more exposed. Its special purpose may be read in the context of a time when Saxon settler-troops were engaged to counter plundering ship-borne bands for whom unregarded waterways were a tempting means of entry. The post seems designed to block the Ouse, one of the principal natural routes into the heart of the southern Midlands. It is not difficult to visualize that the *raison d'être* of its detachment was to deny raiders access in this direction and especially to prevent river pirates infiltrating upstream. An instance of similar tactics in the Viking period comes to mind in the Chronicle's annal for 895 (corrected date) recording a Danish fortress on the Lea 20 miles above London and Alfred's riposte in erecting English forts on both sides of the river to guard a specially made obstruction—probably the weir that gave Ware its name; the Danes were forced to abandon their vessels caught upstream. This incident suggests that traces of something like a weir or strong point may be found on the Ouse near Kempston. If this was the intention behind the choice of location it appears to have been remarkably successful, as there is no sign of Saxon settlement up river before the late 6th century, a phenomenon otherwise difficult to explain.

Further east Sandy, adjoining a major Roman settlement, has produced several urns of 5th-century date including one probably from its first half, and the emphasis on cremation suggests an early date. This site too may be due to tactical siting as it stands beside the Ivel at the junction of the main Roman road and a spur leading towards Kempston.

The Luton I cemetery at Argyll Avenue claims a very early origin. Some of its pottery is late 5th century but a few objects are certainly older. An example of the rare 'Luton type' brooch that belongs to about 400 or not much later, and a broken piece of a buckle of 'military' design found in a woman's grave of the 6th century, perhaps an heirloom belonging to a descendant of a Germanic soldier-settler, give a clear indication of a neighbouring settlement of the pre-Hengist age, another small Saxon detachment comparable with Kempston. The position beside the Icknield Way and not far from Watling Street guarded an obvious gap made by the Lea in the lower Chilterns.

Besides this short roll-call of definite early 5th-century sites the group in the vicinity of Aylesbury merits attention because although only one of its half-dozen small sites is provably early—most if not all the rest are certainly late—they have yielded some noteworthy articles. The Bishopstone plate, an early 5th-century belt piece decorated with animal motif, may have been derived from some local settlement of barbarian *foederati* but was clearly interred generations later. This and an imported glass beaker from Dinton, which dates from the 5th or early 6th century and was also old when buried in a later cemetery, have been taken as proof of a Frankish element involved in Hengist's wars;[4] this far-fetched claim strained too slender evidence. The proximity of these late sites has long been enough to suggest the possibility of an undiscovered earlier local settlement whence both survivals might have come.

That gap now seems to be filled. Recent excavations at Walton on the fringe of Aylesbury itself, just off Akeman Street, discovered a type IB 'military' buckle, which may well be derived from *foederati*; pottery from here 'ranges from the early fifth well into the sixth century, perhaps later', and apparently associated sunken huts were found, the earliest hovelish. We may have here part of the previously suspected primary settlement from which the Dinton and Bishopstone finds could have been handed down.

The cumulative effect of the earliest evidence from Kempston, Sandy, Luton and now Aylesbury reinforces the conclusion that all were quasi-military Saxon settlements of an official character, founded where the requirements of a British government dictated; in an unregulated scramble relics of 5th-century occupation would certainly have been much more widespread. Thus, following the late Roman example of Germanic soldiers with their womenfolk at Dorchester, we can discern four more Saxon settlements of partly military character in the first half of the 5th century that were the result of Vortigern's defence policy. They illustrate our knowledge of political history from written sources, for even if some of the belt equipment was once worn by civil officials it would be equally valid proof of very early contact between Saxon communities at these places and British authorities.

The fate of the early Saxon settlers

About 442 the revolt of Hengist in Kent and allies in regions like East Anglia began a contest of strength between the Britons and their new subjects who were determined to break away and enlarge their territory. We are ignorant how widespread the conflict was; north of the Thames nothing is known of a struggle that lasted half a century and led up to the decisive British victory at Badon which both exemplified and cemented British resistance. Any local effect of this conflict and its sequel must be judged by looking at available archaeological evidence for signs whether the few original Saxon settlements were forcibly extinguished, as Stenton envisaged, or, perhaps reinforced, took an opportunity to begin expanding and founded fresh settlements.

At Dorchester the continuity of a Saxon population can be supported on historical[5] and archaeological grounds, the latter strengthened by recent discoveries at Berinsfield. The town developed as a civil centre and about 634 was important enough to be chosen as Birinus' see. Whatever its eventual fate, the context suggests that after 410 the station would be maintained by one of the provincial authorities, the Verulamium *civitas* whose boundary here was surely the Thames. Yet it is remarkable that in this corner of Oxfordshire with considerable areas of favourable soils there are so few other signs of early Saxon occupation: in fact only outside the limits of this study, at Wheatley and in the Cherwell valley. Local Saxon expansion occurred only on the Berkshire side of the river. These features tell heavily against a suggestion[6] that Dorchester's Germanic garrison seized control before the town emerged into historic times.

That there was no complete break in the exiguous Saxon settlement in the north-east of the region is also fairly clear. Kempston exhibits prolonged occupation, and the only possible time of any interruption is the first half of the 6th century, to which few objects are definitely datable, perhaps because of selective recovery during defective observation. Refoundation on an abandoned site, however, seems most unlikely. The absence of early settlements higher up the Ouse has already been noted, but the absolute lack of early sites representing expansion from Kempston itself is equally obvious. Woefully incomplete evidence at Sandy points to survival into and perhaps beyond the early 6th century, but early expansion thence up the Ivel valley is entirely missing. These places seem to have remained isolated and restricted by effective British control over the district.

Continuity is assured at Walton near Aylesbury and at Luton I where most finds belong to the 6th century. That cemetery extends no further than the late 6th century and its abandonment may have been caused by migration then to the historic site of Luton beside the Lea.

In contrast to Sandy and Kempston there appears to have been some comparatively early expansion in the district west of Luton, for though our knowledge of cemeteries there is too slight for sure dating a few probably did belong to secondary settlements founded before the late 6th century. The single grave at Limbury is inconclusive but the group I burials at Puddlehill can hardly be later than 550. Lamentably the important cemetery at Toddington II, Warmark, was badly recorded and all the finds have gone; according to an eyewitness it contained many cremations, although we need not believe in the reputed thousand burials. Its sheer size might imply foundation as early as the 5th century, but the known objects are much later. A little distance away the Deadman's Slade cemetery at Leighton Buzzard that flourished in the mid to late 6th century may have begun earlier, to judge from the description of the lost pots. The sherd from Totternhoe II could be either side of 500. There is enough collective indication from this district to raise something stronger than suspicion that it contained a few 5th- or early 6th-century settlements, though perhaps none as old as the primary sites.

The only other possible trace of early expansion is the Stevenage hut that produced wares of the late 5th century but nothing later, and a 'military' strap-end that was presumably ultimately derived from an older site, probably Luton. This site may have been abruptly ended and there is no hint of neighbouring growth, unless a puzzling brooch that perhaps came from Hitchin.

Stenton[7] was therefore mistaken in saying that 'the historical evidence ... clashes uncompromisingly with any theory that the country between the upper Lea and the Thames was occupied continuously by Saxon settlers from the fifth century into historic times', for in addition to certain survival at Luton finds imply Saxon occupation further west that began or was active in the early 6th century; the evidence from Warwark, Puddlehill, Deadman's Slade and Totternhoe, while singly inconclusive, supports this.

Yet the archaeological record for the Ouse-Thame basin substantially bears out Stenton's impression that early Saxon settlement there did not prosper, for plainly it long failed to achieve free expansion. Even if Warmark, Deadman's Slade and Puddlehill did not go back beyond 500 they appear to mark the only successful new footholds gained during the century or more after Hengist's time, significantly confined to a limited and exceptional district; why is discussed later. While there is no indication that any settlements were evacuated as Stenton imagined, neither is there a shred of reliable evidence for the foundation of new sites elsewhere in the first half of the 6th century. If we subtract from the archaeological ensemble the Warmark group,the rare oldest sites presumed to continue into the 6th century and those, much more numerous, that began in or after the late 6th century, we are left with a short undetermined list, most of them probably quite late, and a few where no date can be hazarded; none of the problematical sites is large enough to be classed as a cemetery.

We gain the profound impression that apart from the Dunstable district new foundations before the late 6th century can only have been insignificant. Particularly striking is the complete dearth of earlier sites on the Icknield tract that was especially attractive for settlement. The general absence or extreme rarity of new settlements is reminiscent of the observation[8] 'over most of Buckinghamshire there is virtually no Anglo-Saxon pottery on record at all until the last quarter of the 6th century'. Thus instead of Stenton's supposed hiatus an astonishing contrast appears: static occupation and tightly contained expansion entirely absent in the Chiltern zone save for a single spark at Stevenage, and in the Ouse basin restricted to one district—preceding a massive proliferation of new settlements from the late 6th century onwards.

None of this picture is really surprising. Wide failure to create fresh Saxon settlements in the later 5th and early 6th centuries, not only near the original *foederati* stations but almost everywhere in the region, is explained by the ascendancy of British authority over most of England till the late 6th century, manifested in a local regime whose mastery thwarted Saxon colonization until an advanced date. Until its conquest in 571 the Ouse-Thame basin remained an integral part of the British province, not open to immigrants; the exceptional toleration limited to the Dunstable district is explicable without vitiating this verdict.

In absolute terms the earliest local Saxon communities were almost negligible. Amounting to a trifling proportion of the region's population, they were too feeble to challenge British rule unless supported by numerous and powerful compatriots. Otherwise a serious risk of their getting out of hand could only arise in the event of a catastrophic fall in the native population, which seems quite unlikely in a mainly agricultural economy except for some demographic disaster such as the Yellow Plague of about 550, which not long preceded the British collapse and seems to have affected these people much more harshly than their English neighbours.[9]

Isolated acts of communal violence and petty insurrection there may have been, such as could account for the early warrior at Puddlehill, but not the Letchworth casualty who perished in some quarrel or dispute after the British regime came to an end. Probably the only occasion before 571 when the regime might have chanced peril or anarchy was the warfare following the onset of Hengist's rebellion, but if the Chiltern Britons were ever momentarily worsted they must have quickly recovered. The newcomers notably failed to make any encroachment at any time before 571 save for a minor and probably short-lived attempt at Stevenage, a unique exception likely to denote an unsuccessful venture to exploit the rich lands of north Hertfordshire at some moment before Badon when Verulamium was weak or acquiescent, but soon suppressed in favour of a concession in the less desirable country near Dunstable.

It is most unlikely that the early Saxon communities in the valley shared in Hengist's rebellion or revolted during the Badonic wars. Even before Badon the general immunity of the region suggests that British rulers would have no difficulty in asserting their lordship over a sparse Saxon population, even in displacing it if they wished. Except for a possible interval or decline at Kempston early in the 6th century—after Badon— nothing hints the primary settlements were disturbed, nothing indicates the flight of their people. This cannot mean these enjoyed an independent existence, for their inability to acquire fresh sites near Kempston and Sandy plainly shows unbroken control by the British who had once planted them to assist in their own protection. In a frontier zone stalemate might result from the inability of either side to overwhelm the other, but in the Chiltern context the fortunes of these early Saxons must have depended on British dictation, not forbearance.

The survival of these few small communities points to some *modus vivendi* permitting their continuation on a regulated basis. No doubt their dispositions were strictly controlled to prevent them becoming dangerous; the British regimes that outlived Hengist's wars will have learned their lesson and resolved not to let their subjects grow too strong. Their loyalty would be rewarded by being allowed to keep possession of their originally granted lands provided they obeyed British authority, paid tribute and perhaps gave hostages to ensure compliance. Satisfied that such methods would keep a few dubious subjects docile, and reluctant to deprive themselves of a source of food-rents and auxiliary manpower by ejecting people who had been installed with the sanction of their own authority, British rulers in a confident mood overlooked that failure to destroy the Saxon concentrations outside the region incurred the risk of ultimate English domination.

The Dunstable district

The marked disparity of treatment between the isolated northern stations and the favoured Saxon group who used the cemeteries near Dunstable needs accounting for. The remote posts at Kempston and Sandy where a firm hand forbad expansion had a blockhouse and intelligence role, preventing or giving warning of the passage of intruders, that could be fulfilled by small numbers. They were not on the likeliest line of attack; they might be suborned or overawed by powerful Saxon neighbours to the east; but they could easily be watched by wary British liaison officers. From the British point of view it was unnecessary and imprudent to allow expansion there.

It is the anomalous Dunstable district, enjoying different conditions, that requires explanation. Moreover it is quite impossible to regard its settlements as the result of expansion from Luton, which would be too small to provide a sufficient surplus of people. We are therefore driven to acknowledge a peculiar case of permitted post-Hengist immigration or build-up.

The communications of the district offer a clue to the reason for this. It was a strategic position near the crossing of Watling Street and Icknield Way, whence most parts of the region were easily accessible, and one likely to be chosen by a local British government for placing reserves intended to protect its city and counter the formidable menace of the Saxons in Cambridgeshire and East Anglia, not far distant along the Icknield Way which was the most vulnerable approach. Defence priorities changed when these wrested their independence; the need was not for more frontier posts but for more central reserves. If the nearness of potentially unreliable troops to Verulamium seemed to pose an undesirable threat, consideration of the eastern danger must have outweighed it.

One piece of place-name evidence may perhaps corroborate the implied military function of the Dunstable district. A few miles to the south is Studham (*stōd-hām* '*hām* where horses are bred'), a very early type of place-name on which Dr. Cox[10] remarked 'it is possible to see this site as an important one for the mounted cavalry of the Germanic *foederati*'.

Having found a motive for this development we seek an occasion. Savory[11] made the intriguing suggestion that about the time of Badon some defeated Saxon war-bands accepted the status of vassals under British princes. A more likely solution, however, is that newcomers whom the Britons lodged as farmer-warriors near Dunstable were border communities in the Cambridge direction who already owed allegiance to the Chiltern regime and had proved trustworthy, and were deliberately uprooted and resettled in the rear for their own safety as well as state security on fresh grants of land, perhaps from former imperial domains that were still maintained. Such an event is less likely to have happened during the early warfare after Hengist's revolt than in the recrudescence of fighting that led to Badon, when the East Anglian danger would be more developed.

The British frontiers

The limits of local British authority perhaps varied from time to time. Whether any of their Saxon neighbours represented by the Cambridgeshire cemeteries outside this study remained under British subjection is unclear—apparent cultural differences between the people of south-west Cambridgeshire and others may be relevant—but there can be little doubt that the border with hostile barbarians lay not far beyond Royston, at times no further than the great dykes across the Icknield Way. On the south the region was delimited by the Thames and the London territory. A natural northern boundary for a British realm that included the lowland below the Chilterns would be the meandering Ouse, but this would conflict with Myres' suggestion that reinforcements to the upper Thames used that route to the Cherwell. Yet it is hard to believe many Saxons came this way before the late 6th century, for there is not a single earlier Saxon site near the Ouse, but only a small late group at Newport Pagnell and a pair of saucer brooches of about 600 near Buckingham; it seems that Kempston long played its intended part, stopping ingress upstream. Evidently the effective frontier was further north, perhaps on the Nene a dozen miles away, which runs parallel to the Ouse but takes a less sinuous course.

West of the Chilterns, where the upper Thames doubtless formed the bounds of the Verulamium realm, Dorchester seems to have long remained under its lordship, as early Saxon offshoots are unknown in the Thame valley. Reinforcing this belief is the need for strong defences in this quarter because of the remarkable contrast on the opposite bank, where early Saxon villages were thriving; Myres[12] called attention to 'something that looks uncommonly like a political frontier along the Berkshire bank of the Thames'. These communities either succeeded in throwing off the British yoke or made advantageous terms with the provincial capital at Silchester, for unlike Dorchester they were spreading. Pottery distribution convinced Myres[13] that the Abingdon Saxons were heavily reinforced by fresh contingents coming overland from the north-east during a phase of uncontrolled settlement after Hengist's outbreak. Driven to a similar but chronologically imprecise conclusion by the evidence of brooches, Leeds[14] fifty years ago pointed without hesitation to the Icknield Way as the primary route of immigration to the upper Thames.

The Icknield Way theory

As the preceding survey shows, Leeds' views on the role played by the Icknield Way in the migration age need revision. It has become quite impossible to reconcile the archaeological picture of early avoidance with his tenaciously held hypothesis[15] that the Way acted as an early corridor connecting the primary Saxon areas around Cambridge and Abingdon and 'unquestionably' served as the main route of a migration *en masse*[16] to the latter. The awkward lack of intermediate early sites between Luton and Goring on the enticing tract of soils and springs below the Chiltern scarp, as if it were shunned, though exploited in Roman and Norman times, was always a grave objection which Leeds[17] tried to avoid by predicating a double-pronged south-westwards movement with a main thrust via Sandy, Kempston, Toddington, Leighton Buzzard and Ashendon, shedding large numbers of settlers at the first two sites and so leaving conveniently little trace of its path farther west. But as Leeds himself remarked 'it is a weak argument that explains the absence of cemeteries by non-discovery'![18]

Although there are undeniable resemblances between the cultures of Middle Anglia and the upper Thames, even finds at Luton and Abingdon[19] of square-headed brooches cast from the same mould, to account for them it is unnecessary to think of the Way of the scene of any folk movement as Leeds supposed. There is more than one grave objection to the theory and the want of early links connecting Luton and the Thames, though the simplest, is not the most destructive. That the whole northern valley shared the early emptiness of the Icknield tract is far more damaging. In imagining something like a Wild West wagon trail Leeds gave insufficient thought to dating when he advanced his hypothesis.

The mainspring of Leeds' once plausible idea was largely demolished by his own revised dating of the first Germanic burials at Dorchester as late Roman, and by reinterpreting the first Saxon settlers as officially engaged *foederati* stationed at government direction, whose early 5th-century settlements took place not in a

Roman setting but under a British regime. These entirely obviate any need to invent free mass migration to account for their presence.

The *coup de grace* was Myres' demonstration[20] that later immigrants travelled by rivers well to the north—he proposed the Ouse, but the Nene is more likely—and possibly by the lower Thames, which ended the hopeless task of squaring the supposed function of the Icknield Way as a major migration route with the absolute lack of evidence for its contemporary use. A tendency to accept Leeds' solution stultified consideration of riverways, always a feasible alternative since it appears that the invaders normally travelled by this means.[21]

To avoid the obvious difficulty posed by Leeds' theory some[22] imagined Saxon bands travelling the length of the Way unhindered to the safe haven of their Thames colony, yet without daring to establish intermediate settlements because passage was permitted on condition they did not linger—an absurd compromise, for Britons able to harass convoys and forbid Saxon settlement would be too sensible to connive at their own envelopment by such toleration.

Cultural connexions

If the notion of an early folk movement peopling the upper Thames directly from Cambridgeshire collapses, cultural similarities still need explanation. Abandoning Leeds' theory does not entirely rule out social connexions with the Chiltern region at various times, but an acceptable solution must reckon with known political realities. What those links imply can be judged by looking closely at their nature and dating with that framework in mind. Given the historical background any resemblances before the mid 5th century should merely illustrate the integral nature of the British world of which the region formed part; in the succeeding age we might detect whether its small Germanic communities were in contact with and affected by external influences such as 'Saxon' and 'Anglian' fashions, or immune to them; widespread connexions after about 571 would confirm the surmise that the events related by the Chronicle gave the English undisputed possession, and possibly point to the directions whence they came.

Quite another line of interpretation is nevertheless conceivable, with little bearing on political conditions. It is legitimate to ask whether observable patterns of evolution and the spread of brooch designs could be the result of mere fashion, while the Icknield Way and half-derelict Roman roads served as trade routes for pedlars of bronzesmiths' work or the craftsmen themselves. To some extent the popularity of various motifs was clearly a matter of taste, as West Saxon fondness for 'leg' patterns shows. Lethbridge[23] robustly asserted that an object's findspot 'may be merely a question of salesmanship' and visualized 'established firms catering for barbaric taste on a large scale'; the idea cannot be readily dismissed, for it seems unlikely that most Saxon villages contained craftsmen with the skill to produce these neatly cast and tooled articles or capable of passable imitations of new designs. Certainly the most reasonable explanation for the distribution of the distinctive Maltese cross saucer brooches is that they were all sold by itinerant traders from one centre of origin. Imitations tell a different story. The scroll cross brooches from Bishopstone are a clever copy of a design found elsewhere only at Lyminge, Kent, and only close comparison reveals coarser, slightly inaccurate detail and triflingly different dimensions; but although we can credit that the Buckinghamshire ones were made locally, their maker must have carefully studied a perfect original. The Mentmore brooch, however, is so crude that it was probably copied from memory. It is perhaps unsafe to claim that distribution maps convey more than different and possibly shifting trading zones, within the bounds of acceptable taste, with harmless solitary traders being allowed to move freely.

It is easy to under-rate the facility of early trade. To take an example from the Middle Ages when each local potter commonly supplied a dozen neighbouring villages, the products of kilns near Oxford[24] were traded as far afield as Cambridge about 1300, when most roads were probably in little better condition than in the Dark Ages. We should not overlook that objects less cumbrous and fragile than pottery might travel considerable distances to willing buyers if unhindered by effective barriers, and perhaps in the course of time far from their original owners.

Cultural connexions in the Saxon world are exhibited in brooches and pottery, and the former can readily be classified. Saucer brooches, cast and applied, are by far the commonest kind in the region: 105 are known, the majority from Kempston (34), Luton I (20) and Dorchester III (19). Apart from the proto-cruciform of Roman date from Dorchester I there are only six cruciforms, all but one from Kempston, and six each of equal-armed and great square-headed brooches. Ceramic forms are more varied and their ornament protean in its diversity, but the Buckelurn types of the later 5th century and just after and the stamped pendent triangle panel style of the last decades of the 6th may be singled out as easily placed.

The earliest links show up in a few brooches datable to the first half of the 5th century. The extremely early 'Luton' type brooches from Kempston, Luton and Dorchester III and equal-armed ones from Kempston and Dorchester III have continental 'Saxon' connexions. A different tradition associated later with 'Anglian' fashions is seen in the cruciform brooches; at Kempston two come from the mid 5th century and two from later in the century. This particular strain soon fades: Kempston has only one later cruciform, of the later 6th century, and one from Toddington is contemporary. Nowhere in the region are found the florid later cruciforms or ornate wrist clasps that would speak of continuing relations where 'Anglian' styles prevailed. Plainly, whereas Kempston maintained some contact with Middle Anglia until the end of the 5th century it was thereafter isolated; this accords with the harsh political picture of repressed Saxon people inhabiting a British march firmly sealed off against the barbarian world outside after the Germanic reverse at Badon.

The absence of cruciforms at Luton and Dorchester might suggest that early relations with neighbouring Germanic peoples were never really close, and this impression is rather borne out by the Buckelurn pots that occur on four local sites and repeat the story told by brooches. The successive models of these wares seem to have spread from East Anglia. The earliest belong to group I, found at Kempston, Sandy and Luton, and group II which occurs at Kempston and Stevenage. Stylistically later are group III, represented at Kempston, and group IV which has no certain local example though a Luton vessel may belong to it or group III. Finds of group V come from Kempston and Sandy. These urns show early trading between the north-east of the region and East Anglia and to a lesser extent Middle Anglia, and a heavily decorated biconical pot from Kempston reflects the popularity of elaborately stamped wares in the latter.[25] But it seems these links dwindled about 500, because there are seven vessels of the two oldest groups and four of the next two, but only one of the latest, from the early 6th century, which elsewhere is often the most numerous.

Declining contacts with the Saxon world outside can be related to the absence of group V Buckelurn wares in the Thames valley and the south generally, where Myres[26] suspected the British victory at Badon prevented this type developing. Moreover if the presence of these urns was due to trade and not to local imitation—a reasonable assumption considering how widely diffused are the products of the 'Illington/Lackford potter'—they too would imply the imposition of strict control and the creation of a rather rigid post-Badon frontier between British-held territory and hostile independent Saxons. There is no contradiction between the evidence of brooches and urns before that time. Earlier imports could be explained by a modicum of barter or smuggling at a post near Kempston or Sandy, whence Luton could obtain stock; an analogy is Housesteads where traders beyond Hadrian's Wall were admitted to attend the market. After Badon, however, an iron curtain evidently came down.

The saucer brooches at Mitcham,[27] Surrey, which began as a Saxon community installed for the defence of London, provide some comparisons with these relationships and show changing associations. The first phase is marked by brooches with designs found in England and Germany, such as the 5-spiral type common to all Saxon areas; the same complexion is displayed in the Chiltern region where 5-spiral brooches come from Kempston and Dorchester III and a 4-recurved scroll one from Luton, all 5th century.

The Mitcham aspect of the first half of the 6th century was much more insular with some local emphasis; the brooches have few continental parallels and reveal slight contacts with Wessex. Mitcham patterns of this period include a variety of the scroll cross known at Luton and in Berkshire, but the 'leg' fashion popular in Wessex barely penetrated into Surrey and early products of this style are not found in the Chiltern region, which offers few contemporary examples for comparison; but besides the scroll cross from Luton that site and Dorchester III both have 6-spiral brooches and a blunt star to prove that new stock was occasionally received from sources that supplied a large area from Kent to Warwickshire.

In the second half of the 6th century, when saucer brooches were plentiful north of the Thames in great variety of design, Mitcham had local types but only stray specimens of others, betraying an isolation utterly uncharacteristic of the situation throughout the Ouse–Thame basin at that time.

Chapter VIII

'571'

COMPARED WITH THE scanty earlier material in the Chiltern region the volume of later 6th-century evidence is enormous; there is a prodigious heightening of scale, and an explosion in the number of cemeteries which imply new settlements is obvious. The change is plainly shown in the saucer brooches, where types likely to belong to the last quarter of the 6th century far outnumber previous ones. Clearly there had happened some momentous and far-reaching event, which it is impossible to dissociate from the 571 annal. There is also a pronounced change of direction in the affinities of objects of the time.

To cite a typical example from ceramics, the stamped pendent triangle panel style that was widespread between the Thames and the East Riding in the late 6th century is found at Kempston, Moggerhanger, Luton and Kingsey near Thame, and its influence can be seen at Whipsnade and Ippolitts near Hitchin. These finds are matched by extravagantly large late cast saucer brooches, some bearing basketry motifs or wedges in imitation of Kentish garnet brooches, from Dorchester, Buckingham, Ashendon, Stone, Puddlehill and evidently Warmark, but not farther east; several of this type occur on the upper Thames.

In this case the emphasis is decidedly western, but another comparison points eastwards. Rather large applied saucer brooches bearing a Maltese cross pattern, named by Leeds 'the Kempston type' because no fewer than eight specimens came from there, appear to have originated in south-west Cambridgeshire and spread beyond the Ouse valley into Wessex; they have turned up at half a dozen places in Cambridgeshire and Suffolk and as far away as Berkshire and Wiltshire. Kempston is the only certain Bedfordshire findspot but a pair came from Ashwell in north Hertfordshire or somewhere not far away, and another pair from Dorchester. It is surprising that more have not been found locally, but as their fragile frontplates easily perish some unrecognizable fragments and loose backplates may belong to this series. The distribution of this entire family can be satisfactorily accounted for by manufacture in Cambridgeshire and transport thither by trade; this is a likely explanation for the distant occurrences.

Competing late influences are also shown by the great square-headed brooches. From Luton the exemplar of Leeds' B6 group came from the same mould as one from Abingdon, and a similar specimen occurred at Warmark. Leeds' title for this group was a misnomer as the majority come from an area stretching from the upper Thames to Rutland, with an outlier at Mitcham. Here is a case where export from a centre near Oxford can be suspected. However the B2 'southern' group brooch from Dorchester III shows links with Surrey and Sussex where all its fellows were found. The earlier of the Kempston two, from the last third of the 6th century, belongs to the B8 'Barrington' group, thought to have originated in the Cambridge region, which spread to the Midlands and the East Riding. Perhaps this pattern was imitated in the Midlands, but the Yorkshire finds look like imports. The other Kempston brooch, probably of the early 7th century, belongs to the C3 'East Midland' group that Leeds regarded as Middle Anglian productions and occurs also in Cambridgeshire and at Ipswich; the last seems likely to be a case of import, not imitation. Wherever these brooches were made they proclaim that the region was no longer sealed but open to fresh winds from all directions.

Local evidence for the late 6th and early 7th centuries is really much more impressive than mere sampling suggests. Mushroom-like, fresh settlements spring up on previously untouched ground; the Ivel valley, the Icknield tract and the edge of the Oxfordshire Chilterns are opened up, and the Aylesbury cluster comes into view. Among the latter Stone and Bishopstone took advantage of a well-drained outcrop of Lower Greensand that earlier cultivators would not have neglected if they had opportunity. Whereas earlier connexions can mostly be put down to trade, the new sites plainly denote human movements on a large scale. Unprecedented expansion can be due only to considerable immigration, and newcomers to the valley liked fashions that came freely from north, south, east and west; the days of isolation were over. Towards the end of the 6th century the northern basin ceased to belong to a British province and became fully part of English society.

The 571 annal re-examined

It is so impossible to divorce the late 6th-century Saxon explosion from the natural result of the victory related in the annal for 571 that its main import can be taken at face value. From the context of the previous century and a half we can be sure it was the British levies of the Chiltern region that were defeated then. Can the details of that annal be associated with any of the physical evidence?

The annal mentions a battle at *Biedcanford* and Cuthwulf's capture of presumably a swathe of country including Limbury, Aylesbury, Bensington and Eynsham; the last can be ignored for the moment as it lies outside the limits of this study and may not have formed part of the Chiltern realm. The setting and significance of the story need no longer be doubted. Other obstacles to accepting it in its entirety have been the disputed identification of the battle site with Bedford and the English nature of the *tun* names that might connote already existing Saxon communities. The first difficulty hinges upon the name *Biedcanford*; the second disappears when the archaeological background is reviewed.

To begin with we recall the early 5th-century community of *foederati* at Kempston with evidence for continued occupation until the 7th century, and much to suggest that its blockhouse function was long kept up. The place seems significantly close to Bedford for which *Biedcanford* may be intended. The most recent editor of the Chronicle[1] cautiously remarked 'the form of the name does not suggest identification with Bedford', but it is natural to suspect an equation which most historians have accepted despite philologists' objection that *Biedcanford* cannot be ancestral to the modern name derived from *Bedanford* (880).

There are various ways of circumventing this hurdle. Since as Hodgkin[2] pointed out Ethelweard used the acceptable form *Bedanford* in his Latin translation of the 10th century, evidently from a version of the Chronicle different from any now extant, we may allow that he either knew or believed that *Biedcanford* meant Bedford. Copley[3] suggested that the original *Biedcanford* might have been modified by the influence of the neighbouring place-name Biddenham (Biede(n)ham 1086, 'Bieda's *hām*'). The proximity of these names suggests both incorporate the name of a man called Bieda, and so *Biedcanford* may be derived from the pet-form Biedca. The problem might be simply due to poor transcription, for early corruption of the text would equally explain the difficulty and absolve Ethelweard from careless surmise. Asser, writing in 893 only a few years after the original Chronicle was compiled, possessed a text already two stages removed from it. All surviving manuscripts of Tacitus' *Agricola* read *castris Antonam et Sabrinam* which makes no sense, in error for *cis Trisantonam et Sabrinam*—'this side of Trent and Severn'; a slip of one letter. If we combine the arguments of Hodgkin and Copley there is no real objection to accepting Bedford as the place. As Leeds[4] admitted, few historians have pretended that the battle could be located anywhere else, and no alternative has ever been proposed. Many important encounters have been fought at river crossings and the balance of probability is much in favour of Bedford.

Limbury is adjacent to another early *foederati* station near Luton that was certainly occupied till 571. In the immediate vicinity of Aylesbury, centre of a clump of late 6th-century sites whence came the Bishopstone plate, recent finds at Walton seem to have revealed part of the primary settlement of another contingent of early Saxon mercenaries from whom that piece of equipment was inherited. It happens that Limbury and Aylesbury are both significant names, for they contain the element *burh* that implies some kind of fortification. Finally, Dorchester, which attests a Saxon *foederati* station that continued throughout the 5th and 6th centuries, stands within sight of Bensington, now Benson.

Thus at all four places mentioned in the annal there is an astonishing degree of archaeological correspondence, too uncanny to be accounted for by coincidence. All the primary settlements seem to be referred to except Sandy which had perhaps ceased before 571. Although all the seized *tuns* bear indisputably English names it cannot be doubted that even if these were not attached in 571 they were current when the events of that year were still vividly remembered at an English court. The strength of the evidence forbids any idea that the place-names were merely a subsequent geographical indication of the tract conquered then, nor can one imagine how these names could have been guessed three centuries later when the Chronicle was written. We are forced to presume that the mention of these places in the annal was somehow connected with their prior existence, if not the involvement of their Saxon communities.

There is no contradiction between the substance of archaeology and history. At Kempston and at the *burhs* of Limbury and Aylesbury, both specifically designated as defended places, we can visualise garrison settlements still maintained by British authority, their Saxon menfolk retaining as late as 571 the auxiliary military function for which their forefathers were recruited. Whether or not British troops were also present—which seems likely— these places may have been surrendered or betrayed by Saxon defenders who were not anxious to die fighting their own kinsmen; but a determined invader would certainly have aimed to seize British strong points, however manned, which would account for the special boast in Cuthwulf's annal. Such places may at once have been taken into royal hands, a fate that is suggested in the case of Aylesbury by a Kingsbury there.[5]

This explanation will not serve for Bensington, a name without defensive meaning and moreover of a type that as we shall see cannot have been given as early as 571. No certain pagan remains have been found nearer than Dorchester, two miles away. There is reason to believe the place was royal property early in the 7th century;[6] it was certainly a *villa regalis* in 887[7] and remained an important royal manor on which in early medieval times the five Chiltern Hundreds of Oxfordshire were dependent.

Bensington's nearness to Dorchester cannot be overlooked. They are as close as London and Westminster and in early times may have been just as inseparably connected in men's minds. The annal's curious omission of Dorchester might mean that by 571 the West Saxons had already acquired the town, perhaps recently, or that it was an unimportant place which became prominent only when Birinus fixed his see there, possibly because of its Roman associations.The latter is quite unlikely; the probable reason for his choice is that it was then a royal residence, as recorded history and the jewelled pyramid found there strongly suggest.

The fortunes of the town perhaps help to explain why Bensington and not Dorchester is mentioned in the annal. It is exceedingly improbable that they were captured on different occasions, and a reasonable conjecture that Dorchester too fell to Cuthwulf in 571 and was once commemorated in recited tales of his campaign. Bensington's name may have crept in because of its later importance, replacing an original mention of Dorchester in distant recollections after the bishopric there ended about 660. The proximity and common lordship which would make these places almost synonymous might account for the suppression of Dorchester and Bensington's appearance.

Regarding the annal in its full context it is highly credible that its statements are substantially correct and intimately connected: a fight at *Biedcanford*—probably Bedford—destroyed the Chiltern Britons' domination and led to the unobstructed expansion of English occupation; Cuthwulf's conquest freed a few small Saxon settlements that had remained under British sway since the early 5th century. This liberation might explain why the people who used the Argyll Avenue burial ground near Limbury deserted it and moved to the more attractive valley site of Luton; the lack of late brooches of the large cast and Maltese cross types shows this cemetery was abandoned before 600.

This interpretation removes an old perplexity, for we need not suppose that Limbury and Aylesbury were entirely British settlements renamed long afterwards; indeed it is hard to see how English names of much later gift could be cited in the annal, except for Bensington. It explains why both contain the *burh* element, but it cannot determine whether the names existed in 571 or were shortly given by their conquerors. As the subject Saxons who already inhabited these localities presumably had their own names for them, Limbury 'the fort on the Lea' could have been named as early as the 5th century. Aylesbury 'Ægel's fort' may have been called after an early Saxon headman or from some English noble after 571.

There remains the question of Cuthwulf's identity. Although Kempston is not listed among his booty the strong possibility that the conflict took place only two miles away suggests that an attack might have been directed at that place. If events are related in the right order, if Cuthwulf commanded a West Saxon force, and if Bedford was the site of the campaign's initial engagement, he perhaps made a long detour to surprise the outpost and take the Chilterns in the rear, but this manoeuvre would make better sense if he had allies from the east.

It is not absolutely certain, though most likely, that Cuthwulf was a West Saxon, for although his name follows the alliteration of their royal house it was not uncommon and the Chronicle seems rather unsure about him. The early Parker manuscript calls him Cuthwulf but the name appears as Cutha in the E version, where the statement that he was king Ceawlin's brother seems an interpolation founded on tradition or guesswork. Cutha features as Ceawlin's companion in his fight against Kent in the 568 annal, where the F recension adds he was the king's brother. Cutha is in fact a hypocoristic pet-form of Cuthwulf and similar names as well as an independent name.

It would certainly be in character for Ceawlin to attempt conquest in a northern direction, which would consort with an aggressive policy towards all his neighbours —first Kent, then the Chilterns, finally the Cotswolds; yet the Chronicle strangely does not claim Ceawlin's personal leadership of the 571 campaign, and a roundabout approach then, with the risk of premature detection and interception, is not easy to accept. As an alternative Morris[8] proposed that Cutha was a chief of the Cambridgeshire people who introduced the Maltese cross brooches. This suggestion too has difficulties, not least because no West Saxon ruler would take kindly to a rival storming independently through country just across the Thames; Ceawlin's line appears to have come from the Berkshire area. The truth may depend on whether the sequence of events was really from east to west, on which some doubt is thrown by the order of the places taken after Dyrham in 577, which also runs inwards towards Wessex but has a ring of literary contrivance for effect. Perhaps the most satisfactory solution is that the campaign was a combined effort to vanquish the Chiltern regime by a coordinated assault and share the spoils.

It is not of much moment whether Cuthwulf (Cutha) came from Wessex or Cambridgeshire, nor can conflicting views be resolved on inadequate evidence. It was the West Saxons who profited most by the conquest, and they were able to turn their attention north-west where the 571 annal's mention of Eynsham hints they already had designs. If the Chiltern boundary was the Cherwell it would have excluded that place, some miles to the west, but the invaders may have ravaged beyond into territory belonging to another small British state in the Cotswolds which before long fell to Ceawlin after the battle of Dyrham. British resistance still left him some tidying up to do. Whence came the Britons who in 584 fought the West Saxons at *Fethanleag*, evidently with some success, and killed one of their leaders, another Cutha, is impossible to decide. Stenton's identification of the place with a woodland in Stoke Lyne in north Oxfordshire may be confirmed by the place-name Cutslow just north of Oxford, if it was the burial place of that Cutha and not the victor of 571 who died that year; Cuddesdon, east of Oxford, may refer to one of these. After the Chiltern reverse in 571 a force from the Chiltern redoubt is quite unlikely; perhaps these Britons came from the unsubdued north Oxfordshire-Northamptonshire district.

Certain it is that when the Chiltern Britons lost their ascendancy in 571 the Ouse-Thame basin soon passed into West Saxon hands and all their country before long became a bone of contention on the rise of Mercia. The subsequent progress of English settlement in the region and the manner in which its native society perished as a distinct entity are questions where only place-names can shed light.

NOTE ON THE DATE OF CUTHWULF'S CAMPAIGN

Whether the Chronicle's annal for 571 correctly dates Cuthwulf's campaign is debatable. As Frere[9] pointed out, the Chronicle founded its dating of early events in the south-east on Bede, whose reconstruction made the *Adventus Saxonum*—the arrival of Hengist's band—about twenty years too late.[10] However 571 needs no amendment for this reason as the later 6th-century dates are quite independent of Bede's system. Copley[11] thought the Wessex dating from Ceawlin's time onwards was probably based on regnal lists and current sagas which when Birinus came were still fresh enough in memory for the Church to record with reasonable accuracy; 7th-century annalists would have been able to work backwards fairly satisfactorily. If so 571 could be regarded as an absolute date with an error of at most a year or two.

Unfortunately there are grounds for doubting the precision of dating in Ceawlin's reign which different parts of the Chronicle give a length of 17, 30 or 32 years. Moreover some annals are suspiciously placed at intervals of four or eight years 556, 560, 568, 584 and 592—which suggests their arbitrary insertion into the framework of a table of leap-year cycles[12] or Easter dates after Birinus arrived about 634. In that case we could not depend on accuracy to within a decade, even with events in the right order. However as the campaigns of 571 and 577 do not appear to have suffered from this sort of distortion they may be more reliable, and in both cases the true date might have been independently ascertained from British sources in the west, in a way that was not practicable for other events. We should not overlook the availability of the casual kind of dating evidence disclosed in medieval proofs of age by people who were no more literate but could say 'I am 52 years old, and I remember Sir John's son being born in the month I was 30'; in 634 a few men born in 571 and many of their sons would still be alive. It can at least be said that 571 fits quite well with the developments known to archaeology.[13]

Chapter IX

EARLY ENGLISH SETTLEMENT NAMES

ONLY A SMALL PROPORTION of the thousands of place-names created in the region during the last 1,500 years could possibly throw light on early English settlement. We can afford to be selective because the older ones, mainly village and hamlet names, will obviously be the most revealing. Over 800 place-names can be combed out by collecting all those recorded before the end of the 11th century, all other parish names and others containing habitative elements or belonging to other early inhabited places; a handful can be ignored for various reasons such as unknown or definitely medieval origin.

For analysis it is useful to distinguish between parish and minor names. The soundness of this division may be criticized because many small townships only attained the status of civil parish in the 19th century and some are still little more than hamlets, while on the other hand some Domesday vills declined into mere farms or became deserted, but no other simple criterion is available and despite such fluctuations little mass distortion probably results. In a few cases a large village within a parish of another name must be promoted to avoid an obvious anomaly, and places like Northaw, which if it existed before the 12th century was quite insignificant, must be relegated to the minor list.

The region is poor in early sources. Only 93 place-names are recorded before the year 1000, but two-thirds of the rest in the selected list occur in the 11th century. The most frequent elements used in the listed names are shown on the facing page. Some of these terms can only be approximately translated by a single word because their meanings changed. Minor elements[1] bring the total of habitative type names to 383, under half the whole number. Nature names predominate even among parish names.

Before going any further we should notice two recent hypotheses with serious implications for place-name studies and settlement patterns. The potential unreliability of an approach inevitably based on records has been stressed by Sawyer,[2] because of the alarming extent to which minor places are sometimes concealed in early documents, such as Domesday, by tacitly including them in larger units, although other sources reveal they were already in existence. He suggests that England was quite fully exploited in the 7th and 8th centuries and that, instead of the steady process of expansion into the waste causing the foundation of fresh sites, which is usually assumed to explain the continual appearance of new places on record, in reality large early multiple estates were constantly being fragmented—perhaps due to inheritance laws—with the result that the names of their parts began to be used in documents.

Most frequently used elements

		Before 11c	11c	Later	Parish	Minor	% occurring as parish name
tun	farm, village	123	7	81	35	78	45	64
cot	cottage	51	1	18	32	7	44	14
leah	clearing	49	6	33	10	33	16	
dun	hill	43	5	34	4	37	6	
wic	farm, hamlet	41	3	12	26	5	36	12
denu	valley	33	4	26	3	21	12	
worth	enclosure, farmstead	26	4	13	9	14	12	54
ford	ford	26	6	13	7	17	9	
hām	village	(?)23	4	13	6	14	9	(?)61
-ingtun	. . . .	20	2	14	4	15	5	75
wielle	spring	20	3	15	2	12	8	
hamstede	homestead . .	17	3	5	9	8	9	47
burh	strong place	17	3	8	6	11	6	(excluding Iron Age)
feld	open land	15	6	5	4	12	3	
hoh	hill-spur	15	1	11	3	7	8	
hamm	enclosure, meadow	14	3	7	4	12	2	
throp	hamlet	12	—	2	10	1	11	8
eg	islet	12	2	8	2	9	3	
stoc	place, hamlet	10	—	10	—	8	2	80
-ingas	folk group	10	2	3	5	6	4	60
hyll	hill	10	—	8	2	6	4	
healh	nook, corner	9	1	8	—	6	3	
hām or hamm	. . . .	8	—	5	3	5	3	
burna	stream	8	4	4	—	7	1	
hrycg	ridge	8	1	4	3	6	2	
beorg	hill, barrow	8	1	6	1	6	2	
graf	grove	7	—	6	1	4	3	
hlaw	barrow, hill	7	2	4	1	5	2	
stow	place	6	—	4	2	4	2	
heordewic	herd-farm . .	5	—	1	4	2	3	
mere	pool	5	—	1	4	2	3	
ora	bank, edge	5	3	1	1	3	2	
stan	stone	5	1	4	—	4	1	

There are very few early local charters to suggest such extensive properties, but in most of this region the risk of large-scale concealment of early settlements fortunately seems slight as there are few Domesday parallels to the enormous northern estates Sawyer cited, and in many districts vills of that time are too close to leave questionable spaces, but in the Chilterns and south Hertfordshire where some big manors are mentioned the chance cannot be overlooked. We do not know whether Domesday vills were the compact villages typical of the later Middle Ages.

Whether elements like *wic*, *cote* and *throp* could denote long disguised early foundations on an unsuspected scale seems in this region rather unlikely. Sawyer's allegation that a place-name's first occurrence has often been accepted 'as a reliable guide to the date when the settlement was itself established' is exaggerated.

Of course the first surviving record is in a sense accidental, and obviously many places first known in the 13th century, when records became ample, were then centuries old; a third of the *worth* names appear after the 11th century but all must go back well beyond Norman times, and the Celtic personal name in Cadmore (1236) is centuries older than that.

In fact the spread of the first surviving recording of various types of habitation names seems to be a valuable pointer to the *relative* sequence of their formation. For instance the fact that by 1100 71 per cent of the *tun* names are mentioned, but only 37 per cent of the *cote* names, suggests that *tuns* were on the whole founded considerably earlier than *cotes*. Another guide is comparing different average success rates, measured by the proportion of each group that developed into parishes, for we would expect earlier settlements to be usually the most successful because they could choose the best land. Applying these tests supports the traditional view that places bearing names derived from *cote*, *wic* and the like were generally secondary settlements; on marginal land, they lacked the stability and potential of *hāms* and *tuns* that were evidently founded when better sites were available.

Distribution maps confirm that places with 'minor' names do bear the distinctly late character of offshoots that sprang from earlier settlements. While they occur in apparent subsidiary relation to parent villages, in ones and twos, they seldom hint at the extensive hidden estates of Sawyer's hypothesis.

Another recent suggestion[3] is that during the Dark Age period the settlement pattern was constantly changing—'there is every indication that throughout history and prehistory there was never a fixed pattern of settlement', that fluctuations were on such a scale that it is hazardous to assume great continuity of occupation or read too much into Domesday, when the scene may have been very different from one several centuries before. Where however the Domesday picture broadly coincides with the Roman one or fits the indications of soil factors we perhaps need not fear major displacement, despite doubts about the history of individual settlements.

Taylor's mobility theory may have useful applications elsewhere. It could account for the misfit noticed below between the earlier place-names and archaeological traces, by explaining why pagan cemeteries can seldom be associated with these names or later villages, and it probably has some bearing on the disappearance of British names. We can surmise that a shift of site may have been due to the exhaustion of soil fertility, which in Mexico causes the rotation of milpa plots every few years.

It is agreed that *hām* and *-ingas* and the compounds based on them were among the distinctively early elements denoting settlement that were employed in English place-names. Other elements such as *wic* and *cote* long outlasted them, and record evidence shows that *tun* continued into the Norman period, long after *hām* and *-ingas* passed out of currency. In seeking what light place-names cast on the earlier phases of English settlement the latter two seem the most likely to help.

Nevertheless we cannot be sure that habitative names were normally the first to be formed. It is quite likely that simple topographically descriptive terms were employed before permanent English settlement names arose. Dodgson[4] remarked 'it might turn out that quite ordinary nature terms such as *burna* "a stream", *leah* "a wood", *feld* "open land", are the first to be used by settlers in a new land and that habitative names such as *hām* and *tun* and place-names formed from the personal names and folk names of the inhabitants only come into use when the pattern of settlement . . . has evolved to a stage when the need for identification is felt and recognition by neighbours is established'. The ubiquity and long currency of these common elements and others such as *dun* 'hill' and *denu* 'valley' complicate matters, and it has been found that *leah* and *feld* names were sometimes given to early settlements.[5] In this region 33 of the 49 places with names in *leah* and 37 of the 43 from *dun* became important enough to be parishes, but this does not necessarily mean all these were early foundations, because as we shall see towards the end of this chapter in a large part of the region English place-names of this nature type seem to have been formed comparatively late, long after the names in *hām*, *-ingas* and even *tun*. But we cannot exclude the possibility that other terms may be as old as these, and as we have seen the *burh* names Limbury and Aylesbury seem to have existed in 571 or shortly afterwards.

We have moreover to bear in mind a recent demonstration[6] that many places now bear, not their unknown primary names, but others commemorating later Saxon lordship. Nor can we always assume that place names of undubitably English type denoted settlements of English creation. The incidence of these names in Norfolk, compared with the distribution of datable Saxon pottery and the earlier concentration of Romano–Rritish population in certain areas, has led to the conclusion[7] that some were given to native settlements that survived under English rule.

Place-names in hām (Map 5, Appendix IV)

There are powerful reasons for believing that place-names originally ending in *hām*, such as Aldenham and Haddenham, were given very early.[8] *Hām* is often joined with the simple type of personal name, like Luffa and Hicca, that was used before compound names like Ethelwulf, and it is combined with other apparently early elements but not with those in late Old English currency. It is also joined with the early folk-group *-ingas* names in the form *-ingahām* which seems to link the end of the *hām* fashion with the beginning of the *-ingas* period. The only possible example of *-ingahām* in the region is Tyringham, so situated that its origin can be suspected from another element *hamm* 'enclosure, water-meadow' which was often applied to the bend of a river. This case illustrates the constant difficulty of confusion between these elements, because early settlers may often have favoured typical *hamm* locations. Several names ending in -ham border the Ouse and the Ivel and it is impossible to resist the suspicion that most if not all were really *hamms*.

A predominantly valley distribution is an obvious feature of possible local *hām* names. Haversham lies by the Ouse, Bragenham beside the Lovat, both in situations suggesting *hamm*; the Ivel has Newnham; near the Lea feeders are Hixham, Pelham, Hadham, Tednambury and Hartham, the last two probable *hamms*; by the Colne are Aldenham and Denham, perhaps a *hamm*; the Thames has Newnham Murren, Mapledurham, Caversham—a probable *hamm*, Hitcham and Cippenham, with a group of four near—Hicknaham, Burnham, Farnham Royal and Wexham; and Haddenham and Rowsham stand near the Thame. Amersham, Bradenham and Higham in

Chesham—a *hamm*—lie in Chiltern valleys but are probably *hamms*, because the barrenness of this district in other early habitative names raises serious doubts about genuine *hāms* there. Few local *hāms* are remote from streams: Higham Gobion, Puttenham, Studham on the Dunstable Downs, Ingham below the Chiltern scarp and Boreham Wood. Frogmore in Kings Walden is most unlikely to contain hām which rarely survived as a minor name. There are no *hāms* on the Lea or in the north-west quadrant of the region, and most of Bedfordshire is bare if probable *hamms* are dismissed.

Hāms tend to be noticeably missing amidst groups of pagan sites, often standing at a little remove, like Higham Gobion, Newnham and Puttenham. This observation does not necessarily question the common conviction that as a class *hāms* form one of the oldest strata of English settlement. The Chiltern region, however, does not closely accord with Cox's finding that in the Midlands and East Anglia *hām* names 'almost without exception' lie within three miles of Roman roads and ancient trackways. Half the definite *hāms* are unrelated to Roman roads. Although these names do not clearly correspond with patterns elsewhere physical factors would explain aversion to the heavy clays of Bedfordshire, northern Buckinghamshire and south-east Hertfordshire, and a preference for better conditions in other areas. There is however much they do not account for, such as the poor showing in most of east Hertfordshire and the hinterland of Dorchester, with excellent soils.

Let us compare the *hām* distribution with the Roman background and the extent of pagan Saxon sites. *Hām* names are densest in a group of seven north of Slough where three Roman villas and two kiln sites bespeak a considerable earlier population on an assortment of gravels, brickearth and other good soils; the coincidence shows a desirable situation in both Roman and Saxon times. Only Hicknaham is on London clay, but close to the easily tilled Reading Beds. The Taplow barrow and a pagan burial at Hitcham—a *hām*—lie on the edge of this group.

Along the Colne were a number of villas and other Roman sites, but whereas there are no pagan burials here *hām* names occur at Aldenham and Boreham Wood and possibly at Denham. In the western Chilterns there is only the doubtful Bradenham to match a collection of villas, but a barrow burial at Wycombe means early infiltration into a fertile valley. It is uncertain whether any appreciable English settlement took place in this district during the *hām*-forming period. In east Hertfordshire there is no *hām* name near the large Roman site at Welwyn and only at Pelham does one correspond with pagan burial. Sapeham might be a lost example here.

Discrepancies are more pronounced in the northern basin where *hām* names provide extraordinarily little reminder that Saxon settlement began here. Near Kempston there are only the riparian sites that are probably *hamms*, and near Sandy Blunham of which the same can be said. No *hām* stands near Luton. To compare with the pagan sites near Dunstable Studham is a solitary example. The Dorchester district has only Ingham and Newnham Murren. Haversham and Tyringham near Newport Pagnell and Bragenham near Leighton Buzzard are all suspect as *hamms*. Haddenham is the only *hām* that could be associated with pagan burials near Aylesbury. The blankness of the archaeological map in the north-west sector, except for the brooches near Buckingham—a definite *hamm*, is paralleled by a complete dearth of *hāms*.

Almost invariably these *hāms* are outside the margins of pagan settlement, though quite near. Widespread lack of detailed concordance with heathen burial cannot be attributed to the accidents of archaeological discovery; the disparity is too great to dismiss. One conclusion alone is open: throughout the region *hām* names must represent not the earliest or even the abundant late 6th-century phase of pagan archaeology but a later period of expansion overlapping with the decline of heathen burial custom. This decidedly differs from Cox's verdict[9] that the earliest *hāms* were settled 'possibly under the aegis of Roman or regional sub-Roman government' and that they continued to be founded 'throughout the years of migration and the later pagan period'. He was evidently uneasy about awkward exceptions, for his Leicestershire map shows major differences between *hāms* and pagan areas, but he remarked 'lack of relationship between *hām* and pagan burials in a particular county does not invalidate the hypothesis that place-names in *hām* are very early' and thought it necessary to emphasize the often close association of *hām* with pagan burials, especially in East Anglia.

While broad resemblances mean local heathen burials and *hām* names cannot be far apart in time, too few of these names agree well enough with pagan archaeology to represent its period as a whole, and correspondence is limited to its final phase. The meaning of this is plain: the characteristic place-name formulae of the earlier local Saxon settlements of the pagan period have yet to be identified. *Hām* does not fit them. The more advanced stage when many local *hām* names were created, towards the end of or even after heathen practices, may be confirmed by the fact that no place-names near the oldest sites contain *hām*. The explanation may well be Taylor's theory of discontinuity mentioned above.

The local *hām* names are however certainly quite early, because none seems to contain compound personal names of the Ethelwulf type. Moreover, half these names are combined with elements, a type which Cox believed was on the whole earlier than those with personal names.

The date of the hām names

For dating the local *hām* names there is no direct evidence, except the record of Aldenham in 785, only the implications of their distribution. Imperfect correspondence between them and pagan burials provides a rough indication when they were formed: since *hām* is not only applied to places on the pagan margins but stretches beyond it denotes a later but as Pelham and Hitcham show a slightly overlapping phase.

It is significant that *hāms* are nowhere associated with the places known to have been inhabited by Saxons between about 430 and the battle of Biedcanford, which implies that none was founded during that period and that the designation was not used then, at least in this region.

Since archaeology suggests that many new Saxon sites came into existence during the generation following 571 we look to see whether *hām* can be connected with this phase. Some, like Ingham, Rowsham, Puttenham, Studham and Higham Gobion, do lie in districts colonized between 571 and the end of pagan custom. Many such as those in east Hertfordshire and the Slough district are placed where Saxon settlement was prevented until the British regime was overwhelmed in 571 and are certainly later. But it is noteworthy that *hām* is not attached to any of the places with pagan remains in the Aylesbury area, all of them presumably founded soon after 571; Haddenham where no pagan cemetery is known is the only *hām* in the district. Evidently much of the earliest spreading from the presumed Aylesbury nucleus, shown by these cemeteries, took place before *hām* names were formed. It is also hard to detect *hām* period expansion from the early centres near Luton and Dunstable; Studham is the only obvious case, Higham Gobion is more distant.

In the Slough district where *hāms* are most concentrated the wealth of the Taplow burial strongly suggests that the dead chieftain ruled a considerable area, and we can infer that the neighbouring terrain marked by these *hāms*, which as Hitcham shows partly coincide with the pagan age, belonged to his dominions. Taeppa's tomb is dated somewhere about 600—within a decade or two either side, more likely after than before then—and it is not hazardous to think that some of these *hāms* flourished in his time. From these cases we can judge that *hām* names began to be formed in the Chiltern region about 600, but hardly much earlier.

The upper limit of their creation is a difficult question, for though several appear to be later than most of the pagan cemeteries it is not a simple matter to decide when heathen burials ceased. The rarity of graves with late 7th-century articles shows that pagan habits seldom persisted so long, and elsewhere we concluded that active heathenism died out in most districts before 650. In fact few cemeteries contain objects as late as that and pagan burial customs had generally finished well before then. This allows ample time for the latest *hāms* to be founded before the middle of the 7th century, because the *hām* phase seems rather weak in the region. If we put its beginning about 600 a reasonable guess would give it a vogue of not much more than a generation, and by about 650 another term was in use.

Wic-hām names (Appendix IV)

A pioneering study[10] showed that no less than 24 of 28 names in *wic-hām* occur on or within a mile of a Roman road, often at or close to Roman sites, a proportion so far beyond the bounds of coincidence that it argues some intimate connexion. Dr. Gelling concluded that *wic-hām* was used as an appellative, perhaps meaning a place occupied by Saxon mercenaries[11] or 'village near the site of a defunct Roman *vicus*', and that it was probably applied before about 600. She now believes the term may have been given to a surviving post-Roman native settlement.

There are four possible *wic-hāms* in the region. Wickham Hall, [12] a deserted village that was a manor in 1086, is under a mile from a minor Roman settlement at Bishop's Stortford on Stane Street. Wickham Hill near Braughing is the centre of the small Roman town there,[13] and although only late forms of the name are known it seems to be a genuine case of *wic-hām*. Wickham Spring in Standon lies beside a Roman road and a Roman site but there is no pre-modern record of the name. The fourth possible example is Wickhern Field at Toddington, noticed in a report on the Sheepwalk Hill Saxon cemetery there. This 19th-century spelling though not close enough to 'Wickham' may be a corruption of it, and earlier forms of the name which could resolve the point would be welcome; but rather suggestive is a solid concrete platform which can hardly be other than Roman, found on part of the site. No Roman road, however, is known in the vicinity.

All these appear to fit 'a village near a former *vicus*' but Wickhern is the only one that would possibly be associated with any early Saxon community; though Toddington was not certainly a primary 5th-century foundation it is in the unique district where Saxon settlement seems to have expanded before 571. The three Wickham names, remote from any known Saxon occupation of that period, must have been formed after 571, perhaps no later than Dr. Gelling's proposed limit; the *-ingas* name Braughing proves an English presence near one of these by about 650. The *wic-hām* name there might well represent an allusion to a lingering post-Roman site, following her new interpretation, and thus point to some continuity of occupation half a mile from the English village.

Place-names containing -ing

The particle *-ing* which enters into many English place-names has more than one aspect.[14] Sometimes it means no more than 'place'; Clavering is 'place where clover grows'. A complication, however, is that such a simple name might be extended by the later addition of another element, producing a compound that does not look archaic. An analysis by Dodgson[15] of names of the Birmingham and Altrincham type, where *-ing* was once and often still is pronounced as in 'hinge', proposed many instances of this phenomenon. If so, the original uncompounded names in this category must be of great antiquity, for the palatalization of *-ing* which they show betrays an old locative case *-inge*, 'at — ing', which had become obsolete by *c.* 650. Local examples which Dodgson thought display this history are Tingewick, Bucks 'wic at Toting, Tota's place', and Bengeo, Herts. '*hoh* 'hill-spur' at Bening, place by the R. Beane'. It would follow that some names previously regarded as in the *-ingas* series below might be seen as original *-ing* names with a later suffix. This may also apply to some of the apparent *-ingtun* names where palatalization to *-inge* would not persist in front of elements like *tun*, though there is evidence for this at Toddington, Beds.

Place-names from -ingas and inga- (Map 5, Appendix IV)

In some of its applications Old English *-ing* was added to a personal name to mean 'son of'; Alfred Æthelwulfing was Alfred son of Æthelwulf. Place-names tell of early English groups, large and small, who were similarly distinguished by their contemporaries by names like *Readingas* 'Reada's people', and the genitive form of the plural, *-inga-*, was also used for descriptive purposes as in Essendon, Herts. 'the valley (*denu*) of Esla's people'.

In fact, however, these names present some difficulty, for it is often uncertain whether a place-name contains *-inga-* which would later become *-inge-*, a spelling indistinguishable from the locative *-inge* mentioned above. In the four counties, of 40 names that the English Place-Name Society assessed as *-ingas* and *-inga-* only 16 which have *-inga-* spellings definitely belong to the group. Pillinge and Worthy End, Beds., and perhaps others should be discarded as vases containing locative *-inge*;

those now suspect are shown with a question mark in Appendix IV. However, any place-name that in reality is based on locative -inge must have been created no later than c. 650, which justifies their retention in the list.

The distribution of -ingas and -inga- names is so similar and they occur in such close proximity that there is no reason to differentiate between them. Not all such names are early. Hertingfordbury, originally Hertfordingeberi 'the burh of the men of Hertford', which may be identified with one of the English forts raised in 911–12 (corrected date) and surely pertains to the age of the Danish wars, like the well known Fifburgingas 'the men of the Five Boroughs', reminds us that the -ingas construction was still employed in late Old English. If the name Ware recalls the events of 895, Wengeo if it is waringahoh 'hill-spur of the Ware people' must be later. With a few exceptions adopting a topographical description for a folk or like Wing and Wingrave probably recalling heathenism, all the local -ingas and -inga- group names seem to be derived from personal names and can be attributed to an early stage when small pioneer communities were led by the individuals they commemorate. These group names became applied to their settlements, probably soon after they were formed. They are certainly early because all the definite cases and almost all the rest were called after men bearing the simple type of personal name. In most of the -inga- compounds list a folk name is coupled with a variety of topographical terms such as dun 'hill', but among habitative elements worth certainly occurs once, perhaps five times, while there are two doubtful examples of both tun and wic.

These names show a strong tendency to grouping, which may reinforce the traditional view of those which Dodgson would treat as doubtful. There are half a dozen close together in south Bedfordshire, four in the country upstream of Hertford, four near Buckingham and five round Wing: others are scattered near the Thames from Goring to Culham and towards the hills. A few are rather isolated: Wrestlingworth, Tyringham, Halling and Tetchwick in the northern valley, and in east Hertfordshire Wallington, Buntingford and Braughing. In and to the south of the Chilterns such names are rare. Waeclingacaestir (Verulamium) is quite alone, Averingdown is the only one in the Chiltern massif and Basing the sole example in the Slough district, where it stands outside a concentration of hāms and evidently represents a later settlement on the flood plain when higher and easily worked land nearby was already occupied.

Elsewhere -ingas type names broadly occupy territory outside the confines of pagan settlement, though sometimes in the vicinity of a hām. Many of these names signify expansion generally later than the hāms, infilling between them. The congregation of -ingas names in south Bedfordshire—some of them never grew into villages —encroached on the inhospitable sticky clays north-west of an earlier and better placed hām at Higham Gobion. More fortunate were communities that exploited east Hertfordshire with its mixed soils and alluvial valleys, where the widely-spread -ingas names extend well beyond the hāms.

In the Ouse–Thame basin round Wing lie -ingas sites that took advantage of hills of Upper Greensand, and the people of Oving chose a knoll of Portland Beds. North of them Oxford Clay and unfriendly drifts were neglected, but the -ingas near

Buckingham settled on a welcome exposure of Cornbrash in a district that Saxons scarcely touched before heathen burial came to an end, and one where no *hām* is known. In the Dorchester area *-ingas* names colonize the drier soils beside the river and extend beyond the few *hāms*.

Signs of expansion from the early settlements near Dunstable and Aylesbury could be expected. In the latter case *hāms* at Haddenham, Rowsham and Puttenham form an inner ring round the pagan area, and further away *-ingas* names at Halling, Tetchwick, Oving and perhaps Wing and Littleworth might be due to continued expansion. The certain and possible *-ingas* names that might be related to early sites near Luton and Dunstable are Toddington—the village lies between two large cemeteries, Ivinghoe a few miles to the south-west, and perhaps Wing and Littleworth. The strange apparent weakness of expansion here perhaps means that some of the Luton–Dunstable people took an opportunity to move farther afield, away from the shallow chalk soil.

The date of the -ingas names

The *-ingas* formula seldom coincides with pagan archaeology: Toddington and Verulamium, both with cemeteries, and Oving with a stray find are the only instances. Correspondence between *-ingas* names and pagan burials is equally rare in the east Midlands.[16] The divergence, even if the size of some *-ingas* groups means that we should not expect large cemeteries to be linked with them, points to the certainty that most of these pioneer communities belonged to an age when pagan burial practices were past.

That is a feasible explanation for the discrepancies. The almost total absence everywhere of burials that could be those of *-ingas* settlements has often been remarked. Recalling the likely Christian connotation of unfurnished graves outside churchyards like that at Wing—an *-ingas* name—we can surmise that before the close of the 7th century many local inhabitants were buried in Christian graveyards still in use today, so that their remains are concealed; moreover, as pagan burial had been widely abandoned before about 650, some new cemeteries established in the 7th century might have been allowed to remain in use as Christian graveyards without affront to missionary principles. The continuation of unfurnished burials on a pre-Christian site that eventually acquired a church, and new Christian cemeteries, may explain the puzzling 'undiscoverable burials' of the *-ingas* time noted by Dodgson.[17]

The *-ingas* formula reaches into central Hertfordshire and north-west Buckinghamshire where settlement in heathen times is hardly detectable. *Waeclingacaestir*, one of the names by which Verulamium was known to Bede, doubtless contains the name of the folk who were buried in the cemetery outside the walls, which was in use about the middle of the 7th century, when the group name *Waeclingas* had probably been created. The hanging bowl escutcheon from Oving that probably came from the grave of one of 'Ufa's people' almost certainly dates from the early 7th century, and deposition about 650 is likely. Again, the possible origin of the place-name Wing from *weohingas* 'those who worship at the heathen temple' suggests it was given after Christian priests arrived in the neighbourhood, following

Birinus' founding of the see at Dorchester about 634; in any case it could not have been formed until paganism had so waned that an idol shrine caused comment among its neighbours. Such a name could not be much earlier than 650, but it is just possible that it was formed a couple of decades later, for in Germany the pagan term *weoh* was sometimes applied to a Christian church in the missionary period. There is no proof of this usage in England, but it suggests the remarkable possibility that the name Wing may really mean 'people who worship at the church' and contain a contemporary reference to the lately erected minster there (see Chap. V).

These three cases hint that *-ingas* names were being coined before and after the middle of the 7th century. The closely paired Ingham and *englingadene*, Higham Gobion and Shillington, suggest the *-ingas* formula sometimes shortly followed the *hām*-forming phase, but the location of some *-ingas* names in east Hertfordshire and north-west Buckinghamshire presents a more advanced profile. Yet the local *-ingas*-forming movement seems to have lasted for a rather limited time, perhaps only for a couple of generations after the *hām*-founding phase died away. Most of the *-ingas* names probably belong to the years either side of 650, and though some might be as early as about 630 historical factors mentioned later suggest such independent pioneer settlements are unlikely to have been made after about 680. The *-ingas* settlements at Tewin and Essendon were probably in existence when Theodore held his Council at Hertford nearby in 672.

Place-names in -ingtun (Map 6, Appendix IV)

Place-names like Chippenham 'Cippa's *hām*' and Abingdon 'Æbba's hill' that contain personal names in the genitive case no doubt signify some kind of possession. In other place-names, however, a personal name was linked to a word by the connective particle *-ing-*, indicating some kind of association but not necessarily ownership. Many of these names contain the word *tun* 'farm, village', the ancestor of our word 'town'. We should, however, bear in mind Dodgson's opinion above that some apparent *-ingtun* names may be not primary forms but *-ing* names in the locative case *-inge* with *tun* added later; but of those listed in Appendix IV only Toddington shows any *-inge-* spellings, and here they are all treated as a class.

The proper *-ingtun* names must be distinguished from very similar-looking ones like Wallington (*Wandelingetuna c.* 1180) that may descend from the genitive plural of an *-ingas* name. Early recorded forms are the only means of separating them, for later spellings rendered both as -ington. If ancient spellings of one of these names do not include *-inga-* or its usual medieval form *-inge-* it may be regarded as an example of *-ingtun* with connective *-ing-*. Ekwall thought *-ingtun* names were merely *-ingatun* names where the extra syllable happened to drop out too soon to be recorded, but his opinion must be rejected as a rule because the distribution of local -ington names where recorded spellings disclose no trace of the medial vowel that would have betrayed an original *-ingatun* differs distinctly from that of the *-ingas* type; this is fairly conclusive proof that these classes are not related and bears out the orthodox view of the English Place-Name Society.[18] The possibility that a few names surviving as -ington once contained *-inga-* cannot of course be dismissed.

Three-quarters of the 20 local *-ingtun* settlements became parish villages and few remain hamlets. Their success and stability, no doubt connected with the circumstances of their foundation, contrast with the large proportion of *-ingas* places that never thrived or disappeared, like Halling. All but three of their names are based on personal names; the exceptions have topographical references—Bennington, and Norrington and Seddington, 'north' and 'south' of pre-existing sites, do not really belong to the series—and are probably appreciably later.

None of the *ingtuns* is in the higher Chilterns or north-west Buckinghamshire, and east Hertfordshire with a dozen *hām* and *-ingas* names has only two examples. The rest are spread unevenly along the northern basin from Benson to the Ivel, with a group round Thame. The majority are near though seldom actually on rivers, and some seem to show migration from the Dorchester and Aylesbury districts.

Their disposition is more removed than the *-ingas* names from pagan sites. The northern *-ingtuns* evidently arose from expansion after the *-ingas* phase as the first expression of the *tun*-forming age. Newcomers there began to break in the heavier lands, the unappealing clays and drifts that were still mostly forested but in the course of time proved excellent for both corn and stock.

The only *-ingtuns* recorded before Domesday are Watlington in 887 and Bensington in the annal for 571. Since *ingtuns* as a class are not numerous their names were evidently coined over a short period. But could Bensington as a name really be as old as 571? If it belonged to a genuine series of *-ingtun* names it would seem to have been given later than the local *hām* and *-ingas* names which are themselves demonstrably later than 571, which would forbid the idea that Bensington might be a stray formation of an earlier age. If however originally a name with locative *-inge* to which *tun* was subsequently added, the hypothetical primary form *Benesing* could have been created before *c.* 650 when the locative was obsolete. Can we decide between these views? Moreover, is it likely that an English name could have arisen here before the Saxon victory of 571? Unlike Limbury and Aylesbury which contain the *burh* element that may be relevant to the events of 571 the name Bensington has no such significance. On balance it seems preferable to conclude that this name belongs to the main series and arose long after 571, perhaps recalling an early English thegn who held the place from the king; since connective *-ing-* implies only some kind of association the name is compatible with royal property.

The great majority of the main series of *-ingtun* names contain personal names of the early simple type and their strikingly high content of personal names, which reminds us of the *-ingas* groups and suggests they are of almost equal antiquity, contrasts with the slender part personal names played in forming *tun* names. The span of a single generation following the *-ingas* names—which as noted above may have ceased to be formed about 680—might accommodate all the local main series *-ingtuns*. A short vogue of creating these names might explain their absence in the Slough area where several *hāms* show previous development; here expansion may have briefly paused before resuming in the *tun* period. The personal name Ædddi or Eada found in Addington and the adjacent Adstock and Addingrove 18 miles away perhaps points to the formation of a large early estate.

Place-names in tun (Map 7, Appendix IV)

The 123 names derived from *tun* 'farm, village' account for 15 per cent of all local settlements and must have been created over a long span. Luton is on record in 792, Wotton Underwood in 848, five others occur before the year 1000 and 81 in the 11th century, and most of the rest probably existed in 1086 as subsidiary settlements, though hardly on a sufficient scale to support Sawyer's theory of mass concealment. A few, however, like Royston, Patient End and Bishopstone are post-Conquest formations; we can actually watch one name forming in the 13th century as *Uppenende* (1255) changed into *Opton* (1276).

Seventy-eight (64 per cent) are parishes, many others considerable hamlets, few are farms or lost sites. These proportions argue fairly successful settlements, mostly founded when ample good sites were available and therefore before many of the *cotes* and *wics* that were generally of secondary character. Nevertheless a goodly number are comparatively late, for no less than 31 (25 per cent) are distinguished by new, north, south, east, west, middle or up, tell-tale designations which must refer to previous settlements nearby.

While the *tuns* resemble the *-ingtuns* in their success rate, at most only 18 (15 per cent) incorporate personal names, unlike the main series *-ingtuns* that almost invariably do. The common method of coining *tun* names, reference to topographical features or occasionally farming use, implies that most were founded by families or groups of fairly equal status, not by the enterprise of leaders like those whom we glimpse in the *-ingas* and *-ingtun* names; this suggests some kind of social change when few *tuns* had been created.

The *-ingtuns* merge with the mass of *tuns* peppered over the northern basin and the Slough district with a tendency to occur in lines and groups, some of them easily explained, like the chains along the Ouse and Lovat and the fertile Icknield Way strip. But they are very uncommon in the Chiltern zone, fully half the region, and this remarkable scarcity needs specially investigating at the end of this chapter.

Another riddle is the scant trace of *tuns*—only Gilston and Ichetone—in east Hertfordshire which earlier showed four *hāms* and seven *-ingas* formations. What could have checked the creation of English habitative names or slowed down new English settlement? A change in the political setting may explain matters. The *-ingas* groups seem to belong to a chaotic age when adventurous land-taking was rife, but before the end of the 7th century Hertfordshire came under firm Mercian rule and at least a rudimentary administrative system—perhaps implied in the tribute assessments of the Tribal Hidage—was in being. In the face of legal codes and machinery for enforcing them by royal officers private attempts to found new settlements adversely affecting the established rights of existing communities would need express consent and encounter difficulties. If control is the right explanation it would seem that by about 700 most of east Hertfordshire was already well peopled by English or native inhabitants or both, whereas the forested clay lands in the northern basin still had plenty of room to spare. The unusually high density of occupation throughout east Hertfordshire at the time of Domesday, which must to some extent reflect a much earlier situation, supports this view.

The strong contrast with -*ingtun* over the content of personal names suggests that most *tuns* were formed in a protracted later process, but Lidlington and Wallington show that a few *tun* names were given while some of the -*ingas* groups were still recognizable; these could have arisen in the latter part of the 7th century. Two or three more centuries might well elapse while subsidiary villages with names like Newton and Aston were being founded. The majority of *tuns*, antedating most of the *cotes*, *wics* and *throps*, were probably created during the 8th and 9th centuries, though some must be more recent.

Place-names in worth (Map 8, Appendix IV)

Four of the 26 *worth* names occur before the year 1000, the earliest in 962; 13 are first found in the 11th century and 9 later. Fifty-four per cent became parish villages, a success rate below that of the *tuns*. Most of the rest were hamlets or manors but a few sites are lost. It is clear that virtually all the *worths* were established well before the 11th century, and the root meaning of the element—the enclosure of a single holding—may explain why a large proportion remained small. The *worth* formula was used in Middlesex in the 7th century—Isleworth is recorded in 695—and the local names give an impression of greater antiquity than the *tuns*, because like the -*ingas* and -*ingtun* names but in contrast to the generality of *tuns* they contain an extremely high percentage of personal names: only two are definitely without them, four are doubtful. The -*inga*- formula in Wrestlingworth, Littleworth, Datchworth and *Sullingwrthe* suggests the earliest local *worths* probably began a generation or so before about 700.

The distribution of these names looks puzzling, for large parts of the northern basin are devoid of them and none is anywhere near the Ouse. Little groups lie near Sandy and Knebworth, others are spread north and south of Dunstable and between the Chilterns and the Thame. Batchworth faces Rickmansworth across the Colne. Blank areas are the Chiltern range, the vale of St. Albans and east Hertfordshire where Sawbridgeworth and *Sticivesworde* somewhere near Hertford are isolated. Although early avoidance of the Bernwood Forest district is not surprising, saucer brooches and four -*inga*- names near Buckingham and one at Tyringham show that English settlement in the upper Ouse valley had started by the 7th century; and the simple personal names which outnumber the compound and pet forms indicate a generally early date, like the -*inga*- forms. Perhaps in the *worths*, a term conveying a small-scale venture, we encounter a restricted social phenomenon with little further implication.

(Place-names in wic (Map 8, Appendix IV)

The 41 *wic* names occur everywhere except in the higher Chilterns. Only four prospered enough to give their name to parishes and the great majority remain farms or hamlets; six in Hertfordshire rank as deserted villages, elsewhere another six are lost. Two-thirds are first recorded after the 11th century and only three earlier. Ten contain personal names but half of these are of the compound type and do not bear an early complexion. Wick occurs a few times as a simplex name and is not uncommon in the field names of Hertfordshire where it survived in living use into Middle English, when it was often applied to an outlying farm or dependency. Plainly most *wics* do not belong to an early settlement age, but if Tetchwick and Tingewick are genuine *-inga-* formations they would seem to date from the 7th century; if as Dodgson holds these were once early locative forms of *-ing* names then *wic* would be an addition at some later date. The mention of *boiwic* in 785 in the bounds of Aldenham reveals another early one. Most however are probably later than many of the *tuns*.

Place-names in *cote* (Map 9, Appendix IV)

Cote 'cottage' also lived on into Middle English. The great majority of the 51 names belong to minor places and only seven achieved parish status. Only one is certainly mentioned before the 11th century, 18 first occur then and 32 later. Tyrrelcote is named from Humphrey Tyrrel who became its lord about 1500. Clearly these were originally places of little account and the prefixes north, south, east, west, up, nether, out and *burh* in 17 cases, a third of the total, indicating reference to already existing places confirms their secondary character. The poor quality of many of them is shown by the frequency of *ceald* 'cold' which is annexed in seven cases and *hulc* 'hovel' in another. Only 10 certainly and three or four more possibly contain personal names.

It is surprising that an element of such late currency is unevenly distributed. *Cotes* occur thickly below the western Chilterns, in an area densely populated at the time of Domesday, and spread thinly over the northern valley but are absent in the Slough district, the central Chilterns and east Hertfordshire.

Place-names in *hamstede*, *throp*, *stoc* and *stow*

Many of these names probably have little significance for early settlement, although Sandred[19] considered some *hamstede* names appear to be very old. Three of the *hamstedes* are found before the 11th century, five then and nine later. Half are parishes—two well placed on a natural line of communication became towns—but most remain small and two are lost sites. Only one certainly contains a personal name and it is curious that most of those in Hertfordshire were named from trees, plants and birds. Four of them in the St. Albans area—Berkhamsted, Hemel Hempstead, Latimer (*Yselhamstede*) and Rothamsted—correspond with known or suspected Roman sites, but this does not prove a very early date, though Hanstead in that district occurs in the 8th century.

Only two *throp* names out of 12 are recorded by the 11th century; one achieved parish rank, two are lost. A third betray their late origin by combination with east, west and south, and none contains personal names of the simple early type. The distribution, with concentration near Aylesbury but few elsewhere, suggests that *throp* had a very restricted vogue.

All 10 *stoc* names, confined to Buckinghamshire and Oxfordshire, first occur in Domesday. Though it is believed the element denoted once subsidiary places eight of them became parishes. All began as a simplex name except Adstock which may refer to the man commemorated in Addington.

Six local places were called *stow*, the earliest local usage being *St. Albanes stow* in 1007; three more occur in Domesday. The original meaning 'place', especially for meetings or in a religious sense, is borne out by the reference to St. Albans abbey and the fact that Bunsty and Wixamtree were Hundred meeting sites.

Place-names in burh

Names containing *burh* 'fortified place' are scattered over the region but only two are in the Chiltern range. Half a dozen of these sites are known to have been Iron Age forts and others probably were, especially those with 'Aldbury' names that doubtless mean 'old *burh*'—the personal name Ealda cannot underlie them all— but the earthworks were probably in decay by Saxon times and no trace has been found there. Medbury 'maiden fort' which recalls Maiden Castle suggests a legendary rather than an historic site. Perhaps some of these ancient defences were gratefully occupied by early Saxons, just as a few hill-forts were repaired by Britons after the end of the Roman period, but their descriptive names were probably transferred to neighbouring villages.

In a few instances a *burh* name may hint at an English settlement equipped with rudimentary defences; possible examples are Upbury, Padbury, Soulbury and Lathbury which sounds like a derogatory reference to a flimsy palisade. Barley[20] pleaded for the excavation of small settlements whose names incorporate *burh*.

Limbury and Aylesbury have already been encountered in discussing the 571 annal, where it was suggested they mark *foederati* stations established early in the 5th century for British defensive purposes; here some kind of protective work can be suspected.

Another interesting name, Kingsbury, occurs at St. Albans, Benson, Newington and Aylesbury itself. There is no doubt that the first (see Appendix II), a ramparted enclosure of 27½ acres between Verulamium and the abbey which Offa founded, existed before 793, which explains why it is not mentioned among the constructions of the Danish wars. It was royal property until its transfer to the monastery began about 1000. Nothing is known about earthworks at the Benson Kingsbury which probably had a similar history, for this was already a royal manor in 887 and the Kingsbury there was alienated by the Crown about 1235. Benson was an important administrative centre and it can be inferred that the St. Albans Kingsbury played a similar part.

Clearly the latter occupies in time as well as place a position between post-Roman Verulamium and the abbatial town. If a defensible site in the vicinity was required a new earthwork would be a much more manageable proposition than the ruinous Roman city with enormous lengths of dilapidated walls. Why should a stronghold be required before the Danish invasions? The best solution that can be proposed is the rivalry between English kingdoms for this debated territory. Towards the end of the 7th century Mercia was pressing against the conquests of Wessex north of the Thames, though before about 705 Essex had some claim to lordship as far west as Hemel Hempstead, and soon powerful Mercian kings dominated the whole region. The St. Albans Kingsbury may have been erected by the East Saxons and then taken by the Mercians, but more probably it was made by the latter. Such a prodigious work might well have been undertaken by Offa, the great 8th-century dyke-builder who according to St. Albans tradition died at his estate at Offley a dozen miles north of the abbey.

How could this site come into royal possession? The proximity of Verulamium may be relevant. On the British defeat in 571 the *territorium* of the old cantonal capital would have passed into the hands of English rulers and been taken over by the dynasty that displaced them. Other Kingsbury names suggest this also happened at Aylesbury and Benson.

The peculiarity of the Chiltern zone and its meaning

Several *tuns* on the low ground near Hitchin serve to emphasize the almost complete absence of this element in the Chiltern range, which has only Wigginton and Luton, and the positional Norrington which could be quite late. It is this lack which casts doubt on the possible *hām* names in the higher Chilterns. There are few *tuns* in east Hertfordshire, a wide area which discounting the Newton/Aston type and two post-Conquest examples has only Wallington, Watton, Gilston, *Ichetone* and Kimpton. Fawn Wood and Hunton are the only ones near St. Albans, in a district developed by the abbey after Offa's grant in 793. *Tuns* are missing in the Bernwood Forest area of Buckinghamshire. All these gaps significantly coincide with the districts where pagan Saxon traces are scanty or absent. Evidently few English settlements were founded there in the middle Saxon period, though the making of isolated farmsteads by reclamation from the forest in late Saxon times must account for many of the minor names.

The dearth of *tuns* in north-west Buckinghamshire can be explained by the prevalence of thick woodland that deterred early pioneers seeking easy terrain. This simple solution will not do for the Chiltern zone, because it contained much fertile land, previously cultivated and again in Domesday times. Moreover it is not just *tun* that is lacking. Most of the zone exhibits a notable poverty of the typical early habitative elements—*hām*, *-ingas*, *-ingtun* and *worth*—that might be expected to point to extensive English settlement or influence while they were in familiar parlance. What was the reason for the extraordinary scarcity there of these elements and particularly *tun*, in use for so long? Possible theories are that the settlement of largely empty, undesirable land was delayed until even *tun* had gone out of use; that these tracts were occupied by English settlers who did not use the *tun*-naming or earlier formulae; or that this country was already peopled by non-English speakers who did not give such names.

The place-names themselves of the Chiltern zone provide a clue. Here almost all the settlements bear nature names, or much less frequently and mainly in minor names compounds of these and English personal names. We naturally ask whether any positive characteristics can be detected in this area. The answer is none. Careful search has not distinguished any trace of abnormal nomenclature apart from the negative feature noted. The occurrence of endless place-names denoting hills, valleys, streams and woods merely reflects the nature of the terrain. No element not normally used to indicate habitation can be proposed for that exceptional function in the Chiltern zone, where the overwhelming majority of settlements were named after adjacent features.

In the St. Albans district, for example, we have Redbourn on a reedy stream (*burna*), Ridge, Sandridge and Windridge by a *hrycg*, Colney near a river islet (*eg*), Tittenhanger near a wood (*hangra*), Shenley near a clearing (*leah*), Burston by a boundary stone (*stan*), Winchfield in open land (*feld*), Elstree at Tidulf's tree (*treow*). *Tun* occurs twice and there are a few minor names in *wic* and *hamstede*, but nature names predominate.

The same picture greets us at both ends of the Chilterns. In Binfield Hundred at the western end the only settlement names recorded before about 1250 apart from one *hamstede* are from *byxe* 'box tree', *denu* 'valley' (3), *feld* 'open land', *hrycg* 'ridge', *hyth* 'landing place', *lacu* 'pool' and *leah* 'clearing'; not far away are Turville (*feld*), Hambleden (*denu*), Stonor (*ora* 'bank'), Fingest (*hyrst* 'wood') and Cadmore (*maere* 'boundary'). The north Hertfordshire heights at the other extreme offer more variety of the same kind. Here are *denu* (Aspenden, Berkeden, Rushden), *dun* 'hill' (Sandon), *feld* (Broadfield, Therfield), *healh* 'corner' (Clothall, Wyddial, Luffenhall and *Sumersele*—now Hyde Hall, with a personal name), *hoh* 'hill-spur' (Hodenhoe, with a personal name), *leah* (Barley and Wakeley, the latter with a personal name), *ryht* 'rough ground' (Reed), *rith* 'stream' (Cottered), *wielle* 'spring' (Orwell), *anstig* 'narrow path' (Anstey) and *weg* 'way' (Barkway). Habitative elements, on the periphery, are rare: only Wallington (*-ingatun*) and Nuthampstead (*hamstede*).

These names are certainly of pre-Conquest antiquity but their complexion is merely that of standard Old English. We can reject any idea that very many are early forms, for it is a sound presumption that typical habitative elements would surely enter into a large collection of early names, even if early settlements did sometimes use non-habitative names. Considering the very long vogue that *tun* enjoyed it is inconceivable that any English people forsook that formula so commonly employed elsewhere when villages were founded and named by neighbours. It is equally unimaginable that Englishmen familiar with it should here adopt a completely different system and distinguish each other's homes by an entirely novel and so far unrecognized nomenclature based on descriptions like Redbourn 'reedy stream' and Mulsoe 'Mul's hill-spur' to the exclusion of familiar habitative elements; names of the Redbourn type denoted features described before the settlements that borrowed them. The general absence in many districts of the usually abundant *tun* plainly means that most of these names were not coeval with the main *tun*-forming period but created later.

The hypothesis that exploitation of these promising lands was delayed until *tun* was no longer a common designation for a new settlement is rebutted by the fairly even density of Domesday occupation, resulting from a lengthy period of expansion during which nearly every corner received the attention of settlers. If we could regard this as a once unpeopled tract, the names would have arisen as it became occupied at a rather late date when normal habitative elements had fallen into disuse. Given the longevity of *tun* that would imply an incredibly late date. Moreover we have no reason to suppose this large area was entirely unoccupied or very sparsely inhabited in middle Saxon times, which would be contrary to indications from both the Roman and Domesday eras.

So the first two theoretical solutions, late settlement or peculiar English nomenclature, are quite untenable. Cunliffe's recent dictum[21] 'there can be little reasonable doubt that the sub-Roman rural population remained considerable

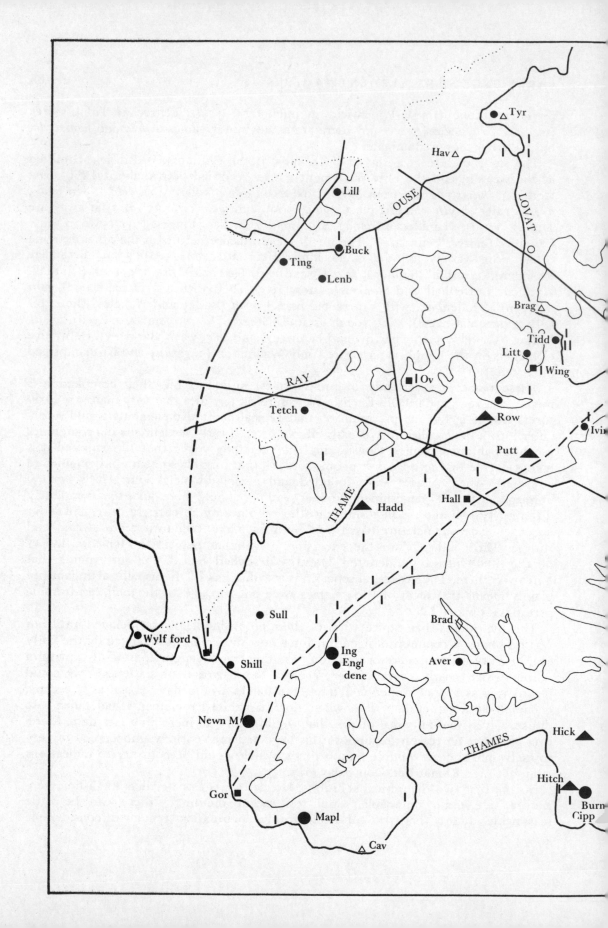

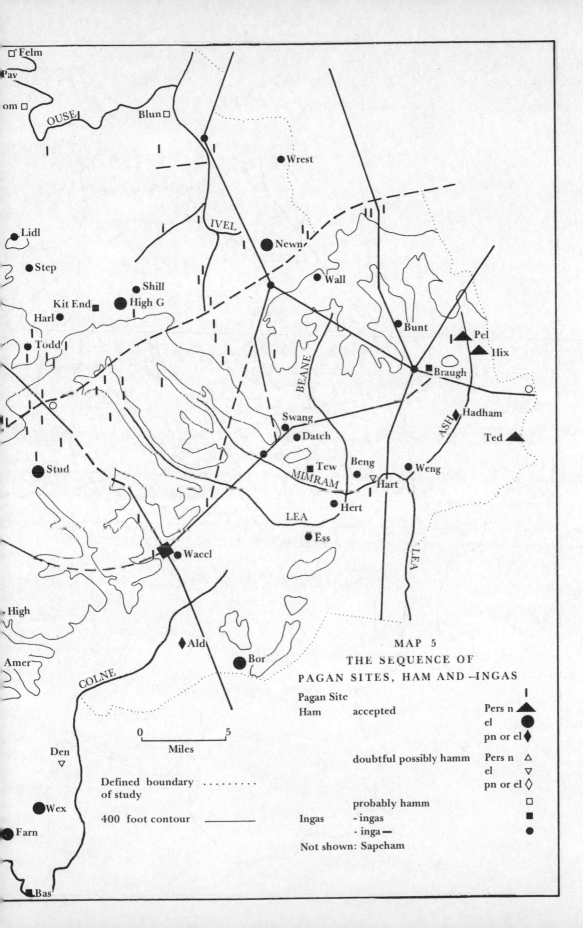

□ Felm
Pav
om □
OUSE
Blun □
● Wrest
IVEL
● Newn
Lidl
● Step
● Wall
Shill
Kit End ■ ● High G
Harl ●
Bunt
▲ Pel
● Todd
▲ Hix
BEANE
■ Braugh
○
Swang ●
ASH
◆ Hadham
Stud ●
Datch
▲ Ted
■ Tew
Beng
● Weng
MIMRAM
▽ Hart
Hert ●
LEA
● Ess
LEA
◆ Waccl
High
◆ Ald
Amer
● Bor
COLNE

MAP 5
THE SEQUENCE OF
PAGAN SITES, HAM AND –INGAS

Pagan Site |
Ham   accepted   Pers n ▲
                                             el   ●
                                             pn or el ◆

0   5   doubtful possibly hamm Pers n △
Miles   el   ▽
                                             pn or el   ◇

Den
▽
                                             probably hamm   □
Defined boundary ....   Ingas   - ingas   ■
of study   - inga —
Wex ●   ●
400 foot contour ————   Not shown: Sapeham
Farn ●

Bas

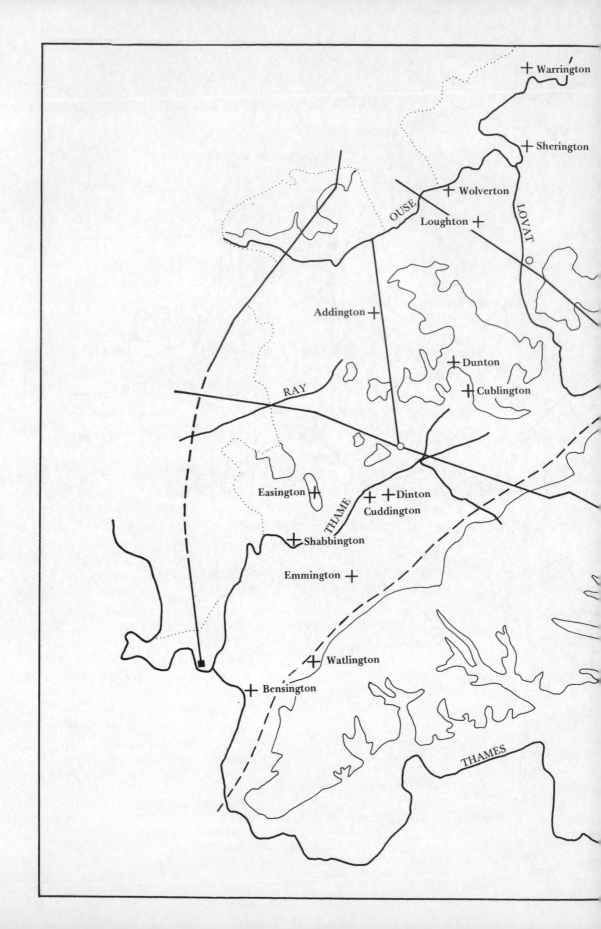

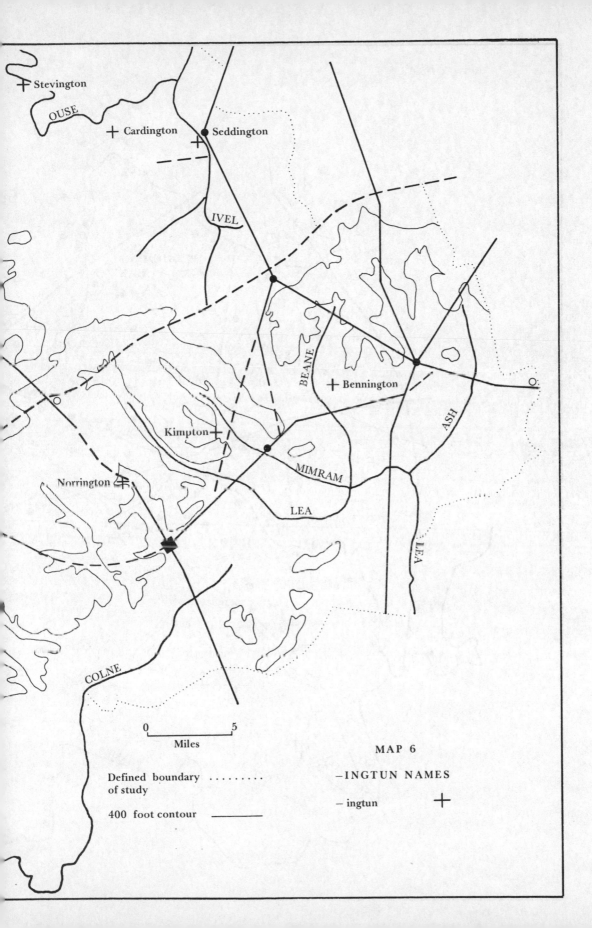

Stevington

OUSE

Cardington

Seddington

IVEL

BEANE

Bennington

Kimpton

ASH

MIMRAM

Norrington

LEA

LEA

COLNE

0   5

Miles

MAP 6

–INGTUN NAMES

Defined boundary · · · · · · · ·
of study

– ingtun

400 foot contour

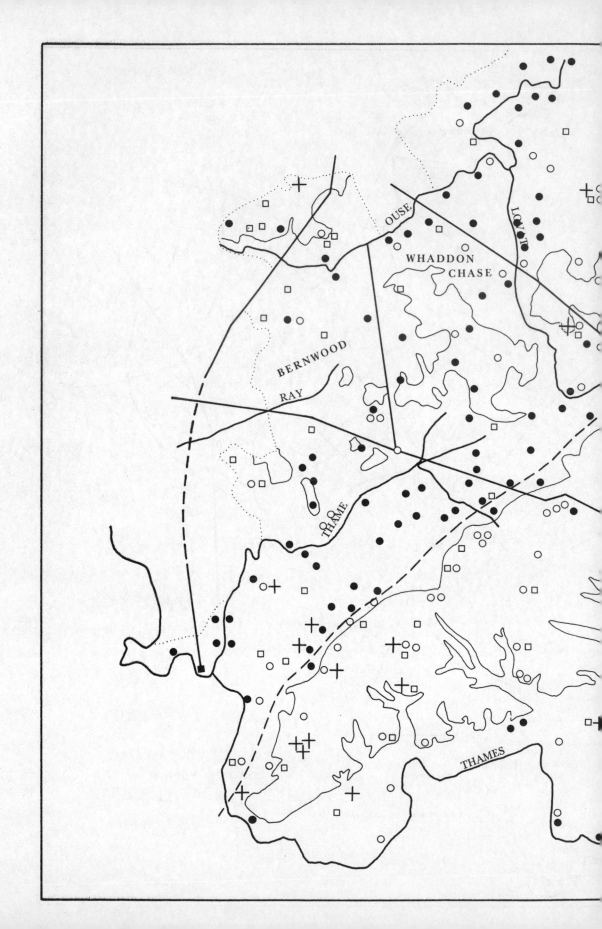

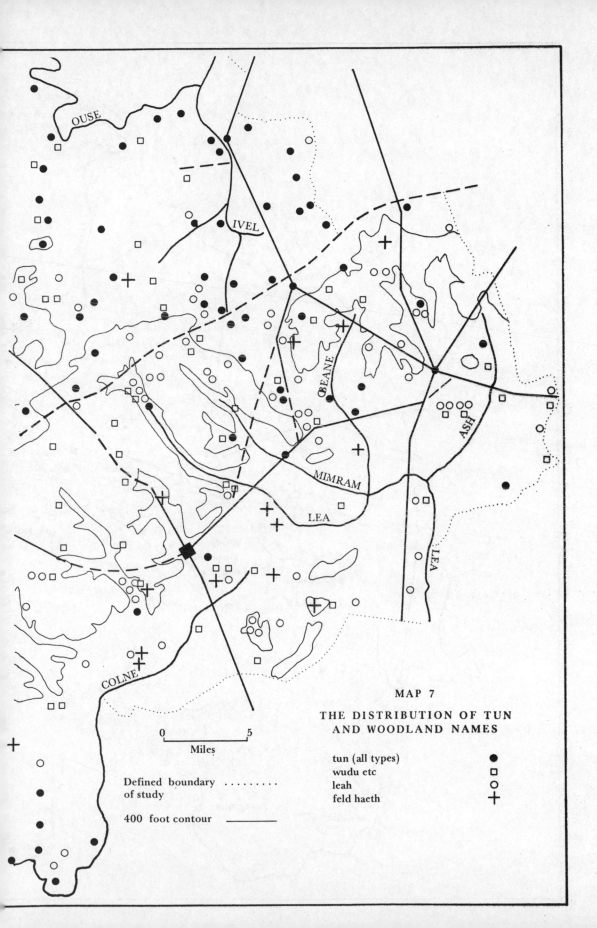

OUSE

IVEL

BEANE

ASH

MIMRAM

LEA

LEA

COLNE

MAP 7

THE DISTRIBUTION OF TUN
AND WOODLAND NAMES

0   5
   Miles

tun (all types)   ●
wudu etc   □
leah   ○
feld haeth   +

Defined boundary . . . .
of study

400 foot contour ———————

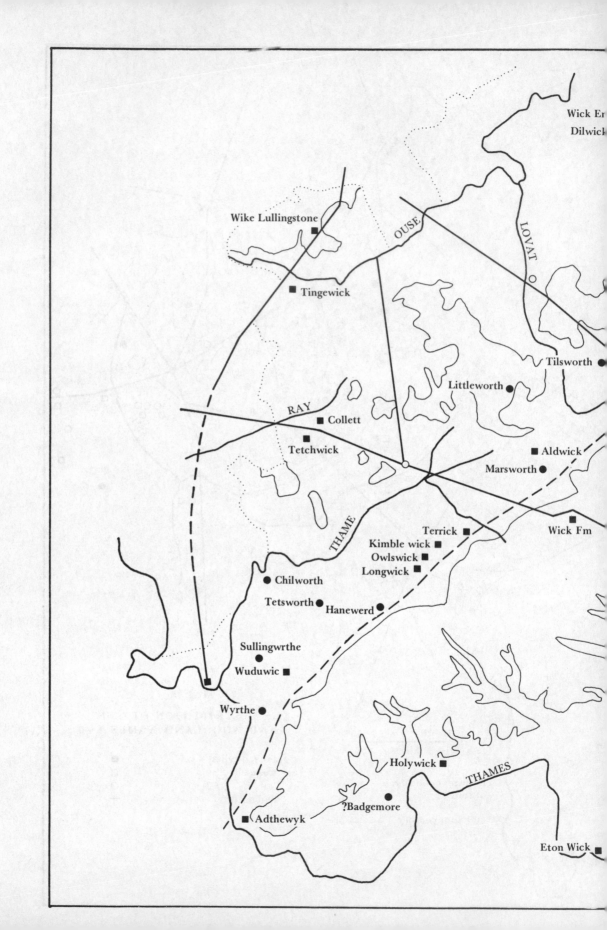

Wick Er
Dilwick

Wike Lullingstone ■

Tingewick ■

OUSE

LOVAT O

Tilsworth ■

Littleworth ●

RAY

Collett ■

Aldwick ■

Tetchwick ■

Marsworth ●

THAME

Terrick ■
Kimble wick ■
Owlswick ■
Longwick ■

Wick Fm ■

Chilworth ●

Tetsworth ● Hanewerd ●

Sullingwrthe ●

Wuduwic ■

Wyrthe ●

Holywick ■

THAMES

?Badgemore ●

Adthewyk ■

Eton Wick ■

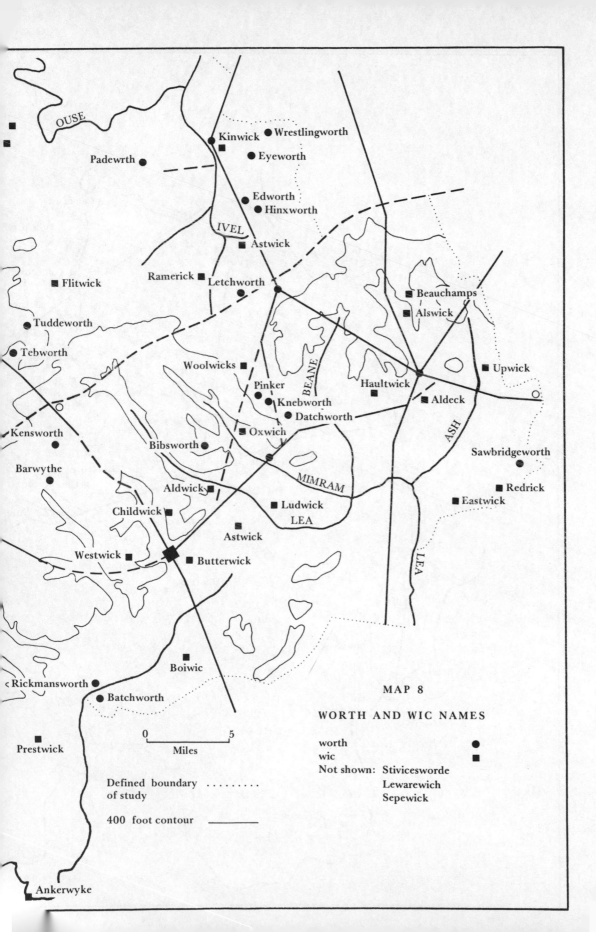

OUSE

Kinwick ● Wrestlingworth

Padewrth ● Eyeworth

Edworth
● Hinxworth

IVEL

■ Astwick

Ramerick ■ Letchworth

■ Flitwick

Beauchamps
Alswick

Tuddeworth

Woolwicks

Upwick

Tebworth

BEANE

Pinker
Knebworth

Haultwick

Aldeck

Kensworth

Oxwich

Datchworth

ASH

Bibsworth

Sawbridgeworth

Barwythe

MIMRAM

Aldwick

Redrick

Childwick

Ludwick
LEA

Eastwick

Astwick

Westwick ■ Butterwick

LEA

Boiwic

Rickmansworth

MAP 8

Batchworth

WORTH AND WIC NAMES

Prestwick

0   5
Miles

worth   ●
wic   ■
Not shown: Stivicesworde
           Lewarewich
           Sepewick

Defined boundary . . . .
of study

400 foot contour ————

Ankerwyke

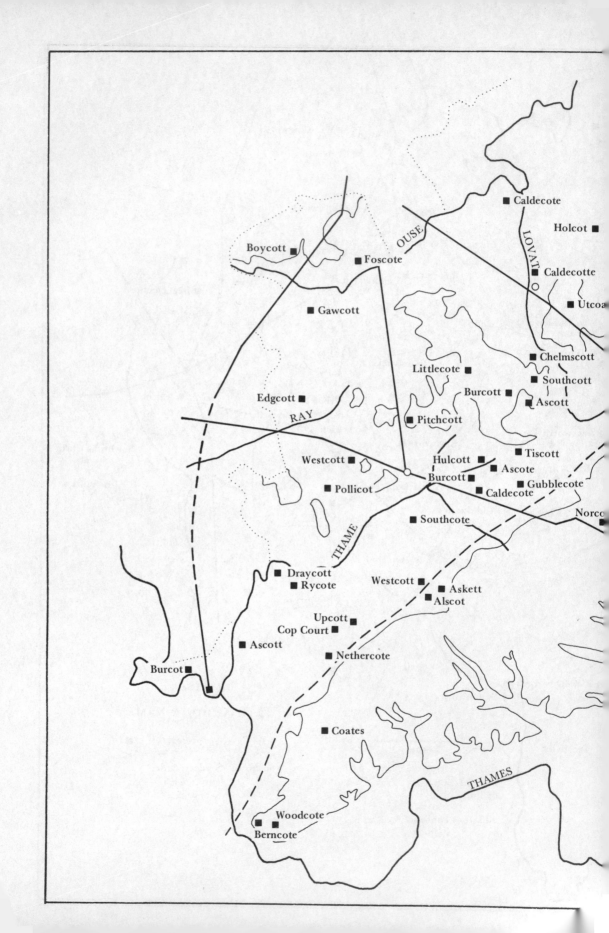

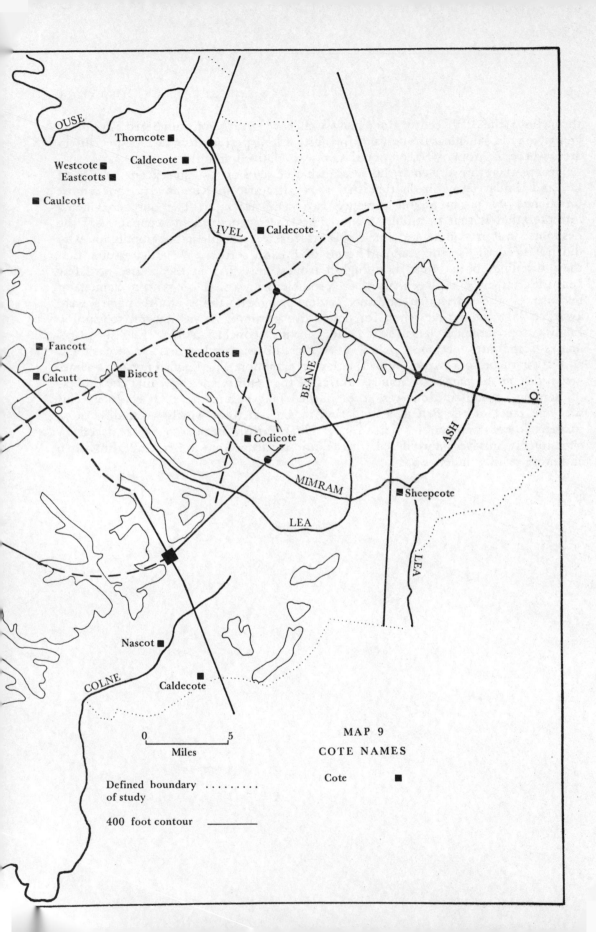

OUSE

Thorncote ■

Westcote ■
Eastcotts ■
Caldecote ■

■ Caulcott

IVEL

■ Caldecote

■ Fancott

Redcoats ■

■ Calcutt

■ Biscot

BEANE

ASH

■ Codicote

MIMRAM

■ Sheepcote

LEA

LEA

Nascot ■

COLNE

■ Caldecote

0   5
Miles

MAP 9

COTE NAMES

Defined boundary ....
of study

Cote   ■

400 foot contour _____

throughout the fifth century and may well have greatly outnumbered the immi-grants' may in fair measure be valid for quite a long period afterwards, especially in areas where the primary Saxon population was relatively minute.

We are therefore driven to an inescapable conclusion by the extreme rarity of *tun* and similar terms in districts that were attractive in Roman days but almost untouched by pagan Saxon presence two centuries later. The only convincing interpretation is that in middle Saxon times there remained in occupation of the desirable Chiltern valleys and much of Hertfordshire a sizable native population who did not need to use the standard terms of English settlers. We must assume that their dwellings bore other, non-English names, and that in the course of a few centuries, either by replacement of the erodible names of Celtic-pattern hamlets or because of the settlement shifting Taylor proposed, these nature names were awarded later at a time when for descriptive purposes it was natural to employ English topographical language.[22] Wade-Martins' conclusion that English place-names sometimes became applied to earlier British settlements—or, we should add, their successors—is no doubt the right explanation. The English personal names embedded in the names of minor features of the countryside show that the process of naming or substitution was accomplished long before the 11th century. This was one facet of the British assimilation to English ways which we shall explore further; there was ample time for residual British names to be replaced or occasionally survive embroidered with additions such as that in Brick-hill, Englished and more readily understood.

Chapter X

CELTIC PLACE-NAMES

CERTAIN KINDS OF place-name are still almost the only hard evidence for the post-Roman British element in most of England. The majority can be regarded as a contribution from the native people, directly or indirectly, while a few others seem to import English allusions to recognizable, still unassimilated Britons in their midst. Because the former category has been strongly challenged as worthless we must consider the validity of the objection and overcome it if we are to invoke these names as evidence.

The late Dr. F. T. Wainwright,[1] who acknowledged that 'one of the most crucial problems of early English history is . . . the extent to which the British population survived the impact of the settlement', was a protagonist of the view that place-names of definite British origin are almost if not quite irrelevant in this connexion. If that were really true it would be hopeless to try to deduce any degree of British survival from place-names alone, even in Cornwall. The reasoning behind this destructive contention can however be contested by considering his arguments.

To disagree with them, however, is not to dissent from a realistic outlook: 'the extreme rarity of Celtic names in Hertfordshire proves that whenever the English occupation of this country took place, it ultimately obliterated the fabric of earlier British life'.[2] Put starkly in Wainwright's words,[3] 'however many Britons physically survived the Anglo-Saxon conquest nowhere in England is there any sign that they exercised an appreciable influence on the language, economy, political arrangements and general way of life of the English. The Romano–British communities were completely broken, and with their language they lost their national identity and their corporate existence. Where they survived it was as alien elements in a society essentially English and essentially Germanic'.

The ultimate emergence of a society of thoroughly English complexion in the historic period is a fundamental reality that cannot be gainsaid, however it might be explained why all traces of the native people were eventually extinguished. But it is important to realize that their disappearance in the light of history no more excludes the possibility of a British component in early English society than the virtually complete medieval assimilation of the Danelaw proves the social extinction of its Scandinavian people. Their language was deeply implanted in the 9th century but by the 13th it had vanished as a living tongue, though the population that spoke it was numerous, compact and largely free. Whereas the Danish settlement bequeathed much in social custom and vocabulary besides plentiful place-names to witness its strength, British society admittedly left a scant legacy; yet their fates are surely in some ways comparable. Disappearance is no adequate ground for maintaining that in no part of England survived an appreciable British element, which the unusual number of British place-names in the Chiltern region suggests was once by no means negligible there.

In a stimulating philosophical work adumbrating a rigorously disciplined approach to various kinds of evidence, Wainwright[4] insisted that the persistence of Celtic place-names could not logically be adduced to prove survival of the native people, even to a meagre extent: 'they do not provide direct evidence for the survival of a British population', and 'those who seek to prove a very considerable British survival in England must find support for their thesis in evidence other than that provided in place-names'.

He expressly admitted other cogent evidence for survival, but curiously did not refer to the nature of sources such as law codes which reveal the existence of recognized classes of 'Welshmen' in late 7th-century Wessex. The omission is surprising, even allowing for the brevity of his remarks and the slant of his reasoning, because the presence of such people implies a likely medium in which place-names of Celtic origin could be handed over and perpetuated in English usage. Such a context cannot be overlooked in understanding place-names; Wainwright's silence on this is remarkable because, despite strictures on the academic misuse of other disciplines, he recognized that facts should be judiciously related to their broad context. It would be silly to handicap ourselves by ignoring these conditions, for the Dark Age historian must cautiously make the most of all the limited material available if he is to extract its full significance. Much of Jackson's *Language and history in early Britain*, an interpretation of linguistic apparatus in harmony with and augmenting the known historical framework, would according to Wainwright's tenets be quite inadmissible.

In Wainwright's opinion the part played by a British element in early England was of minimal importance. His detailed examples claim to show why he reached this conclusion but their selectivity suggests that he approached the question with partiality. An instance of this bias is his assertion that tautological constructions such as Cheetwood—British *ceto-* and Old English *wudu* both mean 'wood'—'imply that the neighbouring Anglo-Saxons had heard but did not know the meaning of these common Celtic words' and 'count heavily against all but the most brief and superficial contact'. This was special pleading, for as Wainwright remarked[5] place-names cease to carry obvious meaning when the words they contain fall out of use; when this happens it is natural for later speakers to embroider them to make sense, by adding a new element describing the feature or distorting a name into something that sounds meaningful.

Finberg[6] pointed out that some of these tautologies are certainly of late formation, and others may well be; Hackpen Hill was still in the 10th century *Hacan pen*, an entirely Celtic name. Others however are early; when king Centwine of Wessex granted Creechbarrow in Dorset towards the end of the 7th century his charter called it a hill 'named *Cructan* in the British tongue, by us *Crycebeorh*',[7] showing how the native word *cruc* 'hill' was absorbed and coupled with an English synonym, perhaps by people not ignorant of its meaning. The Nottinghamshire name Welbeck consists of an English river name to which Old Norse *bekkr* 'stream' has been added, but the only conclusion we are entitled to draw is that Danish men found it convenient to attach their own term to the original. Wensdon Hill in Bedfordshire tells us merely that the meaning of the common word *dun* 'hill' eventually became forgotten by the English themselves. The utter confusion in many medieval spellings between *-don* 'hill' and *-den* 'valley' and even between *-don* and *-ton* 'village' shows that the sense of quite ordinary words could easily be lost. Wainwright's intemperate criticism on this issue will not bear examination.

Because the great majority of Celtic place-names in England signify topographical features Wainwright made much of the fact that Celtic personal names and habitative terms are prominently absent. He overlooked that the contrast with English names, so far as it is valid, arose from different habits of nomenclature and has no bearing on survival. Whereas English place-names often contain personal names and denote their possession or association, Celtic names seldom do: leaving aside frequent dedications to early saints, Welsh place-names are typically descriptive, like Penmaenmawr 'head of the great rock', and naming places from natural features was normal in Roman Britain, as the derivation of those in the Antonine Itinerary and the Ravennas List[8] shows: few contain personal names or habitative terms.

Moreover Wainwright's alleged contrast between Celtic and English fashions was rather exaggerated and should be put in perspective, for nature names were not confined to Celtic people: as already noted the majority of place-names in the Chiltern region are of this type, which was common enough in Germanic place-names. In Bede's *Historia ecclesiastica* names containing habitative elements are far outnumbered by nature names,[9] which became attached to settlements. The eradication of former settlements which Wainwright supposed by no means follows from the rarity of British personal names and terms denoting occupation.

Doubts on the score of the great scarcity of place-names of British origin are a more serious matter. Certainly they are very uncommon except in the west, but there are indications that they were once more numerous. The Chiltern region offers several names that were still current in early medieval times but replaced later —the river name Saferon in Bedford, the older name of the river Ray and others mentioned below. River names of English origin have likewise been supplanted by newer ones, sometimes back-formations from places situated on them, and today even among scholars the artificial modern form Ouzel is ousting the British name of the river Lovat. Disappearance is not confined to river names; among village names Latimer and Chenies in Buckinghamshire and Hare Street in Hertfordshire are replacements, and in the latter county several estate names have changed since medieval times.[10] The loss of a name is undetectable unless we happen to know the original form, but in the whole region the Romano–British names of only five places are known. The replacement of others does not necessarily mean lack of continuity.

Besides names and fragments of definite British origin there are some where the etymology is obscure or puzzling but may perhaps be British. A few British names may have escaped notice, for, warned by the case of York which would be given a perfectly convincing Anglo–Danish pedigree if we had not known its Celtic name *Eburacum*, we may suspect that a concealed though quite small number of apparently

English names really come from an older stratum. If an English or Norse ancestry will serve there is usually no need to seek further. Our place-names have rarely had the benefit of scrutiny by Celtic philologists that might reveal more survivals, but hardly a tenth of them are recorded before Domesday, by which time an original British name could be replaced or twisted into an apparently English one. We must not forget, too, that the vast majority of the great bulk of place-names of all periods that exist today are minor names created by the steady expansion of population over 1,500 years; it is unreasonable to expect British names to exceed a tiny minority.

Examples of substitution illustrate what must have been a constant tendency towards the loss of early place-names. British names were particularly susceptible to this process for a reason that Wainwright ignored. A typical English pattern may always have been the nucleated village, as sites such as West Stow and Sutton Courtenay and the big early cemeteries suggest, but as Caesar remarked and Hoskins reminded us many Celtic people were accustomed to live in single farms and hamlets scattered through the countryside. This must have had differential effects on the preservation of place-names, for village names, those of sizable features and over-whelmingly English or Scandinavian, are fairly resistant to change while minor names are much more liable to replacement or loss.[11] The Celtic pattern of dispersed homesteads would engrave their names less deeply upon folk usage and memory than those of compact settlements, with the inevitable result that they were more vulnerable.

Taylor's proposition[12] that the erosion factor was always active, that throughout the Dark Ages there was a continual shifting of occupation sites, 'part of a long tradition of constantly changing pattern', would mean the uprooting and short-distance migration of many settlements with the loss of some names. This hypothesis may help to explain why Celtic names are scarce, because British founda-tions, being older than the English, would tend to suffer most. The surviving names of British origin, however rare, resemble the visible portion of an iceberg. Most have not endured, but their loss does not deprive the remnant of importance.

Another reason for regarding Wainwright's outlook as excessively cautious is, as Jackson and Reaney stressed, that the accurate form in which some British place-names were transmitted betrays more than casual intercourse between natives and newcomers; Wainwright himself mentioned names like Dover that preserve an original oblique plural. Dover is not a crucial instance as the native word could have been learned before the invaders arrived, but more telling examples betoken a phase when the British learned their new masters' tongue and became bilingual: Wendover is a local name that argues this. It is in this sort of context that we should visualise the transmission of the Celtic elements of topographical meaning that passed early into the English vocabulary; little wonder these are rare, because the newcomers brought terms that were adequate for nearly all purposes. Wainwright rather dismissed these loanwords and did not mention that English place-names themselves contain evidence for a degree of survival: the personal names of British derivation, referred to later, that beyond doubt signify some mingling of the two races.

Surviving British place-names in the region (Appendix V)

As prominent natural features such as hill ranges most tend to keep their original names because they have wide currency, it is not surprising that *Chiltern* is of British origin. *Icknield* is believed to come from the same source, but the other main Roman roads—Ermine, Watling and Akeman Streets—bear English names. The old Buckinghamshire forest name *Morezyf* near Westbury is probably British.

The region's river names are predominantly British, though as usual minor stream names are less emphatically so. *Thames, Thame, Colne, Lea, Ouse, Ivel* and *Lovat* certainly are, and *Hiz* may be in ultimate origin. *Tempsford* probably shows that part of the Ouse once bore the same name as the Thames. Of the Lea tributaries *Beane* is certainly British, and most remarkable because the form *Bene ficcan* (p. 114) points to a formation no earlier than about 600. *Mimram* too is probably Celtic since no convincing alternative has been given, and the Ash was once called *Ysene* which seems to be British; the old name is preserved in Easneye. The lost name *Saferon* for a brook in Bedford is identical with Severn (Welsh *Hafren*) and shows early intake before the initial consonant could change. The Ray now bears an English name but its original *Geht* or *Icht* was remembered well into the Middle Ages. The short Chiltern streams have English names, some of them back-formations like Gade from Gaddesden and Chess from Chesham which perhaps superseded British names within the historic period. Such a name was *Wendover*, a Celtic name meaning 'white waters' which would well fit a chalk stream. The original name of the Chess seems to have been *Isen*, like that of the Ash. Other lesser British river names have been lost, and one now survives only in the first part of the village name *Campton*. Examples such as this, *Saferon* and the old name of the Ray show that many British names now extinct lived on for centuries before being replaced.

In contrast very few names of Romano–British towns in the region lived on. Two lasted into Saxon times: Verulamium was known to Bede as *Werlamceaster* as well as by a new English style, and although the pre-English form of Dorchester is not recorded the British original *Dorcicon* has been reconstructed. The earlier names of Braughing, Dunstable and Dropshort disappeared but that of another Romano–British place may survive in *Bernwood*, perhaps derived from *Brinavis*, a place in the Ravennas List, or from a British cognate of Welsh *bryn* 'hill'.

The impression given by local river names is confirmed by surviving British loan-words and transported fragments: compared with their usual faintness elsewhere their volume in the region is quite impressive. The British elements *brico-* 'hill', *ceto-* 'wood', *camp*[13] 'open space' and *funta*[14] 'spring' all occur more than once, and the incidence of the last is as strong as anywhere outside Hampshire. A particularly interesting loanword found twice in Buckinghamshire is *croh*, denoting the Mediterranean saffron plant which must have survived for some time in the vicinity of Romano–British gardens. Another occurrence in the name of Croydon,[15] Surrey, near the early Mitcham cemetery suggests contact there between the indigenous people and Germanic *foederati*: we can glimpse a situation like that in the Chiltern region and one that makes a *cambo-* 'bend' element in Kempston quite conceivable. The circumstances in which such words as these were absorbed are discussed in Chapter XII.

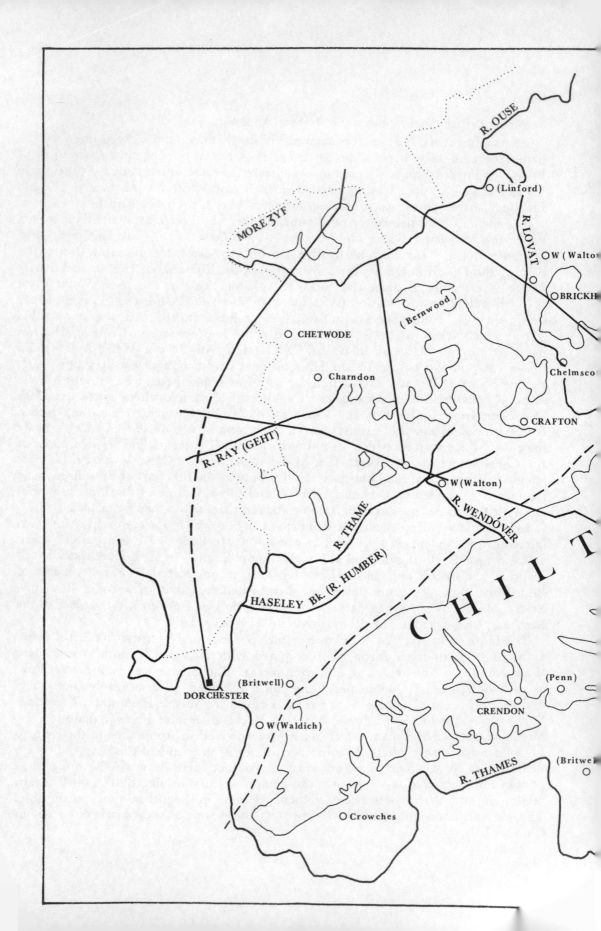

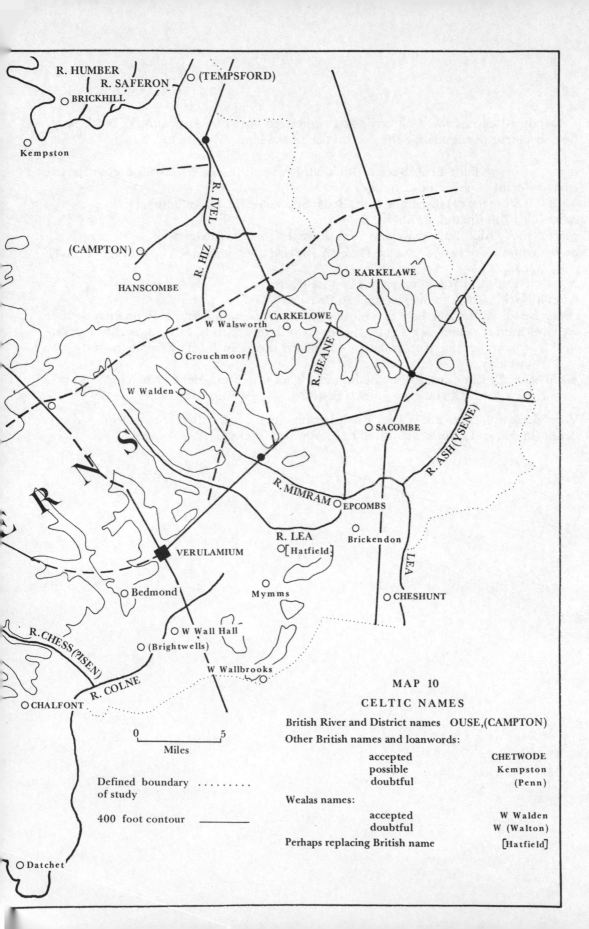

R. HUMBER
R. SAFERON
BRICKHILL
Kempston
(TEMPSFORD)
R. IVEL
R. HIZ
(CAMPTON)
HANSCOMBE
KARKELAWE
W Walsworth
CARKELOWE
Crouchmoor
W Walden
R. BEANE
SACOMBE
R. ASH (YSENE)
E R N S
R. MIMRAM
EPCOMBS
Brickendon
R. LEA
VERULAMIUM
[Hatfield]
LEA
Bedmond
Mymms
CHESHUNT
R. CHESS (?ISEN)
W Wall Hall
(Brightwells)
R. COLNE
W Wallbrooks
CHALFONT

MAP 10

CELTIC NAMES

British River and District names   OUSE,(CAMPTON)

Other British names and loanwords:

accepted	CHETWODE
possible	Kempston
doubtful	(Penn)

Wealas names:

accepted	W Walden
doubtful	W (Walton)

Perhaps replacing British name   [Hatfield]

0   5
Miles

Defined boundary . . . .
of study

400 foot contour ————

Datchet

Details of all possible Celtic survival names are noted in Appendix V, but it may be convenient to summarize the occurrence of the loanwords here:

brico- or *briga* 'hill': Brill, Bucks: Brickhill, Beds and Bucks; ? in Brickendon, Herts.
cambo- 'bend': ? in Kempston, Beds.
camp 'open space': Hanscombe End, Beds; Epcombs, Herts; Sacombe, Herts.
carn 'hill': ? in Charndon, Bucks.
carrec 'rocky hill': Karkelawe and Carkelowe, lost names in Herts.
ceto- 'wood': Chetwode, Bucks; Datchet, Bucks; the compound *penchet* in Panshill, Bucks.
croh 'saffron': Crafton, Bucks; Crendon Lane, Bucks.
cruc 'hillock': Crouchmoor, Herts; ? in Crowches, Oxon.
cumb 'small valley, combe': this passed readily into English and is frequently found in minor names, especially in the Chilterns, but is rare in parish names. Swyncombe and Watcombe in Oxon are the only local examples as early as Domesday.
funta 'spring': Chalfont, Bucks; Bedmond, Herts; Cheshunt, Herts; ? in a lost alternative name of Chelmscott, Bucks. Bedfont, Middx, is not far away.

Very doubtful cases are *hlynn* 'pool, stream' in Linford, Bucks; *pen* 'top, end' in Penn, Bucks; and *prys* 'brushwood' in Pressmoor, Bucks.

Chapter XI

PIECING TOGETHER THE CLUES:
THE ARRIVAL AND EXPANSION OF THE SAXONS

NEARLY ALL THE evidence at our command has been sifted to illuminate the history of the two or three centuries after 410, especially the post-Roman setting and the circumstances of early Saxon settlement in the region. It is time to blend the indications of history, archaeology and English place-names into a synthesis reconstructing the outlines of the period, before trying to understand the most perplexing question of all, the eventual fate of the British population whose country this once was, on which we can draw on a little more evidence of a rather inferential nature.

In 410 when Britain ceased in name to be Roman the Chiltern region formed the greater part of a semi-autonomous state, the Catuvellaunian *civitas* or province governed from Verulamium. Romanized institutions and manners obtained, especially among the upper, landed classes. The city and a hundred villas throughout its territory were not directly affected by the change, and in 429 St. Germanus found conditions normal. Some national framework of government continued and about 425 a noble bearing the title 'Vortigern' attained supreme power. To ward off renewed Pictish menaces and buttress his own position he soon introduced contingents of Germanic soldier-settlers, probably with the status of *foederati*: men bound to serve in arms when required in return for grants of land and provisions. These forces were rapidly built up through the agency of their leader Hengist.

Most of these troops were stationed in the vulnerable east. Few were placed in the region, and in small numbers. One such site was Dorchester, where Germanic personnel accompanied by their womenfolk formed part of the garrison in the last decades of the 4th century and were buried in the town cemetery outside the walls; here continuity is shown by the recently discovered Berinsfield cemetery of entirely pagan Saxon character, which came into use early in the 5th century while the native Christian people were buried in the Queensford Mill ground and perhaps another at Overy.

Similar Saxon *foederati* stations (Chapter VII) were established at this time at Kempston, Sandy, Luton and Aylesbury, at all of which an early 5th-century character is enough to show Saxon communities in occupation in circumstances where the directed settlement of recruited auxiliaries is the only acceptable explanation; land-hungry freebooters had no opportunity before Hengist's revolt.

At Sandy only pottery survives to prove this period, but evidence from Kempston and Luton is fuller and more balanced. Kempston has some early 5th-century wares, and although there are no extant vessels from Luton before the later 5th century the oldest part of the Argyll Avenue cemetery was probably wrecked without investigation. However, Luton, Kempston and Berinsfield are among the extremely rare English sites with specimens of the primitive 'Luton type' brooch that goes back to the very early 5th century, and, most decisively, all three places produced 'military' belt equipment suggestive of contemporary contacts between British officialdom and Saxon mercenary pioneers. Slightly later material—pottery, 5-scroll saucer brooches and at Kempston cruciform and equal-armed brooches—confirms that Saxon communities were soon well established at these sites.

Contemporary evidence at Aylesbury (Walton) is no longer lacking, and here too is a belt fitting; it can be deduced from this, its mention in the 571 annal, and the Bishopstone belt plate and the Dinton beaker both found nearby, that it too was a *foederati* settlement, the putative centre of later expansion whence both objects came. The case for similar status at Stevenage is unproven and its belt fitting was perhaps brought from Luton. Another uncertain candidate is Warmark at Toddington where although much evidence has perished the presence of a big cemetery with plenty of cremations suggests an early foundation. These seven sites— five of them certain—are the only ones in the region with any claim to primary character.

The locations show these forces were mainly reserves on lines of communication between the Cotswolds and East Anglia, placed so that they could readily be switched wherever needed, but Kempston was intended to block the Ouse route from the Fens into the interior. Perhaps because the local authorities disliked barbarian troops or considered them untrustworthy none were placed near Verulamium. This is a remarkable contrast to other important Romano–British cities, such as Winchester,[1] where such Saxon groups were allowed to live in close proximity, and must stem from a deliberately different policy.

Hengist's ambition and growing strength led to confrontation with an increasingly dependent Vortigern and resentful nobles who regretted his taxing bargain once the Pictish danger was over. Insurrection broke out about 442 and despite initially successful British resistance in Kent the Saxons asserted their independence and secured a permanent homeland there and in East Anglia, where further immigration was unchecked. The Britons' struggle was resumed under Ambrosius Aurelianus and fulfilled at Arthur's victory over the Saxons at Mount Badon about 500 in a campaign that put the native side in the ascendant and ensured a peaceful respite for more than two generations, during which hard redrawn frontiers separated the contesting peoples.

The Verulamium canton must have played an active and important part in these wars, for without its resistance the British revival would have been impossible. When Vortigern lost power the separate provinces regained full freedom, but authority doubtless fell into the hands of dynastic 'tyrants' like those castigated by Gildas. Then and long afterwards the region must have shared the post-Roman cultural character and Christianity of the still unconquered greater part of England. The lack of historical mention of this small state is not surprising, but the Welsh evidently preserved some recollection of it under the name *Calchvynydd* and the name of one of its rulers, Cadrawd. The post-Roman decline in living standards, and Christian burial custom, partly explain the failure to recognize more than meagre traces of its indigenous people, to whom we return in the last chapter.

Verulamium was spared disaster, but although the city was undamaged insecurity was felt at some time in the 5th century when corn-drying ovens were built within its stout walls; walls perhaps defended by a local garrison or auxiliaries to whom a buckle scrap swept up with street refuse may have belonged.

The puny and isolated local Saxons no doubt remained obedient and were suffered to stay in possession of their treaty lands where they might still guard the approaches from the large Germanic colony round Cambridge. Some of the great dykes across the Icknield Way are probably connected with border warfare between Verulamium territory and this powerful enemy to the north-east. Kempston, too, long succeeded in denying passage of the upper Ouse.

The few early Saxon villages were not allowed to expand and become a danger. After Badon they were virtually cut off from other Germanic influences by the rigid new frontier and firm British control forbade fresh settlements in the Ouse-Thame valley, where failure to occupy the attractive belt along the western Icknield Way is particularly notable in view of its Roman villas and its heavy population in the 11th century. The whole Chiltern zone was likewise free of early Saxon presence, though much of the terrain was favoured by farmers before and after the Dark Ages. Leeds' theory that the Icknield Way served as an early main migration route to the upper Thames must be completely rejected, both for these reasons and because there is no longer any need to assume uncontrolled mass movement thither at an early date; a later wave did, however, reach the Thames by a more northern route, not by the Ouse but perhaps by the Nene.

This bleak picture admits of an important exception. There seems to have sprung up in the district west of Dunstable, perhaps about the time of Badon, a limited group of new villages—represented by Puddlehill, Sewell, Deadmans Slade at Leighton Buzzard and the cemetery at Warmark if Toddington was not one of the *foederati* stations—which it can be conjectured housed friendly Saxons, driven or evacuated from the Cambridge border, who were designed to play the role of a strategic reserve against any inroads from that quarter. Such relations would explain the unique contrast with the obvious denial of enlarged Saxon settlement elsewhere in the region. Stevenage may have been a short-lived offshoot from Luton, perhaps suppressed in favour of this expansion on poorer land.

There is no sign of any general crumbling of British control before the last third of the 6th century. An efficient regime with ample local manpower—perhaps depleted by the Yellow Plague of about 550 when the British population seems to have sustained severe loss—was well able to defend itself until the events related by the Chronicle under 571, which even if not their true date must be very close to it.

The annal's bald story seems perfectly accurate. Cuthwulf, probably a West Saxon prince from the upper Thames pursuing Ceawlin's forward policy, and perhaps in league with people in south-west Cambridgeshire, led an assault on the Chiltern forces and gained a decisive victory at *Biedcanford* which can reasonably be taken to mean Bedford, and may imply a cutting-out operation aimed at Kempston. The effect was to deliver the entire northern basin into West Saxon hands, and the conquest was associated in English memory with the acquisition of Limbury near Luton, Aylesbury and probably Dorchester, at all of which there were subject Saxon communities that once had, and probably as late as 571 still retained, a partly military role; Dorchester was probably in the original recitation but in later versions displaced by Bensington which grew into an important *villa regalis* within eyeshot. An oratorical flourish, boasting first the furthest conquest, probably accounts for the apparently odd order of names here and in the Cotswold campaign. All these places doubtless became the personal property of the new lord, which would explain the Kingsbury names at Aylesbury and Benson—doubtless part of the *territorium* of Dorchester, where a royal residence hinted at by a piece of fine jewellery may be the reason for its choice about 634 as the first West Saxon see. The lordship of Kingsbury at St. Albans, part of the *territorium* of Verulamium, can be accounted for in the same way.

The immediate result of the conquest was to open the valley to free occupation by the Saxons, whom in this new phase matched throughout England we can now justifiably call the English. New fashions came from all quarters. Dozens of little settlements and a few larger ones sprang up quickly, mostly founded by families and tiny groups of lowly status; sword-bearers were very rare. The bigger cemeteries —Leighton Buzzard, Sheepwalk Hill at Toddington, Marina Drive at Dunstable, Stone, Bishopstone—were situated near earlier centres, suggesting that these had become overcrowded and yearned for expansion. The Ouse and the fertile Icknield strip were soon settled. The British collapse also exposed the Thames frontier where about 600 the Slough district was ruled by a local magnate called Taeppa who was richly buried in a barrow at Taplow, and another noble intruded into the Wycombe area. To the north there seem to have been no leaders of equal rank, though some of the settlers there could afford ornate saucer brooches hawked from Cambridge-shire and their 7th-century descendants possessed objects of silver, but very rarely gold.

Whether the Chiltern zone also succumbed in 571 or by making terms with Ceawlin for a space remained a sub-kingdom preserving some of its integrity remains to be fully considered. Its extensive most desirable land could hardly have escaped explorers, but as the known archaeological traces are almost insignificant and fairly late in the pagan period it may have successfully staved off final breakdown awhile until the dissolution of the old order and its full mergence in an English realm, or weakness of royal control, allowed Englishmen to seize land there.

The last stages revealed by archaeology dovetail with the expansion of English settlement shown by the oldest identifiable place-names. The coinage of local *hām* names—often difficult to distinguish from *hamm* and sometimes suspect for other reasons—probably began about 600 not long before heathen burial customs started to wane, a process that seems to have been complete in most districts of the region before about 650, though a few communities containing a number of comparatively wealthy families occasionally interred articles with their dead until late in the century.

Hām certainly cannot be associated with the primary 5th-century *foederati* settlements, nor even with those founded during the first generation of English emancipation after 571, amidst which *hām* names are not found. No system of nomenclature can be advanced for the earliest Saxon occupation, though Limbury and possibly Aylesbury could be 5th-century names; the shifting settlement pattern proposed by Taylor may be responsible for breaks in continuity that would cause the loss of very early names. Of four probable examples of *wic-hām* only one, at Toddington, might be associated with the earlier phases of Saxon settlement, though the others at Braughing, Standon and Wickham Hall near Bishops Stortford are certainly connected with Roman sites.

The creation of *hām* names appears to have ceased after about a generation, and the *-ingas* names employed in the mid 7th century to describe small groups, and soon the settlements they made under leaders who struck out widely and were the first Englishmen to venture into east and central Hertfordshire, indicate an unregulated scramble.

The *-ingas* phase gave way shortly before 700 to the fashion of *-ingtun* names. Considerable divergence between the distributions of these two types clearly proves that Ekwall was wrong to maintain that *-ingtuns* were originally *-ingatuns*. Like the *-ingas* names, however, *-ingtun* was combined with personal names that recall similar private initiatives, perhaps on a larger scale. But the imposition of Mercian hegemony late in the 7th century and a concomitant administrative framework coincided with the start of a different method of nomenclature in which personal names had little place, for the *tun* element henceforth commonly given to new villages for the next two or three centuries and sporadically even longer eschewed them and attached purely descriptive elements. Names of the Newton/Sutton type, a quarter of the category, evidently denote satellites overflowing from older villages, but in many districts without *hām* and *-ingas* names *tuns* mark the first signs of English presence.

The limited distribution of *tun* names moreover suggests that much of the Chiltern zone was already well populated by indigenous communities whose interests were safeguarded from injurious encroachment by some local administration. In the northern valley, however, where there was evidently plenty of space for fresh occupation and extensive woodlands that could be assarted, a protracted process of infilling was virtually complete by the time of Domesday.

Beside the *hām*, *-ingas*, *-ingtun* and *tun* names that were attached to community settlements, place-names in *worth*—originally meaning 'enclosure'—were given to smaller foundations by family groups whose heads' names were commemorated in these compounds. Some *worth* names combined with *-inga-* probably arose before 700, and their choice of good enduring sites suggests that few date from late in the pre-Conquest period.

Other habitative elements—*wic, hamstede, throp, stoc* and *stow*— clearly indicate secondary and once dependent places; *cote* represented a rather humble dwelling, often on marginal land, and is rather late in the series. Instead of lending support to Sawyer's theory that the existence of many early sites was long hidden by their inclusion in large estates, these names seem to be wholly consistent with a steadily

110   BRITONS AND SAXONS

rising population in the northern basin that gradually forced remoter and less desirable parts of its largely clay forest land into use.

Some *burh* names were transferred from Iron Age forts but others may denote defended villages. Limbury and Aylesbury, both mentioned in the 571 annal, seem to hark back to British defensive sites manned or partly manned by the early *foederati*: the Kingsbury names at Aylesbury, Benson and St. Albans can probably be associated with the royal acquisition of these places on the fall of the British regime, and the great earthwork of this name at St. Albans which was long the seat of royal officials was probably a Mercian construction, perhaps raised by Offa late in the 8th century.

Evidence on the coming of Christianity is confused by the coincident decline of heathen customs before the mission begun by Birinus' establishment of the first West Saxon see at Dorchester about 634 could be effective. A few late 7th-century cemeteries such as Chamberlain's Barn II betray semi-Christian conditions in their orderly arrangement, though gravegoods were still sometimes deposited—usually a knife by the poor but more precious gifts by the well-off, perhaps more from age-old habit than strong pagan belief. The grand church at Wing, if the place-name means 'people of the heathen shrine'—though 'worshippers at the church' is possible, marks a determined mission centred on a community who maintained their pagan faith unusually long, but unfortunately its date cannot be closely narrowed. Here, at Milton Keynes and at Mentmore unfurnished graves may point to successful conversion. There must have been several similar *monasteria*, 'ministers', acting as mission centres. Hertford, chosen for Theodore's synod meeting place in 672, may be an unrecorded site of this kind; Aylesbury where a St. Osyth was buried[2] was probably another, and Braughing, Welwyn and Hitchin also have claims.

Chapter XII

CHANGE AND CONTINUITY:
THE ASSIMILATION OF THE BRITONS

WE NOTICED THAT a remarkably consistent feature of the Chiltern zone is its almost complete rejection of the standard English habitative vocabulary. There are very few reliable *hām* names, *-ingas* names are extremely rare apart from east Hertfordshire where they are not frequent, and even examples of the usually common *tun* are conspicuously scarce: early English exploitation seems to have been minimal and hardly touched the zone until the mid 7th century. In north-west Buckinghamshire this can be ascribed to late settlement in difficult forested land, but both before and after the Migration age the good soils of the Chiltern zone were well populated. From that factor and the poor showing of normal English formulae we must assume considerable native occupation little disturbed by English new-comers and entertain the possibility that social cohesion or favourable terms secured after their defeat in 571 allowed many of these people to remain more or less unaffected, except for a time when a few English pioneers grasped land for their small *-ingas* villages, while elsewhere the march of English expansion continued.

Instead of the typical English mix containing a high percentage of habitative names, especially the ubiquitous *tun*, the nomenclature of the Chiltern zone is distinguished by great weakness in such elements and almost total reliance on nature names which must be mostly of comparatively late creation, either replacements or new gifts by native people who eventually adopted standard English language and descriptive terms.

The problems of the British element: the limitations of evidence

We are reminded that the standpoint of the well evidenced English is really but half the story, for to many of their transactions there was a British side which should also be essayed. The problems this implies involve difficult questions about the survival and ultimate assimilation of the British population, a component of society that within a few centuries had vanished in the sight of history with virtually no legacy and altogether exiguous traces. We enter uncharted waters where an element of speculation is unavoidable in considering the question of continuity in any meaningful sense between Roman Britain and early England; the evidence is patchy and uneven, and calls for the sort of inspired guesswork from which the volume of archaeology and place-names relieve us on the English side.

How the British Chiltern realm came to an end and what happened to its people involve distinct issues susceptible to different kinds of evidence, mainly indecisive. The cessation of recognizable Roman life is a matter for archaeology; the finish of an independent British regime is a political question indeterminable without records, for subjugation of the British Chiltern heartland in 571 with client status is possible; the integration of the mass of its people into the social fabric of English life, with the extinction of their language and separate character, is a complex matter for inference from varied sources. These questions scholarship should resolutely face, however tentative its answers are bound to be.

Future excavations at Verulamium, still little explored, may provide positive material clues that are lacking today. Techniques unknown at the time of Wheeler's work over 40 years ago, such as radio-carbon dating for organic remains, are available. While the city probably remained the provincial capital as long as post-Roman authority endured, because of the prestige bestowed by its proud traditions, its buildings and installations steadily decayed as *romanitas* faded and the urban population became reduced. We can visualize the city wasting to the semblance of a village, its once splendid houses and public edifices crudely repaired and patched, perhaps eventually replaced by the unpretentious but serviceable sort of timber structures traced at Latimer.

Whatever social and administrative functions Verulamium still served in 571 it would have long ceased to look like a Roman city and reverted to a tribal centre, perhaps housing the residences of the ruler and the bishop, the dwellings of officials and court bodyguards, with a few craftsmen, merchants, farmers and priests, a church, a market, barns for storing produce and tribute; reduced to a few hundred souls by natural causes. Yet, recollecting that the *caput* of a well-organised great medieval honor needed little more than the facilities of a manor house, we should beware of mistaking simplicity, even impoverishment, for nonentity. Continuity could remain.

Problems of continuity

Continuity is possible at different levels, and we must differentiate between the periods before and after the great watershed of 571. Until the Saxons broke the British yoke and opened the floodgates of immigration they were a small minority obliged to accommodate itself to the ambient post-Roman society. Thereafter the roles were reversed, and sooner or later the Britons were forced to undergo the prevailing influences of a dominant English milieu, though they cannot at first have faced overwhelming numbers.

Physical continuity as the transmission of the material apparatus of Romano–British civilization beyond 571 is out of the question; no civic or domestic buildings can have long outlived the 5th century, since the skills to maintain them and the monetary basis of higher society passed away. The same is true of utensils and ornaments: post-Roman society was physically reduced and reverted to primitive ways. Roads were perhaps another matter, for much of the network still remains. By their nature the survival of intangible institutions is hardly ever traceable; there are no local monuments or inscriptions of the post-Roman era and any administrative records or legal codes of the time perished. Yet on our reading of the evidence it needs no imagination to believe that a state well organized enough to last from 410 till 571 must have possessed an efficient system, armed forces and the means of taxation to support them. Even illiterate peoples like the Ashanti could organize for war and have facilities for law-giving and enforcement.

Social continuity is a more elusive concept. At lowest it means no more than racial survival, as in the case of Africans transported into slavery with the loss of tribal identity, cultural traditions, even language. Some hallmarks of a society may however linger for a time before they disappear. Within a century or two of their subjection to the Scots the Picts adopted Gaelic, bequeathing only characteristic place-names in *pit* and the like, and perhaps vestiges of their territorial system such as the *davoch* assessment,[1] while the Cornish, under English domination since the 10th century, everywhere left Celtic place-names and kept their language till the 18th century; in neither case is there any doubt about a high degree of social continuity in the face of a stronger alien culture.

Clearly the native population of the Chiltern region, however wracked by disease and civil dissension, survived until 571; the question is what then became of it, and here both the positive evidence of British place-names and the negative, geographically restricted, indications of English place-names are valuable. Nor can economic aspects be neglected, slender though the material is.

For once, however, history is legitimately to be read in the light of the outcome of events: the universal Englishness of later pre-Conquest society which Stenton and Wainwright emphasized. It is crucial to realize that surviving Britons underwent a thorough process of social attrition and assimilation, succumbed as a foregone conclusion to the steady progress of anglicization. Embraced in an English setting, subject to an English king and his elders, governed according to English law, ministered to by a national Church, influenced by English neighbours, encouraged to speak their tongue and generally conform, Britons would find it increasingly difficult to retain their individuality. The forward movement that condensed into the formative kingdoms of the Heptarchy needed neither to eject nor to destroy the native inhabitants; it merely incorporated them into a different system. The task is essentially one of recovering the contemporary evidence for these people and enquiring into the manner of their disappearance as a separate element.

British place-names

British place-names, many of them Anglo–Celtic hybrids, are the surest and—apart from the Chronicle's annals—most direct evidence available for the presence of native people in Dark Age England, pointing unequivocally to the widespread transmission of fragments of their tongue. There are not wanting good reasons to overturn Wainwright's attempt to discredit them as a legitimate form of proof of continuity, as we noted, but perhaps the weightiest argument is that his imagination made no allowance for the inevitable decay of British language and culture under prolonged erosion by a dominant English environment. Once that mechanism is understood it ceases to be astonishing that the Britons finally disappeared from sight; they became mere English. That does not explain why earlier traces are so scanty, but the physical dimension of that dearth is undoubtedly due to their descent into a 'negative culture' and to their Christian religion which, depriving us of tell-tale gravegoods, left little to discover; and the extinction of their regimes in England without heirs equally accounts for historical records being missing.

The disappearance of British place-names is another matter. The immediate impression of their rarity must be deceptive. If we reckon the vast bulk of place-names created during nearly 1,500 years of English coinage we should never expect earlier surviving names to be more than a minute fraction of the total. The constant tendency to replacement that has acted throughout this time, the differential extent to which place-names of the Celtic hamlet-pattern were exposed to this process, the factor of non-recognition through distortion, and then some truth in Taylor's theory of settlement shifting, make it quite understandable that residual place-names of pre-English antiquity are rare.

Place-name losses in the region were certainly high: Sandy, Baldock, Braughing, Cheshunt, Welwyn, Dunstable, Dropshort, Fleet Marston—all the sizable places except Verulamium and Dorchester, where preservation was due to special factors not difficult to guess. Wholesale disappearance is really only an expression of the obvious fact that the economy of the Dark Ages found no use for the urban legacies of a prosperous Romano–British countryside and its markets. Nevertheless the surviving names, which belong to a very different level of existence, like the presence of men with British names in early English society, are not negligible in import.

British place-names through the region are unusually frequent. Chiltern and Icknield are survivals, a score of river names are Celtic or still were in historic times, and over thirty other names, some no longer extant, certainly or possibly contain British loanwords and incorporated fragments of speech. As usual several of these are tautological compounds with *ceto-* or *brico-* where we contested the view that the original meaning 'wood' or 'hill' was no longer understood when the English translation was tacked on, because the Britons went through a bilingual phase which would explain them. In other local examples such as Bedmond where *funta* 'spring' was qualified by *byden* 'depression' and Chalfont where *cealfra* 'calves' was added there can be no doubt the loanword was in living use among English speakers when they were formed. For the use of *croh* 'saffron plant' in two Buckinghamshire names this is the only possible explanation.

The presumption that a good many British names survived the Dark Ages only to be replaced later is borne out by the older names of the Ray, Ash and probably the Chess, as well as Saferon and two Humbers, which show this fate affected river names that are especially resistant to change; another British stream name was camouflaged as a fossil in the village near Campton. Two *carkelows* instance similar loss of the names of minor features and Morezyf perhaps a casualty among forest names. It can only be supposition that some British settlement names were lost in the same way, but Bede's curious reference to the 'English' name of Hatfield more than hints that in 679 it also bore a British name; in the North he knew of current British names such as the *Calcaria* in the hybrid *Kaelcacaestir*, now Tadcaster, that soon became superseded.

British names are as a rule undatable. One fortunate exception gives the most illuminating insight we possess. In 913 the Chronicle calls the Hertfordshire river Beane *Bene ficcan*, the second element of which is 'closely related to, if not identical with, the British adjective represented by the Welsh *bychan* "little"'. The first part, too, is of Celtic origin, but the significance of the idiom is the word order showing a change in the British language, placing the adjective second, which is unlikely to have occurred before the late 6th century. This usage means a current colloquial form in a still living tongue. The local inhabitants' adoption of the late transposition is emphatic proof that they still spoke British and were still in communication with the main western mass of Celtdom as late as about 600 or even afterwards, a conclusion which we may judge is valid for the whole Chiltern zone.

This remarkable evidence corroborates the view that British names were inherited late from surviving natives after they came into broad contact with English people and formed part of a mixed society, however unequally composed. Since that stage did not begin until the English victory of 571 most of these names must have passed later into the English vocabulary and form sound evidence of British survival some time afterwards. The examples of *funta* (3), *camp* (3) and *croh* (2) are all in areas untouched by English settlement before 571. Though both Brickhills lie near early sites they, like Brill, Panshill and Chetwode in late-settled north-west Buckinghamshire, are tautological compounds that must have taken shape after English became the prevailing language.

Late origin need not apply to all such names. The unmutated form Saferon and its propinquity to Kempston, and the archaic order of the elements in Wendover, once the name of a stream joining the Thame near Aylesbury, suggest absorption by Saxon communities there at an early date. Verulamium and Dorchester must fall in this early category. Such cases were perhaps few except for river names, and while those of the Ouse, Lovat, Ivel, Lea, Thames and Thame could have been learned by the earliest Saxons, in their confined situations they were unlikely to become acquainted with remoter streams like the Ray, Beane, Mimram, Colne, Ash and Chess. It is improbable that the *tun* names Campton, which preserved a British river name, and Kempston, which probably contains *cambo-* 'bend', were born before about 700; it would not be surprising if many British forms survived until then.

The land and the villas

Weak early English infiltration into most of the Chiltern zone, shown by the paucity of their typical habitative names, suggests that large numbers of its native inhabitants probably survived on their long-cultivated excellent soils without major disturbance. Agriculture and country crafts must always have provided the means of life for these people, but locally practically nothing is known of their agrarian economy because 'Celtic field' systems and lynchets do not appear on the Wessex scale, since bare chalk is uncommon. The heavy 11th-century occupation of northern Hertfordshire and the Icknield strip which betokens long generations of intensive peasant cultivation in these areas should however not be forgotten.

Villa owners were among the leaders of Romano–British society. A picture of innumerable villa casualties in the havoc of 367 is as false as the prompt expiry of the rest when the Roman link ended. The data are insufficient to justify any sweeping conclusions, and Webster showed how hard it is to derive firm end dating from excavation reports. Catastrophes apart—whether at the hands of raiders or mutinous bondsmen, or by accidental fire—villa buildings were doomed by the inexorable process of economic decline, fading architectural skills and decay; they could no more outlive their time than the way of life they typified.

As self-sufficient estates villas may have lasted much longer. Webster[2] remarked 'it is now widely recognised that some kind of Celtic life survived in England, especially in the areas of the south and west, throughout the fifth and probably into the greater part of the sixth century. It would not, therefore, be unreasonable to suppose that rural life continued, for example, in the Cotswolds, based on the villas, for at least two centuries after 410. Most of the buildings would by then be in ruins, but traces of this long occupation must somewhere survive and may one day be recognised'. Certainly the Chiltern region is another where continuation might be expected. Webster[3] pointed out the variety of fates that could befall villas but which archaeology can seldom hope to distinguish. Rivet[4] also emphasized the role of the villa as a land unit that might survive without its vulnerable and unwanted structures; good land under cultivation would be as valuable to peasant workers as to Saxon settlers: 'it is most unlikely that the cultivated area of the country as a whole was ever abandoned, and the collapse of the centre of an estate does not necessarily imply that all of its land reverted to bush'. The cultivations of Chiltern zone villas and places like Verulamium, Braughing and Welwyn with continuous occupation from Belgic times seem unlikely to have been deserted while reasonable security was maintained.

In the Chilterns Webster's prophecy has materialized at the Latimer villa where lengthy post-Roman occupation and even contemporary pottery are proved. After the ruin of the main building followed four phases, with substantial new timber structures apparently concerned with farming operations, the last placed 'very late in the fifth century if not later'. How far is the poverty of post-Roman archaeology due to concentration on orthodox villa buildings to the exclusion of their surroundings? Branigan remarked 'we should not expect Latimer to be in any way atypical of the Chiltern villa sites in the fifth century', and Applebaum[5] stressed that some of them were flourishing at the beginning of that period. Here we can visualize villas reverting to the farm status from which many of them developed.

Finberg's case[6] for continuity between a Roman villa and an English manor at Withington in the Cotswolds stands unproven. It might be supported by similar field studies with the same drift, and there is a local claimant. The villa at Great Wymondley in Hertfordshire long ago excited Seebohm's attention.[7] The juxtaposition of the villa in its square enclosure, containing a Roman cemetery and a Norman motte-and-bailey castle, doubtless successor to a late Saxon dwelling, and the medieval village on the site of its Roman predecessor, with centuriated fields all around, seemed to demonstrate unbroken continuity. Without the Saxon documentation available at Withington the notion might be dismissed as vivid imagination, but careful study made Applebaum[8] come to the same opinion: 'the medieval field system seems to incorporate within it the fragments of a mathematically laid out "grid" division of Roman date . . . ; the possibility remains that strip fields were found by the English settlers when they reached Britain . . . ; the case of Great Wymondley with its Roman villa standing amid a centuriated field pattern

surviving vestigially as part and parcel of the medieval open fields ... continuity
of settlement here is suggested not only by the survival of the Roman pattern, but
also by the coincidence of the village of Great Wymondley with the Romano-
British village attached to the villa'.

This is a promising case. Moreover the concept of an organized British state with
adequate resources and manpower to endure under dynastic rulers and hereditary
leaders argues that the landed class broadly retained its property and function intact
until 571. It would not be surprising if some villa estates like Latimer survived long
enough to be inherited eventually as going concerns by anglicized Britons or passed
into the hands of Saxon thegns, much as after Hastings expropriated manors were
transferred to new Norman masters without loss of identity, with the social
continuity of the *rustici*.

It is even possible that some of these estates persisted into the Conqueror's reign.
The abnormally high percentage of Domesday serfs in the High Wycombe–Amersham–Berkhamsted district Chenevix-Trench[9] took to show British survival, but he
failed to notice that it corresponds with a locality particularly distinguished by a
concentration of villas. This coincidence, unlikely to be entirely accidental, suggests
that as late as the Conquest some villa estates with descendants of dependent *coloni*
maintained their existence in the Chiltern valleys.

While place-names like Addington, Addingrove and Adstock, and Hitcham,
Hedgerley and Hughenden hint that otherwise unknown Englishmen such as Æddi
and Hycga seized or were granted large tracts, Biddle[10] proposed the likelihood of
early Saxon royal 'palaces' at *villae regales* and important places such as Dorchester,
and we cannot overlook that such sites may have been taken over from native rulers,
as the Kingsbury names themselves suggest; this idea presents archaeology with a
challenge. The region offers a few possible candidates besides Dorchester: Aylesbury
with its Kingsbury, next to Quarrendon where according to ancient tradition[11] a
St. Osyth was born, perhaps king Penda's granddaughter; Dunstable on the royal
manor of Houghton Regis, where Henry I built a house known as Kingsbury on
what had evidently long been royal property;[12] Brill where Edward the Confessor
built himself a house;[13] Benson, a *villa regalis* in 887; perhaps Offley where according to Matthew Paris king Offa died in 796, though here we would have to assume
re-naming.

Without precise evidence impressions of occupational continuity at any level must
be tentative. The settlement pattern of Hertfordshire is however suggestive, for here
Stenton[14] remarked 'it is not the village but the hamlet or single farmstead which
dominates the map', though he did not connect this with the characteristic Celtic
pattern of the south-western counties which it resembles. It suggests that complete
replacement of the earlier people is quite unlikely, even if Saxons who valued
established sites with cultivated land insinuated themselves or took them over.
Moreover, it is impossible to ignore the frequency with which local Saxon sites
coincide with earlier ones; a third of those in the Appendix II inventory correspond.
Coincidence on this scale suggests a degree of continuity, though the evidence is
mainly confined to the Ouse-Thame basin where pagan Saxons left traces. In some
cases this concerns burial, understandably because newcomers might consign their

dead to an ancient cemetery in order to keep all unquiet spirits away from their homes; old barrows, sharper then than now, would be recognizable, but the Saxons obviously learned from natives of other sites not so marked, such as Shefford and Stone.

Christianity and the cult of St. Alban

The most essential feature of post-Roman culture was Christianity, which spread throughout the Celtic lands. Since the Chiltern region belonged to that cultural province until 571 it is not rash to postulate that the faith also obtained there until within a generation of St. Augustine's arrival in England, perhaps even longer. In fact the uniqueness of St. Alban's cult, unparalleled in England,[15] invites the proposition that it was not a revival but a survival due to the continuance of Christian worship at Verulamium throughout the Dark Ages, as Copley[16] envisaged.

By the time of St. Germanus' visit in 429 Verulamium had become a Christian city like its fellows in Gaul, where the religion had been embraced by the nobility in the 4th century and was extended in the countryside in the time of St. Martin of Tours (died 397). Of the old paganism there is hardly a trace in the urban centres of the northern Empire after that, and the Cross appears everywhere triumphant. The cities of Britain where St. Germanus found Christianity so entrenched that the Pelagian heresy had become prominent can have been no exception. Cults like that of Nodens at Lydney were remote and backward-looking. Late Roman Verulamium was no doubt an important centre of Christian worship and it is not surprising that its theatre, which the faithful associated with pagan spectacles, went out of use and became a rubbish dump.

It was customary in the late Empire for each city to have its own bishop.[17] In view of its size and importance Verulamium must have been an episcopal see, and it would be natural for the Church to honour her first British martyr with a worthy edifice there, besides the usual *martyrium* or *memoria*, a commemorative shrine on the site of his death of burial outside the walls. No certain ecclesiastical building has yet been discovered within the partly explored city, though a small basilican structure in the southern quarter[18] may have been a church and an apsed building was found outside the London Gate.[19]

At Verulamium at least there is no reason to assume a violent 'annihilation of urban Christianity, with the wholesale slaughter of bishops, priests and their remaining congregations'[20] in the mid 5th-century strife. Gildas' lurid language suited a terrifying long sermon disguised as a book but was hardly intended to be sober, balanced history.[21] Whatever its grains of truth it is too exaggerated to be universally valid. If the civic order could survive at Verulamium there was no reason why its religious counterpart should perish.

Christianity was not confined to towns, as the house church at the Lullingstone villa, the Hinton St. Mary mosaic and Christian objects often found at other late villas show. It must have gained a hold among the villa owners whose society was closely bound up with Verulamium, though so far archaeology has nothing to say. If the faith continued at the city till at least 571 it must have flourished elsewhere in the province. No doubt superstitions lingered among country dwellers, as they did after St. Augustine's mission, but the Chiltern people were not pagan Saxons and in a post-Roman ambience the only formal religion available was Christianity.

Literary evidence for early Dark Age Christianity in the once British part of England is shadowy, though the *Historia Brittonum*[22] in a passage on Arthur written within three centuries of his time and probably based on much older tradition asserts that he carried a Christian emblem into battle. Until the Britons were submerged their faith was not menaced and widespread in areas not overcome till the English advance late in the 6th century. In places it survived further. In the northern Pennines property that lately belonged to the British Church was taken over by St. Wilfrid about 670,[23] and Finberg[24] noted that two British bishops who joined in the episcopal consecration of St. Chad about that time may well have come not from Wales or Cornwall but from still Christian areas in conquered England. Christianity has always been a tenacious creed, damaged more by internal dissension than persecution, and the Church has outlasted many tribulations. Place-names containing the element *eccles* 'church' prove the existence of some rural Christian communities in the pre-English period; two such names occur in Norfolk,[25] early overrun by the Saxons.

The crux of the question, whether the Christian church locally survived until 571 or a generation longer until the mission begun by St. Augustine could make it secure, lies at Verulamium itself where the cult of St. Alban outside the walls is surely significant.

The evidence is brief but direct. The saint was executed on 22 June 209 as Morris has shown.[26] Later, perhaps about 396-8, a church was built on the spot.[27] Bede, writing about 730, relates: 'The blessed Alban suffered death . . . near the city of Verulamium . . . where afterwards, when peaceable Christian times were restored, a church of wonderful workmanship, and suitable to his martyrdom, was erected'. Bede, whose source was Constantius, the author of a Life of St. Germanus composed about 480, tells the story of his two missions to combat the Pelagian heresy in Britain and says of his first visit with Lupus in 429: 'The bishops sought the tomb of the martyr' where 'Germanus ordered the tomb to be opened'.[28] He adds, as a fact well known, 'in which place there ceases not to this day the cure of sick persons and the frequent working of wonders'.[29]

Did this cult continue unbroken, or was it merely revived as a result of the Roman mission in 597? If St. Augustine's heirs—who had limited success to boast—were responsible they would surely have claimed the restoration of worship at St. Alban's shrine among their brightest jewels, and Bede, who gathered much valuable information from Kentish sources, would certainly have learned of and mentioned this triumph. It is revealing that no such claim was made. Bede's silence, implying that he knew nothing more about the cult, tells decisively in favour of its continuity under the aegis of the British Church; moreover, as he had little fondness for that Church he might have suppressed anything he heard about the cult's British origin.

Two striking facts strongly support the hypothesis of survival. As it can hardly be fortuitous that St. Michael's church stands on the site of the basilica at Verulamium, it seems that in the 10th century abbot Wulsin[30] deliberately placed it where the hall of justice stood because that was still remembered as the spot where St. Alban was sentenced 700 years before. Though Matthew Paris' story of the finding of the saint's relics by Offa in 793 sounds like typical hagiography and is less evidential, he mentions a church dedicated to Alban outside the city as the genesis of the abbey commemorating the place of martyrdom.

There is, therefore, a substantial case for believing that Christianity weathered the British disaster of 571 into calmer times at Verulamium.[31] If so, other surviving Christian communities may possibly explain the siting of the *monasteria* that are known in the 10th century at Braughing and Welwyn;[32] both were important Roman sites closely linked with the city. The extraordinary story of Abingdon, where fortunately existing early records appear to connect a monastic refoundation of the 7th century with a late Roman or post-Roman Christian site that outlived the pagan period—*ubi etiam a primis Britonum temporibus locus fuit religionis*[33]—suggests that some early English minsters may have had equally ancient origins. A prominent perfectly rectangular cropmark near Braughing, visible in an air photograph and clearly antedating the medieval field pattern, may well show the curtilage of a late Roman and post-Roman Christian cemetery serving the town, analogous to the Queensford Mill one at Dorchester mentioned in Chapter III. No study of continuity can ignore the likelihood that Christianity survived in places throughout the Dark Ages among the native people, which would partly account for the success of the reconversion begun in 597 in regions only recently mastered by the English.

The Cilternsaetan

Although the Chiltern territory was dismembered in 571 when the whole northern valley and Thamesside lands passed out of British hands, the marked absence of pagan graves in most of the Chiltern zone and the late date of these encroachments witness that there was no great influx there before the English ceased to be heathen. The loss of an outlying part of the province, clayey forested lands that probably bore a relatively small proportion of the total British population, need not have been fatal to the core of the principality. If the truncated British community succeeded in making terms its position may have favoured its preservation for a time while its neighbours Wessex, Essex and Mercia were too occupied contending for mastery to interfere or even bought British support.

If the Chiltern zone people did manage to retain their identity as a separate unit into the 7th century they might be expected to feature in the Tribal Hidage[34] list of about 670–690, and the folk name *Cilternsaetan* actually found there would be an obvious description. Baldwin Brown[35] found no difficulty in equating them with the Chiltern dwellers but Stenton[36] later assumed they 'occupied the plain beneath the Chilterns'. His identification, strangely deriving a people's name from outside their territory, was most unsatisfactory; Stenton's blindness to the important earlier role of the Chiltern people evidently caused him to dismiss their land as practically uninhabited. It would be less curious if the term denoted the inhabitants of a wider region, but as the formula was a perfectly normal English construction there is really little reason to doubt that it meant those who lived in the Chiltern area. The people of the Ouse-Thame basin must then have borne one or more of the names of the several unidentified folk in the Hidage.[37]

The end of the British regime

The separate character and considerable numbers of the *Cilternsaetan*—their assessment of 4,000 hides, like that of other peoples subject to Mercia, was probably inflated—suggest that at the time of the Tribal Hildage they were governed by their own ruler, appointed by an English king but perhaps a noble of their own lineage, descended from the post-Roman dynasty that had ruled their region until it came under English overlordship. The old regime need not have met its doom in battle; forced into tributary status with the cession of outlying lands, it might have retained some of its former power but withered gradually. English princes frequently married into each others' families, and in Wessex apparently did not disdain ladies of British blood. Whether for politic reasons or under coercion, any Chiltern rulers who kept their place on terms and found themselves obliged to attend the court of an English suzerain may have thought it wise to do the same and soon begun to give their children English names. Their line may have lingered on peacefully amongst the *subreguli*, under-kings who were numerous in early England, and eventually degenerated into mere ealdormen, just as a family of Bernician kings at Bamborough descended to being earls of Northumbria and the partly British royal line of Lindsey[38] became subordinate to Mercia before being lost to sight. The Celtic names in some early Wessex charters may disguise such men of high rank. Apart from the laconic annal of 571 no English tradition bearing on the conquest of Verulamium and the Chiltern territory survived, and on the whole it seems likely that the Chiltern rulers slowly lost their status and were honourably incorporated into the upper ranks of English society.

No more than their subjects would they escape being remoulded and transformed into Englishmen, eventually forgetful of their true heritage. Yet a spark of that memory would have persisted for some generations, and recorded history may guard a faint echo in the statement that before Caedwalla seized the throne of Wessex in 685 he took refuge in the forests of Chiltern[39] and the Weald. The prince, who was not the only member of his house to bear a Celtic name and whose brother was called Mul 'halfbreed', may have sought protection from highly-placed sympathizers likely to succour one of their own kin.

The assimilation of the British people: the question of language

To predicate the likely fate of the highest ranks of society is difficult enough. For the lives of ordinary people early historical sources are even less informative and the obscurity of the Dark Ages presents an almost insuperable problem. Although place-names indicate some degree of survival among the British natives of the region, as the similar intensity of occupation before 410 and in 1086 in certain districts and the weakness of normal English habitative names in the Chiltern zone tend to confirm, it is natural to ask why their vestiges are so faint, why Britons everywhere left no distinctive linguistic imprint, in contrast to the Scandinavian settlers whose legacy is plainly written on the place-name map and persists to some extent in standard English as well as in dialect words.

The British tongue does not survive in any English document, but it is documents on which historians are accustomed to rely. The charters and wills that are extant, in this region none early in the period, are of course in the language of English courts or ecclesiastics, just as the fuller records of the Norman age are—except for the Peterborough Chronicle—written in Latin or Norman French, the media of the Church and ruling minority. We would not expect the British language to be used in any formal record. The name *Bene ficcan*, however, leaves no doubt that it was still spoken in parts of the Chiltern region some time after its subjugation. For several generations after 571 British speech could flourish and then linger for a considerable time in sheltered localities before it was eventually ousted and became completely forgotten save in isolated, barely intelligible place-name fossils.

The question of linguistic fate is worth a digression. A people's language is the essence of its culture as well as the vehicle for it, and if it fails that culture is bound to yield, too. In England the invaders' tongue triumphed, whereas France, Spain and Italy were dominated by newcomers without adopting their speech, in somewhat different circumstances. Not only has no native language survived here, but it is remarkable that English contains hardly a score of British words acquired during the Dark Ages. The victory of English so undiluted seems to contradict the idea that there was more than the slightest contact between the two societies, and at first sight supports Wainwright's grim views. Yet the complete disappearance of a language need not mean the extinction of those who spoke it: Pictish and Etruscan vanished, not their peoples. Linguistic comparisons reveal how the paradox of British racial survival beside the lapsing of their speech can be explained.

Two considerations immediately show that a superficial impression is not the whole truth. The English became the dominant caste whose tongue monopolized the royal courts and administration, but no aristocracy of this kind, even when in a minority, absorbs the language or vocabulary of social inferiors, as the Wessex laws show the Britons there were, class for class. Norman French, spoken by a tenth of the population, reigned supreme in its own field for three centuries; in Bohemia the language of German masters was unadulterated by Slavonic words, though ordinary Czech speech admitted some German, just as English did much French; in Brittany French remains pure while Breton has absorbed French words. The conquered English soon began to give their sons Norman names, never the reverse. These phenomena are a natural function of social stratification where underlings are obliged to adopt or imitate their superiors' ways though the latter are under no reciprocal necessity. Only when a ruling caste loses its cohesion, like the Normans and the Franks, does their language yield to that of their subjects.

Another factor is the process whereby—apart from modern fashions due to travel and mass communications—loanwords get generally adopted only when a language possesses no convenient term. The Saxon vocabulary had no want of everyday domestic, agricultural and military terms, no need to borrow the kind of words— *ffenstr* 'window', *llyfr* 'book'—that survive in Welsh to attest a heritage of Roman civilization. But in their new homeland, very different from the flat lands of north Germany, strange natural features such as rocky knolls and hillside valleys for which they had no distinctive terms necessitated borrowing from the native vocabulary a number of words such as *cumb* 'small valley' that passed into English speech, and a few others such as *funta* 'spring' and *croh* 'saffron' which were current early but died out after use in place-names, so that they are otherwise unknown. These British loanwords and other adoptions show a modicum of broad contact between the old and new peoples.

The accurate form in which certain names such as the plural behind Dover was handed over can be connected with a bilingual phase while the Britons absorbed another language;[40] the replacement of Welsh in modern times took the same slow course. No doubt from the beginning there were men in both communities whose duties obliged them to learn the other tongue, like Vortigern's interpreter mentioned by Nennius,[41] and the English *wealhstōd* who translated the native language may often have picked up his 'Welsh' not in the Marches but in a mixed society. English probably took a considerable time fully to replace the native speech in the deep countryside.

The preconditions for linguistic survival appear from minority languages that still endure or long outlasted conquest. In Wales, Cornwall and until recently much of Scotland Celtic tongues widely persisted, as does Breton across the Channel, while Basque still flourishes near the western Pyrenees, and so does Finnish, bounded by lakes and forests. In Cornwall the old language did not lack tenacity, for it lingered till about 1750, enduring through English conquest and overlordship for eight centuries despite political integration into Wessex and then England. About the same time the old Norn tongue died out in Orkney, ousted by the standard Scots of mainland proprietors and immigrants. Welsh remains the speech of large parts of a fairly large and inaccessible country which maintained its independence into the Middle Ages without losing its squirarchy, and to this day retains a special character. In all these instances the social compactness of a sizable and physically isolated community protected by mountain fastnesses or major barriers favoured linguistic and cultural survival and the development of a strong national consciousness. The larger the society the more inviolate, but even a small population like the Cornish and the Orkneymen was able to retain its native language for a very long period and withstand alien influence provided it was remote and, equally important, preserved its social structure intact.

British was not the only language to disappear here during the historic period. Much of northern and central England—the Danelaw—was heavily settled in the 9th century by Scandinavian people, and these districts, with distinct customs that lasted into the Norman age, once possessed a separate tongue which left a permanent mark. The Danes not only had a strongly individual personality but, unlike most of the Britons who were widely dispersed in separated territories between the Channel and the Cheviots, they had the advantage of a cohesive settlement based on the Five Boroughs; yet they were slowly overcome by prevailing Englishness and within a few centuries became fully assimilated. Although this well documented society held out for some time its eventual end was not very different from that of the Britons who were mastered at a time whence we have no comparable contemporary evidence. We should reflect that if the Danish occupation and eclipse had taken place before a developed administrative system put adequate records at our disposal, leaving only a residue of place-names and words that remain in use, we would be perplexed to understand its nature. If similar records existed in the 7th century we might have seen a distinct British society still in being before it utterly dissolved.

The nemesis of the Danelaw was wrought by social causes, not mere conquest. Its transformation began with the integration of its upper social structure into that of broad England. Jarls became earls and attended the king's court, lesser land-owners and freemen accepted the normal rights and obligations of their English counterparts. Doubtless the process was aided by close affinity between the two tongues and by the invaders' acceptance of Christianity, but it was foreordained because the Danelaw, however large and compact, lacked the geographical isolation that alone could have perpetuated its social entity. Its fairly rapid absorption illustrates the ability of English society relentlessly to erode the different culture of a powerful minority on equal terms. Even this numerous and independent community could not long succeed in maintaining its individuality, surrounded on open frontiers, outnumbered by a well organized society and culturally undermined at all levels: its kings overthrown, its noblemen replaced or anglicized, its leaders induced to behave like Englishmen, its essence constantly assimilated to the pattern of its dominant neighbours.

Whatever their total numbers the Britons' language and culture, without the Danes' massive solidity, were deprived of any chance of long holding out. They were divided between various English kingdoms, mutually separated by deep wedges of intensive English settlement. The essential similarities between the two societies 'facilitated the transformation of British into English society'.[42] Though a Celtic tongue was evidently spoken in Dorset and Somerset long after the West Saxon conquest geography denied it the chance of Cornish. The Chiltern Britons in a small territory detached from their fellows by continuous belts of English villages and open to physical and cultural infiltration would not escape complete assimilation. They were embedded in an English matrix, exposed to its irresistible influence. The language of an English court, pervasive and persuasive, became the medium for administrative purposes and steadily spread everywhere, first no doubt affecting native officials and landowners and ultimately all their people. For a time some might be bilingual, using occasional English just as German was employed through-out the Austro-Hungarian empire; but Czech and Magyar and the vigorous folk culture that went with them could survive indefinitely among solid nations entrenched behind natural boundaries. From a similar threat the common English people were preserved under the Norman minority who, dispersed in an ocean of Englishry and eventually severed from their roots in France, in the end lost their own tongue.

The last stages of assimilation

The Chiltern region lacks the early charters that are valuable in Wessex and the Midlands, and its oldest personal records contain wholly English names. It is only in local place-names that we occasionally discern individual men and communities whose names, thus preserved, betray their British descent.

In Hertfordshire the Cada (British *catu* 'battle') after whom Cadwell and Caddington (now Beds.) were called bore the commonest of these names.[43] Names of this type, which deserve more attention than they have received, could only have been given by parents of British descent. But the attached elements are always English; these place-names are hybrids created in an already basically English society. Personal names of such demonstrably British origin as Cada denote a native population neither intractably hostile nor beyond social recognition, but a British ingredient engulfed in and already well on the way to becoming assimilated to early English society. The place-names that fossilized them were awarded in a mixed society: Caddington was Cada's hill, named by English speakers who knew him. These names portray the widespread adoption of English by native inhabitants by the time they were formed, rather than rigid racial segregation. The British personal names they contain are valuable for revealing a local component for which there is no other evidence and seem to indicate a British element of respectable if not equal status. They go far to prove a process of fusion between the two peoples none the less real because their contributions to the future were most unevenly matched; whatever the numerical ratios, which may have varied much from district to district, the overwhelmingly English character of the toponymy even in the West shows the dominant strain that everywhere imposed a cultural norm. The speech and ways of Cada's forefathers were overshadowed and inexorably doomed to extinction.

Equally valuable are local names showing English reference to Britons in their midst. Although the Saxons brought with them their own term *wealh* 'stranger, Briton' they also learned from the natives their word for one of themselves, *xcombrogos* in primitive Welsh, literally 'fellow countryman', whence come *cymro* 'Welshman', *Cymry* 'the Welsh people' and *Cymru* 'Wales'. The English not only adopted a plural form as *Cumbre* to denote the native inhabitants—Cumberland was once the land of the Welsh too—but used the singular *Cumbra* as an appellative or nickname for a Briton.[44] This term may express an earlier Saxon view of the British than *wealh* below.

A few miles apart in north Hertfordshire are Cumberlow Green in Rushden (Cumbrelawe 1248, from *hlaw* 'barrow, hill') and Cumberton Bottom in Barley (Cumberden *c*. 1470, from *denu* 'valley'). They are matched by two Cambridgeshire names not far away, Comberton (Cumbertone 1086, from *tun* 'village') and Cumberton Bottom in Little Chishill (Comberdeneveld 1387, also with *denu*). These names show recognition of the presence of native people at a time when English was in general use for coining place-names and the designation 'Briton' was unusual enough to serve for distinction.

The association of this word with *hlaw* 'burial mound' in Cumberlow looks at first strange, for as all these names seem to be contemporary references we can hardly translate it as 'barrow of the (old) Britons'. The Briton whom it commemorates was presumably a Christian whose family are unlikely to have given him a pagan Saxon burial; his interment probably belonged to an immemorial tradition still observed in the Dark Ages, for about 500 Carausius, an undoubted Christian, was laid beneath a cairn at Penmachno in Caernarvonshire with the inscription CARAUSIUS HIC IACIT IN HOC CONGERIES LAPIDUM bearing the Chi-Rho symbol.[45]

Other place-name evidence points to recognizable British communities, for the persistence of small islands of unassimilated Britons at a late date is the best interpretation of the names included in Appendix V that contain *wealh* 'Briton,

Welshman' or its plural *wealas*. Place-names that may employ this element have caused no small controversy. It is often impossible to decide from extant forms whether a name incorporates *wealh* or the similar words *weall* 'wall' or *weald* 'wood'. The choice of scholars has given rein to their predilections about British survival and general opinion has it that most of the possible cases do not contain *wealh*.[46]

A graver objection has been that *wealh* meant not only 'Briton' but also 'serf', and usually the latter. Finberg and Morris[47] contested this view, maintaining that a servile sense is a late and peculiarly West Saxon usage and pointing out that in the 7th century Ine's laws applied *wealh* solely to someone of British blood and employed *theow* for 'serf', qualified if necessary by *englisc* or *wealisc*. Now Faull[48] believes the word was never widely adopted to mean 'slave', and recently Cameron[49] has emphatically concluded 'that "a Briton" is the meaning in the Old English period', with Gelling's concurrence. Moreover even if *wealh* changed its meaning rather late after Wessex became dominant it is difficult to imagine the sense 'serf' in place-names, for it was sometimes combined with *tun*, and a village entirely composed of such people seems quite unlikely. The Cambridgeshire Comberton— 'Britons' village'—just cited suggests that a community of *wealas* would not be unknown. In northern England as late as the 9th century some British villages, such as Bretby, were distinguished by a similar term *Bretta* 'Briton' which was borrowed by the Danes. Hence we can now feel justified in believing that *wealh* in place-names does mean 'Briton', and that such names originated at a time when places were inhabited by still recognizably indigenous people.[50]

Four Hertfordshire place-names[51] are accepted as certain occurrences of *wealh* or *wealas*—St. Paul's and King's Walden (recorded in 888), Walsworth in Hitchin, Wall Hall in St. Stephens near St. Albans, and Wallbrooks in Totteridge—and possible other local examples are the two Buckinghamshire Waltons and a minor name Waldich in Crowmarsh, Oxon. Cameron's observation[52] how often minor places named from *wealh* lie close to more important ones and to sites of the Roman period might be applied to the Aylesbury Walton. *Wealh* actually occurs as a personal name, both as a simplex and compounded, and Cameron[53] spells out clearly that here its import must be 'Briton, Welshman'. It is found in the only singular form among the definite four above, Wall Hall, *Walenhale* 'the Briton's nook'. It is interesting that Wallbrooks, *Walebroc*, shows comparatively late formation, after *broc* 'brook' partly superseded the older word *burna* 'bourne', and it is notable that all four certain examples as well as the doubtful Waldich lie in the Chiltern zone. These names were evidently given at a very late stage, long after 571, when English had already been adopted by most people there but a number of British communities remained unassimilated.

When the connotation of *wealas* names as residual communities is accepted, it has nevertheless been held that their rarity tells heavily against British survival in anything but negligible numbers. That reasoning overlooks the erosion of the native culture that was under way before the 7th century and ignores the certainty, as the 9th-century *Bretta* names remind us, that such names could have been formed only when the great majority of the British had become so assimilated to English manners that they were no longer distinguishable. The relatively late date of effective English influence in the Chiltern zone, so obvious from its peculiar nomenclature, confirms that the *wealas* names must belong to a relatively advanced time; earlier, when visibly British communities were more numerous, it would have been pointless for their neighbours to apply the term. It seems rather unlikely that these names were given much before the 8th century, which would not conflict with the question posed by Cameron[54] whether the generality of such names as Walcot and Walworth belong to the late 7th and 8th centuries. In the 9th century a Celtic language may still have been spoken in parts of Wessex.[55]

The Cada type personal names, the *Cumbra* names and the *wealas* place-names proclaim a time earlier than written records when men were still marked by their British character. In the age when they were formed the assimilation of the Chiltern Britons had evidently been almost completely accomplished, their personality obliterated. It was their destiny to become Englishmen and they left no cultural heritage, unless in unexplored folklore; their only legacy was perhaps a distinct racial strain that Beddoe[56] was still able to detect in the Chiltern area a hundred years ago, 1,300 years after its people passed under English overlordship.

NOTES TO CHAPTERS

Chapter I

1. Copley 1954; Brandon 1978.
2. Kirby 1965, 22–9.
3. Biddle 1971, 391–2.
4. Hawkes and Dunning 1961, 1.
5. Applebaum 1972, 250.
6. CBA 1948, 113.
7. Finberg 1972, 401.
8. Germanus may have revisited the city on a second journey to Britain between 440 and 445.
9. Copley 1954, 177, 187.
10. Leeds thought the true date must have been about a century earlier, and Vera Evison would emend it to about 506.
11. Hawkes and Dunning 1961; Hawkes 1972 and 1974.
12. Of the type I and II buckles recognized in a Roman milieu in 1974, 5 came from forts, 24 from walled towns, 12 from rural settlements, 9 from villas.
13. His name may have been Vitalinus (Morris 1973, 55).
14. Gildas' *superbus tyrannus* seems to allude to the meaning.
15. Morris 1965 and 1973, also Frere 1967. Alternative reconstructions are Alcock 1971 (with slight differences), Myres 1951 followed by Hawkes 1956, and Ward 1972. Johnson 1980 and Salway 1981 are the most recent reviews of the period. D. P. Kirby on Vortigern in *B.B.C.S.* 23 (1968) covers the early 5th century. Thompson 1979 on Gildas' historical material believes some parts concern only the north. Sceptical of conventional views is D. N. Dumville, Some aspects of the chronology of the Historia Brittonum, *B.B.C.S.* 25 (1974), and Sub-Roman Britain: history and legend, *History* 62 (1977).
16. Morris 1973, 58.
17. *Historia Brittonum* ch. 31: *urgebatur a metu Pictorum Scottorumque et a Romanico impetu nec non a timore Ambrosii.*
18. As hinted in Webster 1969, 231.
19. Wheeler 1935, 58.
20. *. . . in dicionem Saxonum rediguntur.*
21. Jackson 1953, 17, 26–7: N. K. Chadwick, Early Brittany (1969), ch. 5.
22. Myres 1969, 100–3.
23. Frere 1967, 376; Wacher 1975, 413–4.
24. Myres 1969, 105–12.
25. H. P. R. Finberg, The early charters of Wessex (1964), 215.
26. E. D. C. Jackson and Sir E. (Lord) Fletcher, The apse and nave at Wing, JBAA 3rd ser. XXV (1962), 18–20; Hyslop 1963, 194; Sir E. (Lord) Fletcher, Birinus and the church at Wing, in Studies in church history I, ed. C. W. Dugmore and C. Duggan (1964), 127–31.
27. Morris 1959, 156.

Chapter II

1. Wooldridge 1936.
2. Copley 1954, 185–6.

3. *Ibid.* 118.
4. Branigan 1967, 128, 138.
5. Wheeler 1936; updated by Wacher 1975, 202–25.
6. Branigan 1967 and 1973.
7. The Viatores, Roman roads in the south-east Midlands (1964).
8. Rivet 1969; J. Percival, The Roman Villa (1976).
9. Information from Mr. C. Partridge and Mr. A. G. Rook.
10. Taylor 1974, 6.
11. Collingwood and Myres 1936, 180.
12. Antiq. IV (1930), 95.
13. Frere 1967, 311. A maximum of 4 million in the second century has recently been proposed (Brandon 1978, 4, 225).
14. Darby and Campbell 1962.
15. E. M. Jope, Saxon Oxford and its region, in Harden 1956, Fig. 55, 248.

Chapter III

1. Frere 1966, 97–8; 1967, 376.
2. Branigan 1967, 149–50; 1971.
3. Frere 1962, 114–49; 1966. 93–4; 1967, 244, 250, 252; Durham and Rowley 1972; A. and W. Selkirk, Why is Oxford at Oxford?, *Current Archaeology* 35 (1972), 316–21; Rowley 1974.
4. R. A. Chambers, A cemetery site at Beacon Hill near Lewknor, Oxon. XXXVIII (1973); The cemetery site at Beacon Hill, near Lewknor: an inventory of the inhumations and a re-appraisal, *Oxon.* XLI (1976).

Chapter IV

1. Meaney 1964.
2. Morris 1962.
3. Head 1941–6.
4. Morris 1959, 150–2; 1973, 32–3. Bohme 1974 catalogues the earliest gravegoods.
5. J. N. L. Myres, The Anglo–Saxon cemeteries of Caistor-by-Norwich and Markshall, Norfolk (1973).
6. P. D. C. Brown, Problems of continuity, in Rowley 1974, 17.
7. Hawkes and Dunning 1961; recent reviews in Hawkes 1972 and 1974. Also C. J. Simpson, Belt-buckles and strap-ends of the later Roman Empire: a preliminary survey of several new groups, *Britannia* 7 (1976).
8. M. J. Swanton, The spearheads of the Anglo–Saxon settlements (1973).
9. Meaney and Hawkes 1970, 43.
10. V. I. Evison, Sugar-loaf shield bosses, *Ant. Jl* XLViii.
11. Aberg 1926, 28–56.
12. Leeds 1936.
13. E. T. Leeds and M. Pocock, A survey of the Anglo–Saxon cruciform brooches of florid type, *Med. Arch.* XV (1971). M. G. Welch has contested some of Morris' early datings (*Med. Arch.* XX, 134–6).
14. Morris and Bidder 1959, 80–93.
15. Leeds 1949.
16. D. B. Harden, Glass vessels in Britain and Ireland A.D. 400–1000, in Harden 1956.
17. Myres 1969.
18. *Ibid.* 117.
19. The chief references are R. A. Smith, *Proceedings of the Society of Antiquaries* 2nd ser. XXII (1908), 66–86; Sir T. D. Kendrick, British hanging-bowls, *Antiq.* VI (1932); F. Henry, Hanging bowls, *Journal of the Royal Society of Antiquaries of Ireland* LXVI (1936); Irish enamels of the Dark Ages and their relation to the cloisonne techniques,

in Harden 1956; Irish art in the Early Christian period to A.D. 800 (1965); H. E. Kilbride-Jones, A bronze hanging-bowl from Castle Tioram, Moidart, and a suggested absolute chronology for British hanging-bowls, *Proceedings of the Society of Antiquaries of Scotland* LXXI (1936-7); G. Haseloff, Fragments of a hanging bowl from Bekesbourne, Kent, and some ornamental problems, *Med. Arch.* II (1958); E. Fowler, Hanging bowls, in *Studies in ancient Europe: essays presented to Stuart Piggott*, ed. J. M. Coles and D. D. A. Simpson (1968); D. Longley, Hanging bowls, penannular brooches and the Anglo-Saxon connexion, B.A.R. 22 (1975).

20. T. W. Bagshawe, *Ant. Jl* XI (1931), 282-4.
21. Leeds 1936, 97 et seq.
22. Hyslop 1963.
23. Meaney and Hawkes 1970.

Chapter V

1. *Welei* may contain *weg* 'way' and Wain Wood *waegn* 'waggon' (Gelling 1973, 124).
2. *The Place-names of Surrey*, E.P.N.S. XI (1934), 403-4.
3. Listed in PNBucks, 86.
4. A. Bach, Deutsche Namenkunde (1954, Heidelberg), II, Pt. I, 185. I owe this reference to Mr. J. McN. Dodgson.
5. Gelling 1973, 121.
6. E.P.N.S. XXVII, xxv.

Chapter VI

1. Hyslop 1963, 192.
2. *Ibid.* 194.
3. Bede HE I ch. 30.
4. Stenton's dates are followed.
5. Hyslop 1963, 50.
6. As noted in Appendix II a supposed early pot from Hertford is mistaken. There is no evidence that sunken huts here are early; they might be as late as 10th century.
7. Stenton 1943, 26.
8. A. H. Smith, Place-names and the Anglo-Saxon settlement, *Proceedings of the British Academy* XLII (1956), 85.
9. J. F. Head, Early man in south Buckinghamshire (1955), 96.
10. Davis 1973.
11. Wheeler 1935, 6.
12. Collingwood and Myres 1936, 407.
13. Jackson 1953, 204, 236.
14. Myres 1969, 87.
15. Morris 1965, 172; T. Williams, Iolo manuscripts (1848), 86, 476.
16. In Brittany the once forested inland region is still called *Argoed* (Welsh *coed* 'tree'), contrasting with *Armor*, the tract 'by the sea'.
17. B. H. St.J. O'Neil, The Silchester region in the 5th and 6th centuries, *Antiq.* XVIII (1944).
18. Frere 1967, 377. The form of lettering 'probably precludes a date significantly earlier than the seventh century although the linguistic forms could suit rather better a somewhat earlier date' (G. C. Boon quoting K. H. Jackson, *Med. Arch.* III (1959), 87).
19. Frere *ibid.*
20. Bede HE I chs 19 and 21.
21. Compare the changing interpretations of late Roman Catholic burials at Dorchester cited in Appendix II.
22. PNBucks xii.
23. Hodgkin 1935, I, 146, 188.

24. Stenton 1943, 28.
25. Copley 1954, 184–5.
26. E.g. Blair 1956, 31–2.
27. Frere 1966, 98; 1967, 377.
28. Nennius HB chs. 38, 56.
29. Wheeler 1935, 41.
30. J. Anderson, Scotland in pagan times: the Iron Age (1883), 65.
31. O.S. Dark Ages map, 61, is a convenient note.
32. Reported *Daily Telegraph* June 22, 1970; Thomas 1981, map. on p. 179.
33. K. H. Jackson, The Britons in southern Scotland, *Antiq.* XXIX (1955); The Gododdin: the oldest Scottish poem (1969); Thomas 1971.
34. The Winchester region was discussed by Biddle 1976.
35. Myres 1969, 77, 87.
36. Alcock 1971, 311; Brandon 1978, 222.
37. Blair 1956, 32.
38. O.S. Dark Ages map, 19.
39. T. C. Lethbridge, The riddle of the dykes, *Proc. Camb. Ant. Soc.* LI (1958).
40. O.S. Dark Ages map, 19.
41. Blair 1956, 32.
42. The earliest form is merely 'dyke' and the first element meaning 'fugitives' is not on record before the eleventh century.

Chapter VII

1. Cremation continued for a long time. Without datable artifacts it would be an unreliable guide, as two instances in Appendix II (Moggerhanger, Kingsey) show it was still practised in the late sixth century.
2. The Viatores, Roman roads in the south-east Midlands (1964), 281.
3. Morris 1959, 1953.
4. Evison 1965, 84.
5. Biddle 1971, 394.
6. *Ibid.* 396.
7. Stenton 1943, 28.
8. Myres 1969, 110.
9. Morris 1973, 222–4; Wacher 1975, 414–8.
10. Cox 1972-3, 34.
11. H. N. Savory, Some sub-Roman British brooches from south Wales, in Harden 1956, 58.
12. Myres 1969, 89.
13. *Ibid.* 102, 114.
14. His basic study was Leeds 1912.
15. Leeds 1933 and 1954 rehearse his theory.
16. Leeds 1954, 47.
17. *Ibid.*
18. *Ibid.* 54.
19. Leeds 1936, 34.
20. Myres 1969, 114.
21. J. R. Kirk, Anglo–Saxon cremation and inhumation in the upper Thames valley in pagan times, in Harden 1956, 123.
22. E.g. Copley 1954, 185.
23. Lethbridge 1956, 121.
24. P. V. Addyman, Medieval Cambridge: recent finds, *Proc. Camb. Ant. Soc.* LVIII (1965), 113.
25. Myres 1969, 37, Fig. 15, No. 384.
26. *Ibid.* 114-6.
27. Morris and Bidder 1959, 93-5.

Chapter VIII

1. Whitelock 1961, 13, note 8.
2. Hodgkin 1935, I, 375 note.
3. Copley 1954, 178.
4. Leeds 1954, 56.
5. Copley 1958, 240. PNBucks omits the name.
6. Dickinson 1974, 31.
7. W. de G. Birch, *Cartularium Saxonicum* (1885–93), No. 547.
8. Morris 1962, 61; 1973, 293.
9. Frere 1967, 380.
10. Morris 1965, 153 *et seq*.
11. Copley 1954, 43.
12. Stenton 1943, 15-6.
13. Harrison 1976, 124, 134, 140; Sir F. M. Stenton, Preparatory to Anglo–Saxon England (1970), 120–1.

Chapter IX

1. Rarer habitative elements are: *aern* (1), *beretun* (2), *berewic* (4), *botl* (2), *bur* (1), *hamtun* (3), *leactun* (1), *port* (3), *sele* (2), *wic-ham* (?4).
2. Sawyer 1974, 108–9, 112; expanded 1976, 1–7.
3. Taylor 1974, 8–9.
4. Dodgson 1966, 5.
5. Gelling 1974.
6. Gelling 1978, 184.
7. Wade-Martins 1975, 143, 146, 149–52.
8. Cox 1972-3, 15.
9. *Ibid*. 18.
10. M. Gelling, English place-names derived from the compound *wichām*, Med. Arch. XI (1967); Gelling 1977 and 1978, 67–74.
11. Dr. Gelling referred to *laeti* but no proof of this status is known in Britain. The term *foederati* would be equally appropriate.
12. Misplaced in Essex by Gelling 1967, corrected 1978.
13. J. Holmes, Excavations and fieldwork at Roman Braughing, *East Herts. Archaeological Soc. Trans*. XIII (1950-1).
14. Smith 1956, I, 282–298.
15. J. McN. Dodgson, The *-ing* in English place-names like Birmingham and Altrincham, and following papers, *Beitrage zur Namenforschung, Neue Folge*, Band 2, Heft 3 and 4 (1967) and Band 3, Heft 2 (1968) (Heidelberg).
16. J. Kuurman, An examination of the *-ingas, -inga-* place-names in the east Midlands, *E.P.N.S. Jl* 7 (1974-5).
17. Dodgson 1966, 19.
18. Smith 1956, I, 291-2, Gelling 1978, 178.
19. K. I. Sandred, English place-names in *-stead*, 1963 (Uppsala).
20. M. W. Barley reviewing *The place-names of Derbyshire*, Med. Arch. III (1959), 341.
21. Brandon 1978, 222.
22. Translation of original British nature names is possible (Sawyer 1978, 151).

Chapter X

1. Wainwright 1962, 60. Gelling 1978, chs. 3 and 4, deals with some Celtic place-name elements considered in this chapter.
2. Stenton in PNHerts xv.
3. Wainwright 1962, 64.
4. *Ibid*. 60, 63.

5. *Ibid.* 11.
6. Finberg 1964, 13.
7. Finberg 1972, 389.
8. Sir I. A. Richmond and O. G. S. Crawford, The British section of the Ravenna cosmography, *Arch.* XCIII (1949); A. L. F. Rivet and C. Smith, The place-names of Roman Britain (1979).
9. A. H. Smith, Place-names and the Anglo–Saxon settlement, *Proceedings of the British Academy* XLII (1965), 86.
10. Hare Street was Langeport in Domesday. The withered village of Affledwick became Beauchamps, and at a lower level Sumersele became Hyde Hall and Brocket Hall replaced Waterships.
11. Wainwright 1962, 58.
12. Taylor 1974.
13. Gelling 1977, 5–8.
14. *Ibid.* 8–10.
15. Nicolaisen 1970, 234, 203; Gelling 1978, 81.

Chapter XI

1. Biddle 1976, 326–9.
2. C. Hohler, St. Osyth and Aylesbury, *Rec. Bucks.* XVIII (1966–70).

Chapter XII

1. G. W. S. Barrow, The kingdom of the Scots (1973), 267–77.
2. Webster 1969, 235.
3. *Ibid.* 222.
4. Rivet 1969, 214, 216.
5. Applebaum 1972, 235, 253–4.
6. Reprinted in Finberg 1964.
7. F. Seebohm, The English village community (1883), 431–2 with plan.
8. Applebaum 1972, 42, 90–4, 254, 263, plan 92–3.
9. J. Chenevix-Trench, Coleshill and the settlement of the Chilterns, *Rec. Bucks.* XIX (1973).
10. Biddle 1971, 394, 396, 399–402.
11. C. Hohler, St. Osyth and Aylesbury, *Rec. Bucks.* XVIII (1966–70); not the Essex saint but another of the name.
12. R. A. Brown and H. M. Colvin, The king's houses 1066–1485, in *The history of the king's works*, ed. H. M. Colvin (1963), II, 924–5.
13. *Ibid.* 902.
14. PNHerts xiv.
15. Glastonbury honours no martyr and a Roman origin cannot be sustained; see R. F. Treharne, The Glastonbury legends (1967).
16. Copley 1954, 184.
17. Barley and Hanson 1968, 9. Thomas 1981 now covers the whole field.
18. Wheeler 1936, 122 and pl. xxxv.
19. *Hertfordshire Archaeology* I (1968). Contemporary proof of late Roman liturgical use is rare, even on the continent, because church building was still undifferentiated. It is possible that the large temple next to the Verulamium theatre was converted into a church, as the blocking of the east entrance and the creation of a west door suggest.
20. J. N. L. Myres, Presidential address in Council for British Archaeology Report No. 11 (1961), 43.

21.   Alcock 1971, 355.

22.   On his shoulder says the Latin of ch. 56. Alcock 1971, 52 pointed out that Old Welsh *scuit* 'shield' was probably corrupted to *scuid* 'shoulder'.

23.   *Eddius Stephanus, Vita Wilfridi*, ed. B. Colgrave (1927), ch. 27.

24.   Finberg 1964, 6.

25.   Barley and Hanson 1968, 87–92.

26.   J. R. Morris, The date of St. Alban, *Hertfordshire Archaeology* I (1968).

27.   *Ibid.*   28.   Bede HE I ch. 18.

29.   *Ibid.* I ch. 7.   30.   V.C.H. Herts. IV, 369.

31.   This conclusion is reached in Biddle 1977 which covers the whole ground.

32.   V.C.H. Herts. IV, 289.

33.   M. Biddle, H. T. Lambrick and J. N. L. Myres, The early history of Abingdon, Berks., and its abbey, *Med. Arch.* XII (1968), 33. I am indebted to the late Dr. J. R. Morris for pointing out this remarkable phrase.

34.   Reproduced in Hodgkin 1935, II pl. 53 with transcription p. 389. The list is discussed by C. Hart, The Tribal Hidage, *Transactions of the Royal Historical Soc.* 5th ser. 21 (1971), and by W. Davies and H. Vierck, The contents of the Tribal Hidage, *Fruhmittelalterliche Studien* 8 (1974) .

35.   Brown 1915, IV, 614.   36.   Stenton 1943, 3rd ed. (1971), 43.

37.   The most likely names are *Wiht* and *Oht*, one of which may be connected with the old name *Geht, Giht* of the river Ray. Although the *Wiht gara* are usually identified with the Isle of Wight people who also bore that name the equation seems unsound because the Hidage clearly meant to include the *Wiht gara* among the peoples of greater Mercia. It is possible that *Wiht* refers to the 'raised up land' of the north Hertfordshire heights.

38.   Sir F. M. Stenton, Lindsey and its kings, in *Essays in history* presented to R. L. Poole, ed. H. W. C. Davis (1927).

39.   *Eddius Stephanus, Vita Wilfridi*, ch. 42 (see note 23).

40.   Jackson 1953, 242 *et seq.*; Reaney 1960, 87–8.

41.   Nennius HB ch. 37.   42.   Sawyer 1978, 51–6. 89.

43.   *Cada* occurs in Cadmore End (Fingest), Bucks., 1236; Caddington, Beds., formerly Herts., c. 1000; and Cadwell (Holwell), Herts., 1227; the derivative *Ceatta* is in Chapmore End (Bengeo), Herts., 1294. *Tuda* occurs in Toddington, Beds., 1086. Possible names of this type are *Caeg* found in Cainhoe (Clophill), Beds., 1086 and in Cassio (Watford), Herts., 793; its derivative *Caegin* is in Kensworth, Beds., formerly Herts., 975, and in Kenesway (Gt. Berkhamsted), Herts., 1291. Caddington and Kensworth are adjoining parishes.

44.   Gelling 1978, 95–6; Cameron 1978–79, 11.

45.   Hodgkin 1935, I, pl. 30; V. E. Nash-Williams, The early Christian monuments of Wales (1950), 92 and pl. 8.

46.   Smith 1956, II, 242; DEPN 494.

47.   Finberg 1972, 395–6; Morris 1973, 315.

48.   Faull 1975.   49.   Cameron 1978–79, 3.

50.   Other local names that may connote reference to Britons are Britwell (Burnham), Bucks.; Brightwells (Watford), Herts.; Britwell Prior and Salome, Oxon. These perhaps contain *Bryt* 'Briton' but a stream name is possible (PNOxon 105).

51.   Wallington, Herts., has a different derivation.

52.   Cameron 1978–79, 12, 17.   53.   *Ibid.* 5; Gelling 1978, 95.

54.   Cameron 1978–79, 19.

55.   Finberg 1972, 389 note 1; Jackson 1953, 239 doubted whether Asser's forms of Dorset and Wiltshire names really were 9th century as Ekwall accepted in E.P.N.S. I, part I (1924), 28.

56.   J. Beddoe, The races of Britain (1885), *passim*; H. F. Fleure, *A natural history of man in Britain* (1951), 194 and Fig. 43.

APPENDIX I: KEY TO ROMAN SITES ON MAP 1

Definite and possible villas (D = definite)

1		Tingewick	31	D	Chenies, Latimer
2	D	Foxcote	32		Sarratt, Church Field
3		Shenley Brook End, Dovecote Farm	33		Chorleywood
4	D	Wolverton	34		Rickmansworth, Moor Park
5		Stanton Low	35		Hampermill
6	D	Gayhurst	36		Bushey, Chiltern Avenue
7		Ravenstone	37	D	Aldenham, Netherwild Farm
8		Olney	38		Bricket Wood, Munden
9		Kempston, Thistley Green	39	D	Park Street
10		Bedford, Castle Lane	40	D	King's Langley, Hunting Gate estate
11	D	Little Milton, Ditchend	41		King's Langley, station
12		Mapledurham, Blagraves Farm	42	D	Gorhambury
13	D	Harpsden	43	D	Hemel Hempstead, Boxmoor station
14		Bix	44	D	Hemel Hempstead, Boxmoor House
15	D	Hambleden, Yewden Manor	45	D	Gadebridge Park
16		Hambleden, Flint Hall Farm	46	D	Northchurch
17		Marlow	47		Berkhamsted, Frithsden
18		Bledlow, Wainhill	48		Aldbury, Moneybury
19	D	Saunderton Mill	49	D	Welwyn, Rectory
20	D	Saunderton Lee	50	D	Welwyn, Dicket Mead
21		Little Kimble	51	D	Welwyn, Lockleys
22		Ellesborough, Terrick	52		Datchworth, Bulls Green
23		Ellesborough, Whorley Wood	53	D	Standon, Youngsbury
24		Weston Turville	54	D	Braughing, Mentley Farm
25		Marsworth, Pitstone Green	55		Braughing, Horse Green
26	D	Totternhoe, Church End	56		Little Hadham, Bury Green
27	D	High Wycombe, All Hallows Lane	57	D	Great Wymondley
28		High Wycombe, Great Penn Mead	58	D	Radwell
29		Hughenden, Hazlemere	59		Shefford
30		Amersham, Shardeloes			

Barrows and mausolea

G	Watford, Munden House
J	Harpenden, Rothamstead
K	Harpenden, Pickford Mill
O	Stevenage, Six Hills
P	Stanstead Abbots, Easneye Wood
Q	Broxbourne Bury
R	Thornborough Mounds

Pottery (P) and tile (T) kilns

A	Dorchester, Allen's Pits (P)
B	Stone (P)
C	Fulmer, Duke's Wood (P)
D	Gerrard's Cross, Hedgerley Green (P)
E	Elstree, Bush Inn (T)
F	Radlett, Loom Lane (P)
H	St. Stephens, Blackboy Pits (T)
L	Luton, Waulud's Bank (P)
M	Toddington, Fox Burrow (P)
N	Hitchin Hill (P)
S	Standon, Bromley (P)

APPENDIX II: SUMMARY OF SAXON ARCHAEOLOGICAL SITES

SITES ARE GROUPED by counties in the order Beds., Bucks., Herts., Oxon. and listed in alphabetical order of parishes. Each abstract contains the key number shown on Map 3, the OS 1 inch 7th edition map sheet and grid reference, classification and date of site, followed by notes on significant finds and in some cases discussion. Classification, which differs slightly from the conventions of the Dark Ages map in distinguishing single inhumations from small groups and in separating wholly inhumation cemeteries from those where inhumation is predominant, is shown by the symbols:

SI	Single inhumation
IG	Inhumation group of 2 or 3 graves
IC	Wholly inhumation cemetery
I/CC	Inhumation/cremation cemetery
PCC	Predominantly cremation cemetery
SC	Single cremation
Barrow 1	Primary barrow burial by inhumation
Barrow 2	Secondary barrow burial
Occ	Occupation site
F	Find
B	Burh

The OS category 'predominantly inhumation cemetery' has been abandoned as misleading because it obscures the fact that some cemeteries long in use started with cremation predominant and ended with inhumation only. Doubtful sites are indicated by brackets, e.g. (Arlesey). All sites in the appendix to the Dark Ages map appear in the inventory but the classification of a few has been revised. The summary omits much detail: geology of the site, circumstances and date of discovery, complete find-lists, museums concerned, full discussion and published references. These are given in an earlier version of this book which has been deposited in the Department of Medieval and Later Antiquities at the British Museum.

BEDFORDSHIRE

1 (*Arlesey*)147 TL 18 ?35. Not in OS list. ?IC. Uncertain. 'Bones, spearheads, weapons'.

2 *Astwick* 147 TL 220380. IC. 7c. Finds near a Roman cemetery, including a sword and sugar-loaf type shield-boss, suggest at least 5 furnished inhumations, possibly 8, with others unfurnished.

3 (*Bedford, Russell Park*) 147 TL 061496. ?IG. Uncertain. 3 skeletons in line E–W with spearheads and a sword, perhaps of Viking date.

4 *Chalton, Chalgrave* 147 TL 030260. IC. Uncertain, probably late. 'Large number of Saxon graves ... bodies facing N and S, each with knife at waist', shield-boss.

5 *Clifton* 147 TL 169388. ?SI. 7c. Small sub-globular pot.

6 *Dunstable I* 147 TL 01 21. ?SC. Late 6c. Stamped pendent triangle panel style pot.

7 (*Dunstable II, Five Knolls*) 147 TL 006211. Not in OS list. Uncertain. Nearly 100 bodies inhumed in Bronze Age barrow, mostly later Saxon executions, but in disturbed soil a tapering bronze tube, probably a 'needle case', and Saxon sherds.

8 *Dunstable III, Marina Drive* 147 TL 001213. IC. 7c. Near Totternhoe RV. At least 49 burials round a Bronze Age barrow, many in orderly rows, most with heads to E or NE, 12 unfurnished. Finds included hanging bowl escutcheon, earrings and necklace parts of silver wire, silvered bronze work-boxes, silver locket, necklaces. Except for a damaged small-long brooch most cannot be earlier than late 6c and many are certainly 7c. Lack of orientation makes it difficult to place the cemetery in the Christian period; it was probably used from *c.* 600 until soon after the mid 7c.

9 *Eggington, Gault Hill* 147 SP 960254. IC. Late 6c. Roman occupation on site. Few finds included a 'needle case'.

10 *Fancott, Brickworks* 147 TL 018279. IG. Uncertain, probably late. Small pot without early characteristics.

11 *Henlow* 147 TL 17 38. Not in OS list, probably same site as Clifton. ?SI. Typical 7c. pot.

12a *Houghton Regis I, Puddlehill* 147 TL 003237, 011237. IC, Occ. Early 6c and *c.* 600. Belgic–Roman occupation on same ridge. Cemetery consisted of 2 adjacent groups: I with 8 graves, only 3 furnished, including warrior with mortal wound, with coin of Gratian and few finds: II of 4 graves, 1 furnished, with finds including a pair of large saucer brooches, the easternmost of a type of *c.* 600 or a trifle later. A grave of II cut into one of I after its site was forgotten, suggesting an interval of hardly less than 50 years and so indicating *c.* 550 or before for I. Village 250 yards away with at least 7 sunken-floored huts; finds included cowrie shell, beads, inlaid box lid, sherds of bag-shaped ware and coins of Constantine I: belongs to *c.* 600.

12b *Houghton Regis II, Sewell* 147 SP 991225, 998231, TL 003235. Occ. Late 6c. Two small groups of sunken-floored huts with sherds of baggy vessels, some with stamps suggesting late 6c.

13 *Kempston* 147 TL 031471. I/CC. Early 5 to late 7c. Probably about 300 burials; 161 certain including 35 cremations. Finds include 6 swords, 86 brooches, several late luxury objects—bronze workboxes, gold and silver pendants, silver wire pieces. Six bronze bars and 2 semi-tubular bars are *military belt fittings* like those from Dorchester I. An early '*Luton type*' brooch was dated by Roeder *c.*425; a silver gilt *equal-armed brooch* is *c.* 450. Of 5 *cruciform brooches* 2 of Aberg group I are probably mid 5c, another group I and a group II are late 5c, the last is a plain group V of the very late 6 or early 7c; there are no florid types. 34 *saucer brooches* run from the 5c to the early 7c; the few early ones include a 5-scroll motif; 8 are late 6c medley designs, 8 are the Maltese cross 'Kempston' type. Of 2 fine *great square-headed brooches* one, incomplete, is late 6c of Leeds' B8 group, the other early 7c of C3. The main emphasis of the datable *pottery* is early: from the first half of the 5c come several vessels (some with a 'very Romano–British look'—Myres) and a window urn; the later 5c is represented by the long-boss style and 5 urns of

Buckelurn groups I, II and III; a group V Buckelurn is early 6c; 4 urns show the late 6c stamped pendent triangle panel style; 3 plain vessels with tall necks are 7c. Few objects belong with certainty to the early 6c, perhaps because of the lack of distinctive ceramic styles of that period, perhaps because of selective recovery during gravel working.

14 (*Kensworth, Dyers Hill Farm*) 147 TL 042180. F. Uncertain. Reputed 'several fine specimens of Anglo–Saxon earthenware' but site reference may be misplaced.

15 *Langford* 147 TL 18 40. F. Late 6/7c francisca.

16 *Leagrave, Sarum Road* 147 TL 065238. SI. Uncertain, probably late. Skeleton with knife and comb.

17 *Leighton Buzzard I, Deadmans Slade* 146 SP 927263, I/CC. ?late 5 to 6c. Near tumuli. Inhumations and cremations are inferred. Finds include a mid 6c saucer brooch and lost globular urns, some with bosses and 'zigzag patterns interspersed with dots and circular lines' which may suggest the late 5c or the late 6c stamped pendent triangle panel style.

18 *Leighton Buzzard II, Chamberlain's Barn I* 146 SP 927263, IC. Early 7c. 500 yards south of Deadmans Slade which it may have replaced. At least 19 poorly furnished inhumations, one surrounded by a ditch. The few datable finds—buckle with triangular chape, bronze-rimmed wooden cup, small lugged pot—and absence of brooches favour early 7c rather than late 6c.

19 *Leighton Buzzard III, Chamberlain's Barn II* As No. 18. 7c. Iron Age occupation on site. 68 inhumations, nearly all with heads to WSW, many carefully spaced in rows, a few in shrouds; 2 graves surrounded by ditches. 30 burials were bare, several others had few gravegoods. Finds included a quoit brooch of probably c. 625, twice broken before burial, a composite brooch of Sarre I type (garnetted bosses, small cells decorated with gold plates and filigree) of c. 650, and distinctively late 7c objects—a tall sugar-loaf shield-boss, small wooden chests with metal fittings, silver wire rings with beads, linked silver pins, stamped silver disc pendent, gourd-shaped pots. Layout and assemblage are typical of new semi-conformist cemeteries established soon after the Conversion, and the site is only 4 miles from the 7c church at Wing. The cemetery probably replaced No. 18.

20 *Limbury, Leagrave Marsh* 147 TL 056243 (corrected by OS). IG. Late 6c. Near Waulud's Bank, Neolithic henge monument. Bronze disc brooches.

21a *Luton I, Argyll Avenue* 147 TL 081229. I/CC. Early 5 to late 6c. Near a Roman site. During a partial rescue dig amidst building work about 40 inhumations and 7 cremations were distinguished, of a probable total of 70–80 or more. Many unassociated finds came from destroyed graves, some of them probably the oldest. Many objects included a damaged *military buckle* of the late 4/early 5c type found in a 6c woman's grave; a primitive '*Luton type*' *brooch* dated by Roeder c. 400; an *equal-armed brooch*; 20 *saucer brooches* extending from the late 5c (quadruple recurved scroll) to the late 6c, many of types unknown at Kempston: a *great square-headed brooch* of B6 group, late 6/early 7c; an iron weaving sword of a type indicating high status and confined to women's graves; *pottery* from the 5c to late 6c, beginning with 2 of Buckelurn groups I and III or IV and ending with an urn of the stamped pendent triangle panel style. There are no cruciform brooches or saucer brooches of the Maltese cross or late cast varieties.

21b *Luton II, vicinity* 147 TL ?08 23. F. 6c. Saucer brooch probably but not certainly from Luton I.

22 *Luton III, Biscot Mill* 147 TL 079231. IC. 7c. 500 yards north of Luton I.

At least 11 inhumations round a Neolithic long barrow, only 4 furnished, meagrely. Finds include 7c pot, according with absence of brooches.

23 *Luton IV, Dallow Road* 147 TL 082215. SI. Late 6/7c. Cowrie shell.

24 *Moggerhanger* 147 TL 138491. ?SC. Late 6c. Globular urn with stamped pendent triangle panel style.

25 *Sandy* 147 TL 177488. PCC. Early 5 to early 6c. Near major Roman settlement. Finds indicating at least 10 cremations and probably some inhumations include a silver bracelet and 14 pots, half of them 5c, the earliest perhaps a dimpled carinated bowl; there are 3 later 5c vessels of Buckelurn group I and a few early 6c wares including a group V urn.

26 *Shefford* 147 TL 135387. ?SI. Late 6c. Near a walled Roman cemetery. A pair of medley design cast saucer brooches.

27 *Shillington, Pegsdon Common* 147 TL 133310. Barrow 2. Uncertain. In a (?) long barrow one burial, and possibly others as a shield-boss, spear-heads and sherds in Hitchin Museum may come from this site.

28 *Sundon, Cement works* 147 TL 037275. SI. Uncertain.

29 *Toddington I, Sheepwalk Hill* 147 TL 02 29 (corrected: most finds came from the hill near Old Park). I/CC. Late 6c. probable Roman building (buried concrete platform) on site. Loose finds suggest considerably more than 17 reported skeletons, and urns nearby indicate cremations. A few graves were moderately furnished. Both saucer brooches are lost, but the complexion of numerous bronzes is neither 5 nor distinctively 7c. It is more likely that a group IV cruciform brooch of the third quarter of the 6c 'from Toddington' came from this site than from Warmark.

30 *Toddington II, Warmark Farm* 147 TL 002283. I/CC. ?5 to late 6c. Accounts of 1829 spoke of a reputed 1,000 burials, with bones and numerous urns filled with (burnt) bones and what must be very large late cast saucer brooches. Everything has gone but illustrations depict a B6 group great square-headed brooch of the late 6c. The apparent size of the cemetery and high proportion of cremation may point to 5c foundation.

31 *Totternhoe I* 147 SP 988228. F. 7c. Equal-armed brooch.

32 *Totternhoe II, Roman villa* 147 SP 987207. F. Late 5/early 6c sherd.

33 *Whipsnade* 147 TL 01 17. F. Late 6c sherd showing relationship to the stamped pendent triangle panel style.

BUCKINGHAMSHIRE

34 *Ashendon* 146 SP 705142. SI. *c.* 600 or very early 7c. Pair of late very large cast saucer brooches with basketry motif and garnet setting.

35 *Aylesbury I, Cemetery* 146 SP 829135. F. Late 6 or 7c. Seax knife.

36 (*Aylesbury II, Holman's Bridge*) 146 SP 818153. F. Spearhead on reputed scene of Civil War engagement.

37 *Bishopstone I, Church site* 146 SP 807101. IC. Late 6c. The only fairly complete saucer brooch resembles the medley one from No. 38.

38 *Bishopstone II, Causeway Field (Cursley Hill)* 146 SP 799110. IC. Late 6c. Near supposed tumulus. At least a dozen and perhaps twice as many inhumations, most with heads to N. Finds included a bronze belt plate decorated with stylized beasts, of late Roman military type, clearly a survival; 2 swords; 4 shield-bosses; 5 saucer brooches including a cast pair with scroll cross design and an applied one with medley pattern. The belt plate, probably an heirloom, was old when buried;

it cannot be preferred to the general complexion which strongly favours initial use of the cemetery *c.*570.

39 *Bledlow I, The Cop* 159 SP 774010. Barrow 2, I/CC. ?7c. Secondary burials in a Bronze Age barrow. Two or 3 inhumations and 5 or 6 cremations, proportions that normally mean an early date, but the rite of cremation continued late locally (Kingsey) and small groups in the upper Thames area tended to conservatism. Pottery rather resembling the globular shapes of the late 6/7c, a composite brooch that may be late, and the absence of brooches may point to the 7c.

40 *Bledlow II, The Warren* 159 SP 775014. IG. 7c. Poorly equipped burials.

41 *Buckingham, near* F. *c.* 600/7c. A pair of very large late cast saucer brooches.

42 *Dinton* 146 SP 765114. IC. ?7c. At least 19 inhumations, mostly without gravegoods. An imported glass cone beaker of the 5 or early 6c, evidently a survival, does not fit the complexion of the cemetery which produced few finds and was probably later than 600.

43 *Ellesborough* 159 SP 845070. IG. 7c. A cowrie shell suggests late 6 or 7c and the lack of brooches makes the latter likely.

44 *High Wycombe, Castle Hill* 159 SU 866931. SI, ? Barrow 2. 7c. In a barrow, probably secondary. A gold disc pendant with gold wire and (missing) garnet centre is of Kentish type and belongs to the first half of the 7c.

45 *Hitcham, Windmill Field* 159 SU 921811. SI. Uncertain, probably late. Near a Roman villa. The shield-boss is not of a distinctively late type. Hitcham is a *hām* place-name.

46 *Kingsey, Tythrop Park* 159 SP 741072. I/CC. Late 6c. There were two bone-filled urns, and finds suggest a few inhumations. The roughly made pots broadly belong to the stamped pendent triangle panel style, and a cast saucer brooch said to come from the site, with imitated garnet lozenges and medley infill, could be as late as *c.* 600.

47 *Little Kimble* 159 SP 82 06. SI. 7c. A francisca and spearhead, probably from a inhumation.

[*Note:* a pot from *Loudwater*, referred to by Head and Meaney, is definitely not Saxon.]

48 *Mentmore* 146 SP 906196. IC. Late 6 to 7c. On site of Roman cremation cemetery. Three separate inhumation groups probably represent a considerable span of time. One group of 10 burials lying E–W, near the church, was almost unfurnished and may be of the early post-Conversion period. The only surviving find is a coarse 'spider's legs' design cast saucer brooch of the late 6c.

49 *Milton Keynes* 146 SP 890392. IC. 7c. Not in Dark Ages map list. Seven orientated unfurnished burials near the church.

50 *Newport Pagnell I* 146 SP 887453. IC. Late 6c. Several skeletons arranged in two circles with feet pointing inwards. Finds included 3 swords, 2 (lost) applied saucer brooches with a star design, probably late 6c, and a claw beaker of that date. It is doubtful whether a Roman mould-blown beaker came from this site.

51 *Newport Pagnell II, Tickfordfield Farm* 146 SP 887442. IC. Uncertain. The site adjoins No. 50 and may have formed part of it.

52 *Newport Pagnell III, Kickle's Farm* 146 SP 863448. SI. ?late 6c. Roman finds from site. Sword only.

53 *Oving* 146 SP 78 21. F. 7c. Enamelled hanging bowl escutcheon with degenerate 'developed trumpet pattern', perhaps from an inhumation.

54 *Pitstone* 159 SP 947148. IG. Uncertain, probably late. No finds.

55 *Quarrendon, Bicester road bridge* 146 SP ?796153.F. Late 6/7c seax.

56 *Stone* 146 SP 779122. IC. Late 6 to 7c. On site of extensive Roman cremation cemetery next to pottery kilns. Numerous inhumations, with a shield-boss (lost) and a very large late cast saucer brooch with basketry motif, imitation garnets and a cross divided into tiny squares like cloisonne work, clearly influenced by fine Kentish brooches.

57 *Taplow* 159 SU 906821. Barrow 1. *c.* 600. A barrow burial with many luxurious objects approaching Sutton Hoo in magnificence: sword, 2 shield-bosses, silver-rimmed cups, buckets (one with embossed bronze plates), bronze Coptic bowl, 4 claw beakers, over 30 bone draughtsmen, a lyre, 4 drinking horns with silver- and bronze-gilt mounts, fabric with gold-woven edging, gold buckle set with garnets, a pair of bronze-gilt clasps. The place-name—'Taeppa's burial mound'—probably preserves the dead chieftain's name, which is not known in any surviving royal genealogy.

58 *Upper Winchendon, Eythrope* 146 SP 771141. IC. Late 6c. Three shield-bosses, one with silver rivets which point to late 6c.

59 *Walton* (*Aylesbury*) 146 SP 824133. Occ, IC. Early 5c to 7c and later. Not in Dark Ages map list. Roman coins and pottery on site. Random finds in vicinity of several inhumations with spearheads (one perhaps late 6-7c.), knife, loomweights and urns (lost). Domestic: the earliest of 5 sunken huts were small and crude, later ones larger, with 3 later 'halls'. Floor deposits included silver ring, iron buckle, combs, knives, crucible, pottery (dated by Myres early 5c to 6c and perhaps later) including a few vessels with stamps or small bosses and grass-tempered wares. From a medieval gully a late Roman 'military' type IB buckle; also unstratified, a small-long brooch and quoit brooch. Pits contained rotary quern, carbonized wheat, barley and oats. Many cattle and sheep bones.

60 *Wing* 146 SP 881215. IC. 7c. Not in Dark Ages map list. Several skeletons adjoining the churchyard, with no mention of finds, suggest a new post-Conversion Christian cemetery, entirely conformist due to the oversight of the great mission church here.

HERTFORDSHIRE

61 *Ashwell I, Odsey* 147 TL 298386. IG. Late 6c. Most objects said to have come from a cemetery are undatable, but a pair of applied saucer brooches 'probably' from Ashwell bear the Maltese cross pattern of the late 6c and a goose-shaped bronze shield mount is consistent with this.

62 *Ashwell II, Slip End* 147 TL 28 37. Not in Dark Ages map list. IC. Uncertain. A puzzling recently discovered site. One grave had a body laid with head to W, another contained 3 complete burials (2 largely disarticulated) and 2 skulls, and in ditch between them lay 1 or 2 incomplete skeletons, all without gravegoods. Saxon sherds on the site, not yet assessed, may be late 5/early 6c.

63 *Furneux Pelham* 148 TL 431279. IG. Uncertain, probably late. Roman material on site. Pelham is a *hām* place-name.

64. *Hertford, Foxholes Farm* 160 TL 345123. Not in Dark Ages map list. Occ. Uncertain. Seven sunken Saxon huts, without finds, in a complex of Bronze Age, Iron Age and Roman ditches.

[*Note:* The cited provenance of a cremation urn of *c.* 500 'from Hertford' is incorrect, as its label has been changed.]

65 *Hitchin I* 147 TL 17 29. F. 7c. The 2 surviving escutcheons of a complete hanging bowl, probably from a burial, bear developed trumpet pattern spirals; the presence of yellow enamel as well as the usual red favours 7c rather than 6c for manufacture.

66 (*Hitchin II*) 147 TL ?18 29. F. The attribution to Hitchin of a curious kind of brooch, possibly late 5 or early 6c, is undependable.

67 *Ippollitts I, Millfield Lane* 147 TL 193268 (corrected: not at Pound Farm). SI. Late 6/7c scramasax.

68 *Ippollitts II, Vicar's Grove sandpit, Gosmore* 147 TL 187270. F. Late 6c. Gourd shaped pot with decoration faintly akin to stamped pendent triangle panel style.

69 *Kings Walden, between Breachwood Green and Darley Hall* 147 TL 140220. SI. ?late 6c. Applied saucer brooch fragments suggest late 6c which would fit the bronzework, but a sherd of a pot with rudimentary bosses and decoration could be earlier.

70 *Letchworth, Blackhorse Road* 147 TL 233336, not in Dark Ages map list. IC. 7c. Nine burials including one of a man with a fatal wound, all poorly or not equipped. Absence of brooches and a scramasax point to the 7c.

71 *Redbourn* 147 TL 10 12, not in Dark Ages map list. ?Barrow 1. Late 6/7c. Ten burials in 2 barrows opened in 1178, with ?scramasax.

72 (*Royston, Briary Lane*) 147 TL 35 40. ?IG. Uncertain. Three skeletons with ?a knife only.

73 *St. Albans, King Harry Lane* 160 TL 131067, not in Dark Ages map list. IC. 7c. Adjoining large Roman cemetery. 32 graves, most with head to NW, of which 21 were furnished, some with a knife only and few well equipped. Two scramasaxes, a silver pendant, 2 elaborate chatelaines and the complete lack of brooches clearly tell 7c.

— *St. Albans, Kingsbury* 160 TL 14 07. B. ?8c. The *burh*, directly opposite Verulamium across the Ver, was a sub-rectangular ramparted enclosure of 27½ acres with a salient to the SE. In places the banks are still 20 feet high but most is built over, and Fishpool Street winds along the S side with its N footpath raised on the edge of the partly demolished rampart. Tree trunks are said to have been found in the N scarp, with remains of a palisade. Renn (D. Renn, *Medieval castles in Hertfordshire*, 1971) wrongly believed Kingsbury was 'an open settlement contructed by levelling a hillock' but the scale of the works and the *burh* element proclaim a defensive motive. The *burh* is clearly post-Roman and must have been founded by 793 when Offa pointedly excluded it (and Verulamium) from his great endowment to the abbey. It long continued to be governed by royal officials, and the name and history suggest the possibility here of one of the royal 'palaces' mentioned by Biddle; it is potentially a site of great archaeological interest. The proximity of royal and abbatial jurisdictions caused constant friction between the monks and the *burh* men who depended on the fishponds below. Edgar sold these to the abbey, and under Ethelred II his chancellor Ælfric acquired most of the *municipium* which he demolished when he became abbot, but the salient remained the residence of royal officers until *c.* 1152 when Stephen allowed it to be razed.

74 *Stevenage, 444 Broadwater Crescent* 147 TL 263217, not in Dark Ages map list. Occ. Late 5c. One sunken hut. A bronze strap-end is of late Roman military type but wares of the second half of the 5c, including at least one group II Buckelurn, must be contemporary with occupation.

75 *Therfield, Five Hills* 147 TL 341401. Barrow 2. 6/7c. In a Neolithic long barrow. A bronze buckle may be as early as 5c but this type of burial suggests 6 or 7c deposit.

76 *Therfield II, Therfield Heath* 147 TL 340403. Barrow 2. 6/7c. In a long barrow. Spearhead only, remarks as for No. 75.

77 *Wheathampstead* 160 TL 170140. IG. 7c. A Coptic bronze bowl and glass palm cup give the date.

OXFORDSHIRE

78 (*Benson*) 158 SU 615908, not in Dark Ages map list. An extremely doubtful site: of several burials none from their manner seems to be Saxon, some clearly are not, and 'Saxon spearhead and knife' was a guess.

79 (*Chinnor I*) 159 SP 750010. ?IG. No finds.

80 *Chinnor II* 159 SP 765002. Barrow 2. Uncertain, finds are lost.

81 *Dorchester I, Dyke Hills* 158 SU 577934. IC. Late Roman to *c.* 600/7c. The Dyke Hills earthwork outside the Roman town was 'full of Saxon burials'. This classic site needs segregation of the 2 oldest graves which must be linked with a contemporary one at No. 82.

(1) The 2 earliest graves were in a normal late Roman inhumation cemetery. A male burial was accompanied by bronze military accoutrements—bars strengthening the belt, buckle, strap-tags, disc attachments. A female burial had a similar buckle with confronted animal heads and a proto-cruciform brooch, the earliest found in England. The evaluation of these graves and their contents is a long story. Sixty years ago their dating presented an acute dilemma, for though Brown realized the woman's brooch could be no later than *c.* 400, Aberg, constrained by Bede's dating of the Adventus Saxonum, believed it could not have been deposited before *c.* 450, though made earlier. When it became obvious that the military equipment meant that was too late for the burials Kendrick suggested that the relics belonged to a nest of river pirates and Myres that the graves were those of raiders, despite the presence of a woman. In 1953, when the place of Germanic mercenaries with womenfolk in the late Roman world was realized, Kirk and Leeds recognized that the burials did not belong to the invasion period 'but to *feoderati* in some Roman detachment stationed at Dorchester'. The military equipment is of the types described in Chapter IV; it does not follow that all who wore such belts were Germans. The barracks of these troops were probably the crude dwellings within the town, mentioned in Chapter III. The last decade or two of the 4c is the most likely date for these burials.

(2) Other graves contained a pair of very large late cast saucer brooches with basketry motif which show the burial ground was still used *c.* 600/early 7c.

82 *Dorchester II, Minchin recreation ground* 158 SU 577948. IG. Late Roman and ?later. A woman's burial was accompanied by several Roman objects and a pair of applied brooches of a kind in fashion in north Germany under the late Empire; the design seems to be ancestral to the 5-coil spiral found on the earliest saucer brooches. The grave is obviously from the same horizon as the early Germanic ones at No. 81 and probably came from a similar late-Roman extra-mural cemetery. Another burial on the site, with a spearhead and ? shield-boss, was probably later.

83 *Dorchester III, Berinsfield* 158 SU 580957, not in Dark Ages map list. I/CC. Early 5c to *c.* 600. Bronze Age cremations and late Roman ditches on site. At least 91 inhumations, most with heads to S or W, including 18 unfurnished, 15 with only one article and 8 well provided; 3 or 4 cremations, one surrounded by post-holes

as if for a canopy. Finds included 16 shield-bosses (2 of a late type); a *military belt-end* (found with a shield boss) similar to a late Roman one at No. 81; a very early '*Luton type' brooch*; an *equal-armed brooch* of developed form, probably later 5c; 19 *saucer brooches*, including 2 pairs of 5c 5-coil spiral pattern and a pair of 6-coil spirals of *c.* 500, the rest mainly late 6c including a cut-down pair of the Maltese cross design of *c.* 600; 2 late 6c *great square-headed brooches*, one of the B2 'southern' group, the other unplaced. The military belt piece, though late 4c, was evidently interred later in a purely Saxon context in a cemetery of *foederati* founded in the early 5c and used until *c.* 600, only some decorated buckets could be a little later. (Berinsfield is an artificial modern name, not derived from Old English *byrgen*.)

84 *Dorchester IV, Amey's gravel pit* 158 SU 570956. IC. 6/7c. At least 13 burials round a Bronze Age barrow, with few objects.

85 *Dorchester V, Bishop's Court* 158 SU 573954, not in Dark Ages map list. IC. 7c. Ten inhumations, one with 2 seaxes, all with heads to W.

86 *Dorchester VI, in the town* 158 SU 57 94. F. 7c. A lost gold stud of blunt pyramid shape with a garnet and intricate cloisonne work, perhaps from a scabbard strap or sword harness, was found with gold coins of Valentinian I (4c) and Mauricius Tiberius (582–602) and a runic gold coin probably contemporary with the Crondall hoard of *c.* 640/50. Similar studs from Sutton Hoo and Broomfield are dated to *c.* 625. The stud suggests someone of princely status at Dorchester at that time, and the coins, of types often mounted in pendants, may have belonged to a goldsmith working for a rich patron; both buttress the argument that Birinus chose or was given the site for his see because it was then a royal centre.

87 *Ewelme* 158 SU 644929. IC. Late 6/7c. 'Prehistoric urns' found nearby. About 15 skeletons without gravegoods in nearly all cases, most spaced in rows and some with heads to W, but 5 in one pit. Cremation is uncertain as bones found with a bronze bowl may not have been human but perhaps a funeral feast or offering. A bronze-bound bucket is likely to be late 6 or 7c. The bronze bowl superficially resembles normal hanging bowls but is of thicker metal and made of two sections telescoped together, and is of a strange shape, strongly nipped in to form a low neck. It has plain escutcheons and the base has plain discs inside and outside. The bowl is probably of two periods, an early vessel being added to and rebuilt into an improvised hanging bowl, and deposit in the late 6 or more probably the 7c is likely. A pot found nearby is probably not Saxon.

88 *Lewknor I, The Knapp* 159 SU 716971, not in Dark Ages map list. IC. 7c. One or 2 scramasaxes.

89 *Lewknor II, Postcombe* 159 707994, not in Dark Ages map list. IG. Late 6/7c. Near Bronze Age barrow. Very poorly furnished.

90 *Lower Shiplake* 159 SU 775795. I/CC. 6c. Two pots with 6c ornament seem to be cremation urns, and other finds including a sword probably denote some inhumations.

91 *Sydenham* 159 SU 730010. SI. Uncertain. The shield-boss is lost.

92 (*Whitchurch*) 158 SU 622781. ?SI. Probably Roman, as a Roman coin in the mouth was Charon's traditional fare.

APPENDIX III: HEATHEN PLACE-NAMES

Worship

hearg	Beds	Harrowden (Eastcotts)	1086
weoh	Bucks	Weedon	1086
		Wing	1012
	Herts	?Wain Wood/*Wayndene*)	14c
		?*Welei* (lost)) (Ippollitts)	1086
heafod	Beds	Manshead Hundred	1086
	Herts	*Hertesheved* (Bushey)	13c
Woden	Beds	Wenslow Hundred	1086
?*Thunor*	Herts	?Thundridge	1086
		?Thunderfield (Cheshunt)	1728
?*Tiw*	Herts	?Tewin	944–6
?*Grimm*	Herts	?Grimes Brook, Grymescroft (Cheshunt)	N D

Burial sites

ād	Herts	The Node (Codicote)	1426
byrgen,	Bucks	Burn Hill (Stone)	1276
byrgels		?Bernwood	*c.* 950
	Herts	?Barley	*c.* 1050
		Kinsbourne Green (Harpenden)	1201
	Oxon	Berins Hill (Ipsden)	1657
		Cowberry Lane (Watlington)	*c.* 1220
		haethenan byrigels (Crowmarsh)	966
		haethenan byrigels (Pyrton)	10c
hlaw	Beds	Bucklow Hundred	1086 Bucca
		Goldenlow (Dunstable)	1286
		Wadlow (Toddington)	1200 Wada
		Wenslow Hundred	1086 Woden
	Bucks	Bledlow	1012 Bledda
		Cottesloe (Wing)	1086 Cotta
		Culley Farm (Hartwell)	1320 ?Cusa
		Taplow	1086 Taeppa
		Winslow	792 Wine
	Herts	Betlow (Tring)	1203 Betta
		Cumberlow Green (Rushden)	1248 Cumbra
	Oxon	*cudan hlaewe* (Cuxham)	995 Cuda

Superstition

	Herts	Bastow (Anstey)	1362
		Berdestaplesholme (Stanstead)	13c

APPENDIX IV: ENGLISH HABITATIVE PLACE-NAMES

I   Possible hām names

BEDFORDSHIRE

Regarded as certain

Higham Gobion 1086 *heah* 'high' Studham 1053–66 *stōd* 'breeding stud'

Probably hamm

Blunham 1086 ?Bluwa Felmersham 1086 Feolumaer
Bromham 1086 Bruna or *brom* 'broom' Pavenham 1086 Papa

BUCKINGHAMSHIRE

Regarded as certain

Burnham 1086 *burna* 'stream' Hicknaham (Dorney) 1199 Hicca
Cippenham (Burnham) *c.* 1110 Cippa Hitcham 1086 Hycga, Hicca or Hwicca
Farnham Royal 1086 *fearn* 'fern' Rowsham (Wingrave) *c.* 1130 Hrothwulf
Haddenham 1086 Haedda or Headda Wexham 1195 *weax* 'beeswax'

Doubtful, possibly or probably hamm

Amersham 1066 Agilmund, Agilmond Haversham 1012 Hacfer or *haefer* 'goat'
   or Ealgmund Higham (Chesham) 1287 *heah*
Bradenham 1086 Brada or *brad* 'broad' Tyringham 1086 Tir, Tir- or Tidhere
Bragenham (Soulbury) 1178 ?Bracca
Denham 1066 *denu* 'valley'

HERTFORDSHIRE

Regarded as certain

Aldenham 785 Ealda or *eald* 'old' Newnham 1086 *niwa* 'new'
Boreham Wood (Elstree) 1188 *bor* 'hill' Pelham, Furneux, Brent and Stocking
Hadham G. and L. 957 *haeth* 'heath' or   1086 Peola or Peotla
   Haedda or Headda Puttenham 1086 Putta
Hixham Hall (Furneux Pelham) 1086
   Theodric

Doubtful, possibly hamm

Hartham (Hertford) 1324 *heorot* 'hart' Tednambury (Sawbridgeworth) 1307
Sapeham (lost, Edwinstree Hundred) 1086   Tyda

Rejected

Burnham Green (Digswell) 1380 probably manorial.
Frogmore (Kings Walden) *c.* 1270 *focga* 'reeds' or Focga.

147

Welham Green (North Mymms) Edw. II *withing* 'withy'.

OXFORDSHIRE

Regarded as certain

Ingham House (Watlington) 887   Mapledurham 1086 *mapuldor* 'maple'
  ? element meaning 'hill'   Newnham Murren (Crowmarsh) 966

Doubtful, possibly hamm

Caversham 1086 Cafhere

II   *Names in -ingas and -inga-*

BEDFORDSHIRE

-ingas

Kitchen End (Pulloxhill) 13c. Cycci.

-inga-

? Harlington 1086 Herela   ? Steppingley 1086 Steapa
? Lidlington 1086 Lytel   ? Toddington 1086 Tuda
? Shillington 1060 Scyttel, Scytla   ? Wrestlingworth *c.* 1150 Wraestel

BUCKINGHAMSHIRE

-ingas

Basing (Ankerwyke in Wraysbury)   Oving 1086 Ufa
  c. 1150 Basa   Wing 1012 ? *weoh* 'temple'
Halling (Stoke Mandeville) *c.* 1200 Heall

-inga-

? Averingdown (W. Wycombe) 1222 Haefer   ? Littleworth (Wing) 1227 Lytel
Buckingham 918 Bucca   ? Tetchwick (Ludgershall) 1086 Tota
? Ivinghoe 1086 Ifa   ? Tiddingford (Linslade) 966 Ytta
? Lenborough 1086 *hlith* 'slope'   ? Tingewick 1086 Tida
? Lillingstone Dayrell, Lovell 1086   ? Tyringham 1086 Tir, Tir-, Tidhere
  Lytel   Wingrave 1086 from Wing

HERTFORDSHIRE

-ingas

Braughing 825–8 Breahha   Tewin 944–6 Tiwa

-inga-

? Bengeo 1086 R. Beane   ? Swangleys (Knebworth) 1278 Swan
? Buntingford 1185 Bunta   Uaeclingacaestir (Verulamium) *c.* 730
Datchworth 969 Daecca   Wacol
Essendon 11c Esla   ? Wallington 1086 Waendel
Hertingfordbury 1086 from Hertford   ? Wengeo (Ware) 1307 from Ware

OXFORDSHIRE

-ingas

Goring 1086 Gara

-inga-

englingadene (Pyrton) ? 10c. Engel.
Shillingford 1156 ?Sciella,
   Scilling, scyling 'parting'

? *Sullingwrthe* (? Chalgrove) 1278–9
   ?Sciella, Scilling, scyling
   wylfinga ford (Culham) 940 Wulf

(Watlington occurs once as Huuaetlingatune 11c but is regarded here as a case of *-ingtun* which spellings support.)

III   Names in *-ingtun*
BEDFORDSHIRE

Cardington 1086 Caerda or Cenred
Seddington 1306 *suth* 'south'

Stevington 1086 Styfa or Stif

BUCKINGHAMSHIRE

Addington 1086 Æddi or Eada
Cublington 1086 Cubbel
Cuddington 1115/25 Cuddi or Cuda
Dinton 1086 Dunn(a) or Dynne
Dunton 1086 Doda, Duda or Dudd(a)
Easington (Chilton) 1086 Esa or Esi

Loughton 1086 Luhha
Shabbington 1086 Sc(e)obba
Sherington 1086 Scira
Warrington c. 1175 Wearda, Wearheard
   or — weard
Wolverton 1086 Wulfhere

HERTFORDSHIRE

Bennington 1086 R. Beane
Kimpton 1086 Cyma

Norringtonend Farm (Redbourn) 1296
   north

OXFORDSHIRE

Bensington c. 870 (annal 571) Benesa
Emmington (Chinnor) 1086 Eama

Watlington 887 Wacol or Waecel

IV   Names in *tun*
BEDFORDSHIRE

Beeston (Sandy) 1086 *beos* 'bent grass'
Campton 1086 British river name
   Camel
Carlton 1086 *ceorl* 'churl'
Chalton (Muggerhanger) 1086 *ceorl*
Chalton (Toddington) 1131 *ceulf*
   'calf'
Chellington 1242 Ceolwynn (fem.)
Clifton 944–6 *clif* 'cliff'
Clipstone (Egginton) 1195 Clip
Dunton 1086 *dun* 'hill'
East End (Flitwick) Eston 1321 *east*
Eaton Bray 1086 *eg* 'islet'
Etonbury (Arlesey) 1667 *eg*
Everton 1086 *eofor* 'boar'
Flitton 1086 *fleot* 'stream'
Houghton Conquest 1086 *hoh* 'hill-spur'
Houghton Regis 1086 *hoh*

Kempston 1060 probably British *cambo-*
   'river bend' rather than Cemmi
Lidlington 1086 Lytel, *-inga-*
Luton 792 R. Lea
Marston Moretaine 969 *mersc* 'marsh'
Milton Bryant 1086 *middel*
Newton (Dunton) 1504 *niwe* 'new'
Potton c. 960 *pott* 'pot'
Shelton (Marston Moretaine) 1086 *scylf*
   'shelf'
Stratton (Biggleswade) 1086 *straet*
   'street'
Sutton 1086 *suth* 'south'
Upton End (Shillington) Uppennende
   1225, 1294, Opton 1276
Westoning 1086 *west*
Willington 1086 *welig* 'willow'
Wootton 1086 *wudu* 'wood'

BUCKINGHAMSHIRE

Aston Abbots 1086 *east*
Aston Clinton 1086 *east*
Aston Mullins (Dinton) 1215 *east*
Aston Sandford 1086 *east*
Bierton 1086 *burh* 'town'
Bishopstone (Stone) 1227 *biscop*
    'bishop'
Bourton (Buckingham) 1086 *burh*
Broughton 1086 *broc* 'brook'
Broughton (Bierton) 1086 *broc*
Calverton 1086 *cealf* 'calf'
Chilton 1086 *cild* 'young person'
Clifton Reynes 1086 *clif* 'cliff'
Crafton (Wing) 1086 *croh* 'saffron'
Ditton Park (Stoke Poges) 1086 *dic* dyke
Dorton 1086 *dor* 'door, narrows'
Drayton Beauchamp 1086 *draeg* 'slipway'
Drayton Parslow 1086 *draeg*
Emberton 1086 Eanbeorht
Eton 1086 *eg*
Fleet Marston 1086 *mersc*
Halton *c.* 1038 *healh* 'corner'
Hoggeston ?*c.* 1000, 1086 Hogg or
    hogg 'hog'
Horton (Ivinghoe) 1086 *horh* 'dirt'
Horton 1086 *horh*
Ivinghoe Aston (Ivinghoe) 1086 *east*
Maids Moreton 1086 *mor* 'moor'
North Marston 1086 *mersc*
Milton Keynes 1086 *middel*
Monkton (Marlow) 1535 monk
    (Medmenham Abbey founded 1204)

Moreton Farm (Dinton) *c.* 1218 *mor*
Moretons (lost, Marlow) 1284 *mor*
Newton Blossomville 1175 *niwe*
Newton Longville 1086 *niwe*
Preston Bisset 1086 *preost* 'priest'
Quainton 1086 Quen-
Ravenstone 1086 Hrafn
Shalstone 1086 Sceald or *scealdwelle*
    'shallow well'
Shipton (Winslow) 1279 *sceap* 'sheep'
Simpson 1086 Sigewine
Slapton 1086 *slaep* 'slimy place'
Snelson (Lavendon) 1272 Snell
Stantonbury 1086 *stan* 'stone'
Sutton (Iver) *suth* 'south'
Thornton 1086 *thorn*
Turweston 1086 Thurulfr, -fastr
Upton (Dinton) 1086 *up*
Upton (Slough) 1086 *up*
Walton *c.* 1218 *weall* 'wall', *weald*
    'wood' or *wealh* 'Briton'
Walton (Aylesbury) 1237–40 as
    preceding
Water Eaton 1086 *eg*
Weston Turville 1086 *west*
Weston Underwood 1086 *west*
West Town (Taplow) Weston 13c *west*
Woolstone 1086 Wulfsige
Wormstone (Waddesdon) *c.* 1200
    Waermund or Waermod
Wotton Underwood 848 *wudu*
Woughton on the Green 1086 Weoca

HERTFORDSHIRE

Aston 11c *east*
Bearton Green (Hitchin) 1086 *burh*
Charlton (Hitchin) 1086 *ceorl*
Fawn Wood (lost, St. Albans)
    Thwangtune 11 c *thwang* 'thong'
Gilston 1197 Gydel or Gedel
Glitton (lost, Ashwell), 1313 ?*gleoda*
    'kite'
Hainstone (lost, Odsey Hund.) 1086
Hexton 1086 Heahstan
Hunton Bridge (Abbots Langley) 1391
Ichetone (Layston) 1086
Long Marston (Tring) 1287 *mersc*
Newton Wood (Stevenage) W. de N.

1281 *niwe*
Norton 1007 *north*
Patient End (Furneux Pelham) 1434
    Payn
Pirton 1086 *pirige* 'pear'
Preston 1185 *preost*
Royston 1286 Crux Roaisie 1184
    Roesia
Wallington 1086 Waendel, -*inga*-
Waltonesford (lost, Hitchin) 1294 *wealh*
    'Briton'
Watton at Stone 969 *wad* 'woad'
Weston 1086 *west*
Wigginton 1086 *Wicga*

OXFORDSHIRE

Aston Leys (Kingsey) 1385 *east*

Aston Rowant 1086 *east*

Chislehampton (Stadhampton) Hentone 1086 *heah* 'high'

Clifton Hampden 1146 *clif*

Drayton St. Leonard 1146 *draeg*

Henton (Chinnor) 1086 *heah*

Kingston Blount (Aston Rowant) 1086 *cyng* 'king'

Milton, Gt and Little 1086 *middel*

Moreton (Thame) 1152 *mor*

Newington ?997, *c.* 1045 *niwe*

Pyrton ?766, 987 *pirige*

North Weston (Gt Haseley) 1200 *west*

South Weston 1086 *west*

V Names in worth

BEDFORDSHIRE

Barwythe (Studham) 1086 Baere or *bar* boar

Edworth 1086 Edda

Eyeworth 1086 Æga or *eg*

Kensworth 975 Caegin

Padewrth (lost, Northill) 1282 Pada

Tebworth (Chalgrave) 962 Teobba

Tilsworth 1086 Tyfel

Tuddeworth (Toddington field name) 13c Tuda

Wrestlingworth *c.* 1150 Wraestel, -*inga*-

(*Note:* Ducksworth (Stagsden) is probably a manorial name).

BUCKINGHAMSHIRE

Littleworth (Wing) 1227 Lytel, -*inga*-

Marsworth 1012 Maessa

HERTFORDSHIRE

Batchworth (Rickmansworth) 1007 Baecci

Bibsworth (Kimpton) 12c Bibbe

Datchworth 969 Daecca, -*inga*-

Hinxworth 1086 *hengest* 'stallion' or Hengest

Knebworth 1086 Cnebba

Letchworth 1086 *lycce* 'enclosure'

Pinker Wood (Knebworth) 1363 Pinca

Rickmansworth 1086 Ricmaer

Sawbridgeworth 1086 Saebeorht

Stivicesworde (lost, Hertford Hund.) 1086

(*Note:* Herringworth Hall (Gt. Munden) is probably manorial).

OXFORDSHIRE

Chilworth (Gt. Milton) 1086 Ceola

Hanewerd (lost, Chinnor) *c.* 1220–30 Hanna

Sullingwrthe (lost, ?Chalgrove) 1278–9 Sciella, -*inga*-

Tetsworth *c.* 1146 Taetel

wyrthe (lost, Benson Hund.) 996

VI Names in wic-hām

BEDFORDSHIRE

?Wickern Field (Toddington)

Early forms not noted by EPNS.

HERTFORDSHIRE

Wickham Hall (Bishops Stortford) Wicheham 1086

Wickham Hill (Braughing) Wicombs 1626

?Wickham Spring (Standon) No forms; see Gelling 1978, 68, 74.

VII   *Other place-names*

A selection only need be given of other types of place-name referred to in the text, many examples of which clearly have no relevance to early settlement. Some are obviously of post-Conquest formation, such as Ankerwyke (Wraysbury) and Holywick (Hambleden) which refer to monasteries founded *c.* 1160 and 1204.

Wic The only names recorded before Domesday are *Boiwic* 785 (?Kemprow Farm, Aldenham) and Westwick 944–6 (St. Michaels), both in Herts., and a lost *wudu wic* (Cuxham) in Oxon. Names that first occur in Domesday are: Beds.— Astwick, Flitwick, Kinwick (lost, Sandy); Bucks.—Tetchwick and Tingewick, both perhaps containing *-inga-*; Herts.— Alswick, (Layston), Beauchamps (formerly Affledwick, Layston), Eastwick, Lewarewich (lost, near Much Hadham), Oxwick (lost, Codicote) and Woolwicks (lost, Stevenage).

Cote Holcot in Beds. is the only one recorded before the 11c. Codicote in Herts. occurs in 1002. First found in 1086 are: Beds.— Biscot (Limbury) and Cotton End (then Westcote, Wilshamstead); Bucks.— Boycott (Stowe). Caldecote (Newport Pagnell), Edgcott, Foscott, Littlecote (Stewkley), Pollicott (Ashendon) and South-cote (lost, Stone): Herts.— Caldecote, Gubblecote (Tring) and Tiscott (Tring): Oxon.— Draycot (Waterstock), Nethercote (Lewknor) and Rycote (Gt. Haseley).

Hamstede Three Herts. names occur before the 11c.: Gt. Berkhamsted 966–84, Hanstead House 793 (St. Stephens) and Wheathampstead *c.* 960.

Throp The only pre-Domesday recordings are Helsthorpe (Wingrave) in Bucks. and Tythrop (Kingsey) in Oxon.

Stoc All the names occur in Domesday: Bucks.— Adstock, Stoke Goldington, Stoke Hammond, Stoke Mandeville and Stoke Poges; Oxon.— Littlecote (Checkendon), North Stoke (Crowmarsh), South Stoke, Stoke Talmage and Waterstock. Adstock is the only one that did not start as the simplex name Stoke.

Stow In Domesday are Elstow and Wixamtree Hundred in Beds. and Stowe in Bucks., but Bunsty Farm (Gayhurst) though not on record till 1241 was a Hundred meeting place.

Burh Excluding names of medieval and manorial origin there are 24 *burh* names. Apart from Limbury and Aylesbury mentioned in the 571 annal the only pre-Conquest records are Kingsbury (St. Albans), *Wendlesbiri* and Willbury (Norton) in north Herts. and reference to a lost *ealdan byrig* (Crowmarsh) in Oxon.

Full lists and derivations of all the place-names discussed in Chapter IX, with references, are included in the unpublished work mentioned in Appendix II.

APPENDIX V: CELTIC PLACE-NAMES

Chiltern (Cilternsaetna (gen. pl.) 7c., Cilternes efes 1006): derived from a British adjective *ᵡcelto-* meaning 'high'.

Icknield (Ic(c)enhilde weg 903): etymology unknown but generally thought to be British. It is difficult to resist the conjecture that it refers to the Romano–British Iceni to whose territory this ancient way led.

River names

Ash (Herts.): present name no older than 1750. Previously called *Ysme* 1275, Isenwater, Yseney *c.* 1400, also found in Easneye (Stanstead Abbots) Herts., Isneye 1253; related to the Northants river name Ise, a derivative of the British name Ouse.

Beane (Herts.) (Bene ficcan 913): certainly British. The first element, related to Welsh *bun* 'woman' and *benyw* 'female', perhaps meant 'goddess' and hence a divine stream. The second part which survived into the 13c in *Beneficche* is closely related to Welsh *bychan* 'small'. The adjective follows the noun, after a late change of order in the Brittonic languages.

Campton (Beds.) (Chambeltone 1086): a village name preserving the British name, cognate with Camel (Cornwall), of a branch of the Ivel.

Chess (Bucks.): a quite modern back-formation from Chesham. An earlier name is apparently compounded in *Isenhamstede* 1195, now Chenies. It has been suggested this refers to a chalybeate spring (Old English *isen* 'iron') but as it resembles the old name of the Ash where no such spring is known a British origin is more probable.

Colne (Bucks., Herts.) (Colenea 785): identical with Clun (Salop.) and certainly British.

Hiz (Herts.): a back-formation from Hitchin no older than *c.* 1750; earlier called Cadwellbroke 13c. Ekwall thought the tribal name *Hicce* which lies behind Hitchin was perhaps 'derived from an old name of the river Hiz, which may belong to Welsh *sych* "dry", a word common in stream-names'. The explanation fits a chalk stream and is strengthened by the British origin of the Ivel and Campton nearby.

Humber (Beds.): the old British name of a brook north-west of Bedford, 'formerly a common name of streams in England' (Ekwall).

Humber (Oxon.): the Haseley Brook which joins the Thame bore this name.

Ivel (Beds.) (Givle *c.* 1180): a British name identical with that of the R. Yeo and Yeovil (Som.), meaning 'forked' which describes its two main branches, and connected with Welsh *gafl* 'fork'.

Lea (Herts.) (Lig(e)an 880): certainly of British origin, from the Celtic root *lug–* in Welsh *goleu, lleufer* 'light'; meaning 'bright river' or 'river sacred to the god Lugus'.

Lovat (Beds., Bucks.) (Loviente 1193): identical with the British river name Lavant (Sussex), derived from the same root as Latin *labor* 'glide'.

153

Mimram or *Maram* (Herts.) (Memeran 913, Ma(e)ran 913): etymology unknown, but there is little reason to doubt it is Celtic. It may be related to the British river name Mint (Westmorland).

Ouse (Beds., Bucks.) (on Usan 880, Use 937): certainly British, through $^{x}udso$- from a widespread Indo-European root found in English *water*.

Ray (Bucks., Oxon.): present name first found 1363. Forms of the earlier name are *Geht* 845, *Giht* 983, *Ychte* 1185, probably cognate with the Welsh river name Ieithion, from Welsh *iaith* 'language, speech'. Yeat Farm in Wotton Underwood possibly preserves the name.

Saferon (Beds.) (Seuerne, Sauerna 13c., Saferondiche): a lost British name of a Bedford stream, identical with the Severn (called Sabrina by Tacitus *c*. 115). The name probably passed early into English, before the initial consonant could suffer the mutation which happened in the case of the Severn (Habren *c*. 800, modern Welsh Hafren).

Tempsford (Beds.) (Taemesford 921): Ekwall suggested 'ford on the way to the Thames', i.e. to London, which would be a curiously oblique reference to the capital, but the statement that a Danish chief who died at Tempsford in 921 was killed *apud Tamensem fluvium* shows this stretch of the Ouse once bore the name Thames.

Thame (Oxon.) (Thame town Tamu 675): a British name identical with that of the rivers Tame and Taf, and probably with the Thames.

Thames (Oxon., Bucks.) (Tamesis 51 B.C.): a river name given by Caesar and cognate with the Sanskrit Tamasa, a tributary of the Ganges probably meaning 'dark river', befitting one laden with silt.

Wendover (Bucks.) (aet Waendofron *c*. 970): originally the British name of a clear chalk stream, with elements corresponding to Welsh *gwyn* 'white' and *dwfr* 'water', from the root $^{x}dubro$- in a plural form.

(*Note:* It is now certain that the river Wye (Bucks.) is not a survival. The name seems to be a late back-formation from Wycombe, but was once believed to be the common British river name Wye.)

Other names

BEDFORDSHIRE

Bedford—*Brickhill* (Brichull 1276) British $^{x}brico$- 'top, hill' with English *hyll* added tautologically.

Kempston (Kemestan 1060, Coembestun Edw. Conf., Camestone 1086) Ekwall suggested that as the place is situated at a sharp bend of the Ouse the first element might be connected with the British $^{x}cambo$- 'crooked'. The presence of a 5c *foederati* station here, which might have borne some such name as Cambodunum, and the survival of British names not far away (Saferon, Campton, Brickhill), favour Ekwall's solution as against the alternative proposal of an unrecorded personal name Cymmi.

Shillington—*Hanscombe* (Hanescamp 1222) contains the loanword *camp*.

BUCKINGHAMSHIRE

Ashley Green—*Pressmore* Farm (Preesmoor 1826). The first element could be the British word found in Welsh *prys*, *pres* 'brushwood', but no early forms are known.

Aylesbury—*Walton* (Walton 1159) The first element may be *wealh* 'Briton', *weald* 'wood' or *weall* 'wall'.

Boarstall—*Panshill* (Pansehale 1230) The British forest name *penchet* with *healh* 'nook' added.

Botolph Claydon—*Bernwood Farm* (Byrnewudu *c.* 950) The name recalls the once extensive forest of Bernwood where a surviving British name would not be unexpected. It was associated with Bicester (Bernecestre 1086) as both appeared to contain *byrne* which it was thought might perhaps be a British word corresponding to Welsh *byrn* 'hill', but Old English *byrgen* 'burial place' was also proposed, and more recently Bicester has been interpreted as 'fort of the warriors' (*beorna*) or 'of Beorna', which would serve equally for Bernwood. Some doubt remains because when Richmond and Crawford discussing the Ravennas list sequence *Tamese-Brinavis-Alauna* agreed the last was Alchester and *Brinavis* probably Woodeaton they did not remark the odd omission of a name for Dorchester, an important place on the route that the list presumably followed, and these identifications are therefore uncertain. It remains possible that the name is derived either from *Brinavis*, if that is not Woodeaton, or from a British word similar to *bryn*.

Brickhill, Bow, Great and Little (Brichella(e), Brichelle 1086) British *ˣbrico-* 'hill, top' with tautological *hyll*.

Brill (Burhella, Bruhella 1072) The first element is British *ˣbriga* 'hill' which lies behind Welsh *bre* and is closely related to *ˣbrico-* in the preceding name, again with *hyll*.

Chalfont St. Peter, St. Giles (?Ceadeles funtan (dative) 949, Celfunte, Chelfunde 1086) This contains the British loanword *funta* 'spring'. The 949 form with the personal name Ceadela (an anglicized diminutive of the British name Cada) is more likely to refer to Chadshunt, Warws. If so the later forms mean 'calves'.

Charndon (Credendone 1086, Charendone 1227) The 1086 form may be corrupt in which case *Caerdan-dun* 'Caerda's hill' is possible; Caerda is a short form of the British personal name Cerdic. Ekwall's suggestion that the first element might be British *ˣcarn* 'cairn, heap of stones' also suits the position on a marked ridge, so *dun* may be tautological.

Chetwode (Cetwuda (dative) 949) Another instance of tautology, with *wudu* added to British *ˣceto-* 'wood'.

Datchet (Deccet 10c., Daceta 1086) Ekwall suspected this contains British *ˣceto-* 'wood'. It may be a British name identical with *Decetia*, now Decize, in the Nièvre department of France.

Linford, Great and Little (Linforde 1086) The situation hardly entertains Old English *hlynn* 'torrent' and derivation from British *ˣlindo-* 'pool, stream' seems more likely, but *hlyn* 'maple', *lin* 'flax' and *lind* 'lime-tree' have also been proposed.

Penn (Penna 1188) Perhaps British *pen* 'head, end' as the place stands on a pronounced hill, but Old English *penn* 'enclosure' is possible.

Soulbury—*Chelmscott* (Chelmediscot 12c.; Chaumundesfunt occurs 1200) Most forms combine Ceolmund and *cote*. The exceptional -funt in 1200, unlikely to be a scribal error as the ending is so rare, may indicate an alternative name containing the British loanword *funta*.

Walton (Waldone *c.* 1218) As for the Aylesbury Walton.

Westbury—*Moreȝyf* (lost, Moreȝyf, Moreyf 13c.) Mawer (Problems of place-name study (1929), 2) remarked that the name is analogous to Morfe, Staffs. (Moerheb 736), a recognized British forest name.

Wing—*Craflon* (Crouslone 1086, Croftone 1200) This is *croh-tun* '*tun* where saffron grows', *croh* being a loanword through British from Latin *crocus* for the cultivated saffron bulb which is not native to Britain but must have been introduced in Roman times.

Wycombe, High—*Crendon* Lane (Cruendena *c.* 1220, Cronden' 1227) Another *croh* name, with *denu* 'valley'.

HERTFORDSHIRE

Abbots Langley—*Bedmond* (Bedesunta 1331, Bedfunte 1433) The original form contained the loanword *funta* 'spring', later confused with Old French *mont*. The first element, *byden* 'tub, depression', suggests tautology.

Brickendon (Brikandun 959) This may be 'Brica's hill' but the first element is possibly British *ˣbrico-* or *ˣbriga* 'hill'.

Cheshunt (Cestrehunt(e) 1086) The first element is *ceaster* which refers to the Roman site now known to exist here. Evidence shows that most names in -hunt really go back to the British loanword *funta*; the lack of forms in -f- presents no difficulty, as the oscillation between -f- and -h- spellings of Chalfont bears out.

Hatfield (Haethfelth *c.* 730) The name is clearly English, *haeth*, *feld* 'heath-covered open land', but Blair pointed out (Transactions of the St. Albans and Herts. Architectural and Archaeological Soc. 1938, 224) that Bede's remark that the Synod of 679 met in *loco qui Saxonico vocabulo Haethfelth nominatur*—'the place called Hatfield in the English language'—reveals that it was also known by a British name.

Hertingfordbury—*Epcombs* (Thepecampe 1086) The second element is the British loanword *camp* 'open space', the first perhaps the name Eoppa.

Hitchin The possibly British origin of the tribal name Hicce (7c.) is mentioned under the river name Hiz above.

Hitchin—*Walsworth* (Waltonesford 1294, Walssworth 1523) The place was the ford of a lost Walton, and some local field names (le Walwey 1460, Walhamsted, Welshemancroft 1556, Walcot 1608) and proximity to an important early estate favour *weala-tun* '*tun* of the Britons'.

Mymms, North (Mimmine 1086, Mimmis 1138; South Mymms is Mimes 1086) Skeat's suggestion of a folk name Mimmas is highly improbable in a scantily populated clay forest area developed late. Stenton once thought the name an unsolved problem and noted similar field names in Herts, but later forgetfully listed the supposed Mimmas among early Middlesex groups. South Mymms, in 1086 an outpost of Edmonton 8 miles away, seems to have been a late foundation named like its neighbour. Both villages probably took the name from the brook that runs through them, and for this an original British name is likely as English etymology has made nothing of Mymms, some connexion with the river name Mimram above is possible.

Offley—*Crouchmoor* Farm (Crychmer 1567, ?Robert atte Cruche 1314) In view of 16c. forms the first element seems to be British *cruc* 'barrow, hillock', not medieval *crouche* 'cross'. A small pool explains *mere*.

Sacombe (Sueuechamp, Sueuecampe 1086) The final element is the British loanword *camp*, the first probably the personal name Swaefa.

St. Albans—*Verulamium* (Verulamium A.D. 50, Verlamacaestir sive Uaeclinga-caestir *c.* 730) The British name was preserved by the English who qualified it by *ceaster* 'chester' often given to a Roman site, but also formed an alternative from the personal name Wa(e)col and -*inga-*.

St. Stephens—*Wall Hall* (Walenhale 1218, Walehale 1269) If -n- in the first form is correct the name means 'Weala's corner' (*healh*), otherwise it is from *weala*, genitive plural of *wealh* 'Briton'. *Wealh* is recognized as a personal name meaning 'Briton'.

Sandon—*Karkelawe* (lost, Karkelawe 13c.) This probably contains a British word related to Welsh *carrec* 'rock', with *hlaw* 'hillock' added, rather tautologically.

Totteridge—*Wallbrooks* (Walebroc, Walebrokesfeld 1227) This is accepted as a definite example of *wealh* 'Briton', with *broc* 'stream' which occurs later than *burna*.

Walden, Kings and St. Pauls (Waleden(e) 888) This is certainly *weala denu* 'valley of the Britons'.

Weston—*Carkelowe* (lost, Carkelowe) As for the Karkelawe in Sandon.

OXFORDSHIRE

Crowmarsh—*Waldich* (lost, Waldich *c.* 1216) The first element is thought to be *weald* 'wood' or *wielle* 'spring', but *wealh* 'Briton' is not impossible in this late form.

Dorchester on Thames (Dorcic, Dorciccacaestrae *c.* 730) The second element *ceaster* alludes to the Roman town. The first is British *Dorcicon*, perhaps from the root *derk-*, found in Welsh *drych* 'aspect' and Old English *torht* 'bright', which occurs in some river names.

Eye and Dunsden—*Crowches* (Crechfeild, Cruchfeild 1603-4) Not from medieval *crouche* 'cross' but perhaps from British *crouco-* 'hill'.

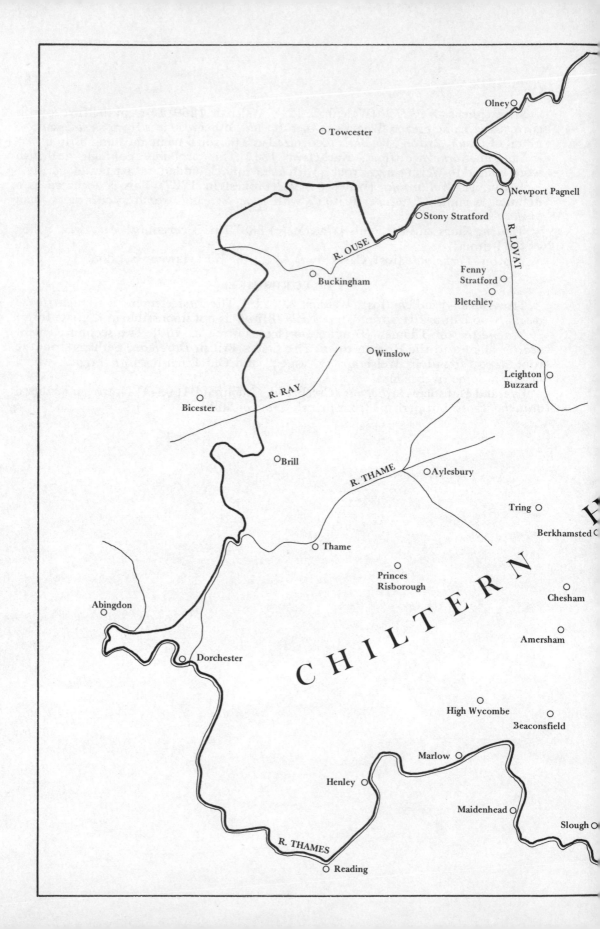

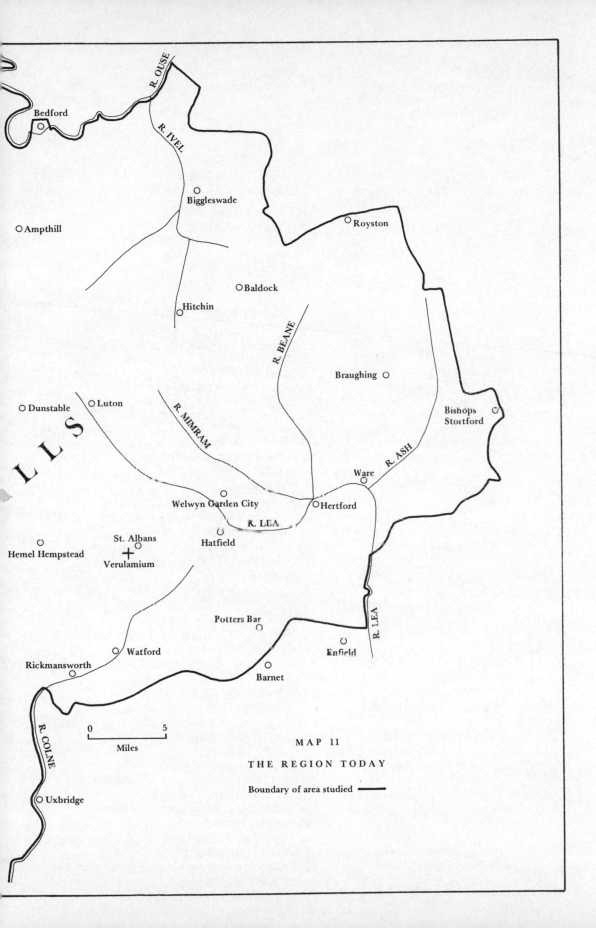

R. OUSE

Bedford

R. IVEL

Ampthill

Biggleswade

Royston

Baldock

Hitchin

R. BEANE

Braughing

Dunstable   Luton

R. MIMRAM

Bishops
Stortford

L L S

R. ASH

Ware

Welwyn Garden City

Hertford

R. LEA

Hemel Hempstead

St. Albans

Hatfield

Verulamium

Potters Bar

R. LEA

Enfield

Watford

Rickmansworth

Barnet

R. COLNE

0   5

Miles

MAP 11

THE REGION TODAY

Boundary of area studied ▬▬▬

Uxbridge

BIBLIOGRAPHY

Abbreviations

Antiq.	Antiquity
Ant. Jl	Antiquaries' Journal
Arch.	Archaeologia
Arch. Jl	Archaeological Journal
B.A.R.	British Archaeological Reports (Oxford)
B.B.C.S.	Bulletin of the Board of Celtic Studies (Cardiff)
E.H.R.	English Historial Review
E.P.N.S.	English Place-Name Society
E.P.N.S. Jl	English Place-Name Society Journal
Med. Arch.	Medieval Archaeology
OS	Ordnance Survey
Oxon.	Oxoniensia
Proc. Camb. Ant. Soc.	Proceedings of the Cambridge Antiquarian Society
Rec. Bucks.	Records of Buckinghamshire
V.C.H.	Victoria County History

Most works mentioned only once or twice in the Notes to Chapters are excluded

Aberg 1926 N. Aberg, *The Anglo-Saxons in England.*

Alcock 1971 L. Alcock, *Arthur's Britain*

Applebaum 1972 S. Applebaum, 'Roman Britain', in *The agrarian history of England and Wales*, I, part II, ed. H. P. R. Finberg.

Barley and Hanson 1968 Christianity in Britain 300–700, ed. M. W. Barley and R. P. C. Hanson.

Bede Historia ecclesiastica gentis Anglorum, in *Bedæ Venerabilis opera historica*, ed. C. Plummer (1896); with translation, Bede's ecclesiastical history of the English people, ed. B. Colgrave and Sir R. A. B. Mynors (1969).

Biddle 1971 M. Biddle, 'Archaeology and the beginnings of English society', in *England before the Conquest: studies in primary sources presented to Dorothy Whitelock*, ed. P. Clemoes and K. Hughes.

Biddle 1976 M. Biddle, 'Hampshire and the origins of Wessex', in *Problems in economic and social archaeology*, ed. G. de G. Sieveking, I. H. Longworth and K. E. Wilson.

Biddle 1977 M. Biddle, 'Alban and the Anglo-Saxon church', in *Cathedral and city: St. Albans ancient and modern*, ed. R. Runcie.

Blair 1956 P. H. Blair, An introduction to Anglo-Saxon England.

Böhme 1974 H. W. Böhme, Germanische Grabfunde des 4 bis 5 Jahrhunderts zwischen unterer Elbe und Loire (Munich).

Brandon 1978 The South Saxons, ed. P. Brandon.

Branigan 1967 K. Branigan, 'Romano-British rural settlement in the western Chilterns', *Arch. Jl* CXXIV.

Branigan 1971 K. Branigan, Latimer: Belgic, Roman, Dark Age and early modern farm.

Branigan 1973   K. Branigan, Town and country: the archaeology of Verulamium and the Roman Chilterns.

Brown 1915   G. Baldwin Brown, The arts in early England, vols. III and IV.

C.B.A. 1948   Council for British Archaeology, A survey and policy of field research in the archaeology of Great Britain: I—Prehistoric and early historic ages to the seventh century A.D.

Cameron 1978–9   K. Cameron, 'The meaning and significance of Old English *wahl* in English place-names', *E.P.N.S. Jl* 12.

Collingwood and Myres 1936   R. G. Collingwood and J. N. L. Myres, Roman Britain and the English settlements.

Copley 1954   G. J. Copley, The conquest of Wessex in the sixth century.

Copley 1958   G. J. Copley, An archaeology of south-east England.

Cox 1972–3   B. H. Cox, 'The significance of the distribution of English place-names in *hām* in the Midlands and East Anglia', *E.P.N.S. Jl* 5.

Darby and Campbell 1962   H. C. Darby and E. M. J. Campbell, The Domesday geography of south-east England.

Davis 1973   K. R. Davis, The deserted medieval villages of Hertfordshire.

D.E.P.N. 1960   The Oxford dictionary of English place-names, 4th ed., ed. E. Ekwall.

Dickinson 1974   T. M. Dickinson, Cuddesdon and Dorchester-on-Thames: two early Saxon 'princely' sites in Wessex, B.A.R. 1.

Dodgson 1966   J. McN. Dodgson, 'The significance of the distribution of the English place-name in *-ingas*, *-inga-* in south-east England', *Med. Arch.* X.

Durham and Rowley 1972   B. Durham and R. T. Rowley, 'A cemetery site at Queensford Mill, Dorchester', *Oxon.* XXXVII.

Evison 1965   V. I. Evison, The fifth-century invasions south of the Thames.

Faull 1975   M. L. Faull, The semantic development of Old English *wealh*, Leeds Studies in English XVIII.

Finberg 1964   H. P. R. Finberg, Lucerna.

Finberg 1972   H. P. R. Finberg, 'Anglo-Saxon England to 1042', in *The agrarian history of England and Wales*, I, part II, ed. H. P. R. Finberg.

Frere 1962   S. S. Frere, 'Excavations at Dorchester-on-Thames, 1962', *Arch. Jl* CXIX.

Frere 1966   S. S. Frere, 'The end of towns in Roman Britain', in *The civitas capitals of Roman Britain*, ed. J. S. Wacher.

Frere 1967   S. S. Frere, Britannia: a history of Roman Britain.

Gelling 1973   M. Gelling, 'Further thoughts on pagan place-names', in *Otium et negotium: studies in onomatology and library science presented to Olof von Feilitzen*, ed. F. Sandgren (Stockholm).

Gelling 1974   M. Gelling, 'The chronology of English place-names', in Rowley 1974.

Gelling 1977   M. Gelling, Latin loan-words in Old English place-names, *Anglo-Saxon England* 6.

Gelling 1978   M. Gelling, Signposts to the past: place-names and the history of England.

Gildas   Gildae sapientis de excidio et conquestu Britanniae, ed, T. Mommsen, *Mon. Hist. Germ., chronica minora*, vol. iii (1896); with translation, Gildas: the ruin of Britain and other works, ed. M. Winterbottom (1978); translated in J. A. Giles, The works of Gildas and Nennius (1841); historical parts translated in A. W. Wade-Evans, Nennius' 'History of the Britons' etc. (1938).

Harden 1956   Dark Age Britain: studies presented to E. T. Leeds, ed. D. B. Harden.

Harrison 1976   K. Harrison, The framework of Anglo-Saxon history to A.D. 900.

Hawkes 1956   C. F. C. Hawkes, 'The Jutes of Kent', in Harden 1956.

Hawkes 1972   S. C. Hawkes, 'A late Roman buckle from Tripontium', *Trans. Birmingham and Warwickshire Archaeological Soc.,* LXXV.

Hawkes 1974   S. C. Hawkes, 'Some recent finds of late Roman buckles', *Britannia* V.

Hawkes and Dunning 1961   S. C. Hawkes and G. C. Dunning, 'Soldiers and settlers in Britain, fourth to fifth centuries', *Med. Arch.* V.

Head 1941–6   J. F. Head, 'Buckinghamshire A.D. 450–700' *Rec. Bucks.* XIV.

Hodgkin 1935   R. H. Hodgkin, A history of the Anglo-Saxons.

Hyslop 1963   M. Hyslop, 'Two Anglo-Saxon cemeteries at Chamberlain's Barn, Leighton Buzzard', *Arch. Jl* CXX.

Jackson 1953   K. H. Jackson, Language and history in early Britain.

Johnson 1980   S. Johnson, Later Roman Britain.

Kirby 1965   D. P. Kirby, 'Problems of early West Saxon history', *E.H.R.* LXXX.

Kirby 1967   D. P. Kirby, The making of early England.

Kirk and Leeds 1952–3   J. R. Kirk and E. T. Leeds, 'Three early Saxon graves from Dorchester, Oxon.', *Oxon.* XVII/XVIII.

Leeds 1912   E. T. Leeds, 'The distribution of the Anglo-Saxon saucer brooch in relation to the battle of Bedford, A.D. 571', *Arch.* LXIII.

Leeds 1913   E. T. Leeds, The archaeology of the Anglo-Saxon settlements.

Leeds 1933   E. T. Leeds, 'The early Saxon penetration of the upper Thames area', *Ant. Jl* XIII.

Leeds 1936   E. T. Leeds, Early Anglo-Saxon art and archaeology.

Leeds 1939   E. T. Leeds, 'Anglo-Saxon remains', in V.C.H. *Oxon.* I.

Leeds 1949   E. T. Leeds, A corpus of early Anglo-Saxon great square-headed brooches.

Leeds 1954   E. T. Leeds, 'The growth of Wessex', *Oxon.* XIX.

Lethbridge 1956   T. C. Lethbridge, 'The Anglo-Saxon settlement in eastern England', in Harden 1956.

Meaney 1964   A. L. S. Meaney, A gazetteer of early Anglo-Saxon burial sites.

Meaney and Hawkes 1970   A. L. S. Meaney and S. C. Hawkes, Two Anglo-Saxon cemeteries at Winnall, Winchester, Hampshire, *Med. Arch.* monograph series IV.

Morris 1959   J. R. Morris, 'A gazetteer of Anglo-Saxon Surrey', Surrey Archaeological Collections LVI.

Morris 1962   J. R. Morris, 'The Anglo-Saxons in Bedfordshire', *Bedfordshire Archaeological Journal* I.

Morris 1965   J. R. Morris, 'Dark Age dates', in *Britain and Rome: essays presented to Eric Birley*, ed. M. G. Jarrett and B. Dobson.

Morris 1973   J. R. Morris, The age of Arthur: a history of the British Isles from 350 to 650.

Morris and Bidder 1959   J. R. Morris and H. F. Bidder, 'The Anglo-Saxon cemetery at Mitcham', Surrey Archaeological Collections LVI.

Myres 1951   J. N. L. Myres, 'The Adventus Saxonum', in *Aspects of archaeology in Britain and beyond: essays presented to O. G. S. Crawford*, ed. W. F. Grimes.

Myres 1969   J. N. L. Myres, Anglo-Saxon pottery and the settlement of England.

Nennius   Historia Brittonum cum additamentis Nennii, ed. T. Mommsen, *Mon. Hist. Germ., chronica minora*, vol. iii (1896); translation by A. W. Wade-Evans, Nennius' 'History of the Britons' etc. (1938). Nennius' British History and The Welsh Annals, ed. and trans. J. Morris (1980).

Nicolaisen 1970   W. F. H. Nicolaisen, The names of towns and cities in Britain.
OS   Dark Ages map Ordnance Survey, Map of Britain in the Dark Ages, 2nd ed. (1966).
OS   Roman map Ordnance Survey, Map of Roman Britain. 4th ed. (1978).
PNBedsHunts   Sir A. Mawer and Sir F. M. Stenton, The place-names of Bedford-
    shire and Huntingdonshire (E.P.N.S. III, 1926).
PNBucks   Sir A. Mawer and Sir F. M. Stenton, The place-names of Buckinghamshire
    (E.P.N.S. II, 1925).
PNHerts   J. E. B. Gover, Sir A. Mawer and Sir F. M. Stenton, The place-names of
    Hertfordshire (E.P.N.S. XV, 1938).
PNOxon   M. Gelling, The place-names of Oxfordshire (E.P.N.S. XXIII–XXIV,
    1953–4).
Reaney 1960   P. H. Reaney, The origin of English place-names.
Rivet 1969   A. L. F. Rivet, 'Social and economic aspects', in *The Roman villa in
    Britain*, ed. A. L. F. Rivet.
Rowley 1974   Anglo-Saxon settlement and landscape, ed. R. T. Rowley, B.A.R. 6;
    includes R. T. Rowley, 'Early Saxon settlements in Dorchester on Thames'.
Salway 1981   P. Salway, Roman Britain.
Sawyer 1974   P. H. Sawyer, 'Anglo-Saxon settlement: the documentary evidence',
    in Rowley 1974.
Sawyer 1976   P. H. Sawyer, Introduction, in *Medieval settlement: continuity and
    change*, ed. P. H. Sawyer.
Sawyer 1978   P. H. Sawyer, From Roman Britain to Norman England.
Smith 1956   A. H. Smith, English place-name elements (E.P.N.S. XXV–XXVI).
Smith 1902   R. A. Smith, 'Anglo-Saxon remains', in V.C.H. Herts. I.
Smith 1904   R. A. Smith, 'Anglo-Saxon remains', in V.C.H. Beds. I.
Smith 1905   R. A. Smith, 'Anglo-Saxon remains', in V.C.H. Bucks. I.
Smith 1923   R. A. Smith, A guide to the Anglo-Saxon and foreign Teutonic
    antiquities in the British Museum.
Stenton 1943   Sir F. M. Stenton, Anglo-Saxon England (3rd ed. 1971).
Taylor 1974   C. Taylor, 'The Anglo-Saxon countryside', in Rowley 1974.
Thomas 1971   A. C. Thomas, The early Christian archaeology of north Britain.
Thomas 1981   A. C. Thomas, Christianity in Roman Britain to A.D. 500.
Thompson 1979   E. A. Thompson, Gildas and the history of Britain, *Britannia* 10.
Wacher 1975   J. S. Wacher, The towns of Roman Britain.
Wade-Martins 1975   P. Wade-Martins, 'The origins of rural settlement in East
    Anglia', in *Recent work in rural archaeology*, ed. P. J. Fowler.
Wainwright 1962   F. T. Wainwright, Archaeology and place-names and history.
Ward 1972   J. H. Ward, 'Vortigern and the end of Roman Britain', Britannia III.
Webster 1969   G. Webster, 'The future of villa studies', In *The Roman villa in
    Britain*, ed. A. L. F. Rivet.
Wheeler 1935   Sir R. E. M. Wheeler, London and the Saxons, London Museum
    Catalogue 6.
Wheeler 1936   Sir R. E. M. Wheeler and T. V. Wheeler, Verulamium: a Belgic and
    two Roman cities.
Whitelock 1961   D. Whitelock, The Anglo-Saxon Chronicle: a revised translation.
Wilson 1976   The archaeology of Anglo-Saxon England, ed. D. M. Wilson.
Wooldridge 1936   S. W. Wooldridge, 'The Anglo-Saxon settlement', in *An historical
    geography of England before A.D. 1800*, ed. H. C. Darby.

INDEX

(Excluding references in Appendix I and minor names in Appendix IV)

Abbreviations: Bd = Beds., Bk = Bucks., Ht = Herts., Ox = Oxon.

Aberg, N. 27
Abingdon, Berks. 8, 58, 62, 120
ād element, 36
Addingrove Bk, 79, 117
Addington Bk, 79, 117, 149
Adstock Bk, 79, 82, 117
Aetius, 9
Agilbert 11, 12
Akeman Street, 2
Alban, St., cult, 12, 118-9
Aldenham Ht, 71-3, 147
Ambrosius, 8
Ambrosius Aurelianus, 10, 18, 106
Amersham Bk, 71, 147
Anglo-Saxon Chronicle, xiii, 10, 46, 49, 52
    annal 571, 4, 5, 10, 45, 63-7, 107, 120
    annal 577, 4, 66
Anstey Ht., 36, 85, 146
Antonine Itinerary, 99
Applebaum, S., 3, 116-7
Arlesey Bd, 137, 149
Arthur, 10, 48, 106
Ash river, former name, 101, 114, 153
Ashendon Bk, 62, 140
Ashwell Ht, 20, 39, 62, 142, 150
Aspenden Ht, 85
Asser, 64
Aston Ht, 150
Aston Abbots, Bk, 150
Aston Clinton, Bk, 150
Aston Leys, Ox, 151
Aston Mullins, Bk, 150
Aston Rowant, Ox, 151
Aston Sandford, Bk, 150
Astwick Bd, 137
Augustine, St., 11
Averingdown, Bk, 76, 148
Aylesbury, Bk, 4, 20, 52, 64-6, 74, 83, 105, 106, 108-110, 117, 140; and *see* Walton
Badon, Mount, 10, 45, 106
Baldock, Ht, 17
Bamborough, Northum., 121
Barkway, Ht, 85
Barley, M. W., 83

Barley, Ht, 36, 85, 125, 146
Barwyth, Bd, 151
Basing, Bk, 76, 148
Batchworth, Ht, 81, 151
Beane river, Ht, name, 42, 101, 114-5, 153
Bearded posts, 36, 146
Bearton Green, Ht, 150
Beddoe, J, 127
Bede, xiii, 11, 99, 114, 119
Bedfont, Middx., 104
Bedford, 4, 63, 65, 101, 108, 137; and *see* Biedcanford, Brickhill, Saferon
Bedmond, Ht, 104, 114, 156
Beeston, Bd, 149
Bengeo, Ht, 75, 148
Bennington, Ht, 79, 149
Benson (Bensington), Ox, 4, 65, 79, 83, 108, 117, 144, 149
beorg element, 36
Berdestaplesholme, *see* Stanstead
Berins Hill, Ox, 36, 146
Berinsfield, *see* Dorchester
Berkhamsted, Gt. Ht, 18, 82
Berkeden, Ht, 85
Bernwood, Bk, 16, 36, 84, 101, 146, 155
Betlow, Ht, 146
Bibsworth, Ht, 151
Biddenham, Bd, 64
Biddle, M. 1, 2, 117
Biedcanford, 4, 63-5, 107
Bierton, Bk, 150
Bilingual phase of Britons, 100, 114, 123
Birinus, 11, 23, 53, 110
Bishop's Stortford, Ht, 17, 74; and *see* Wickham Hall
Bishopstone, Bk, 26, 52, 53, 59, 63, 80, 106, 108, 140, 150
Blair, P. H., 50
Bledlow, Bk, 36, 141, 146
Blunham, Bd, 72, 147
Boarstall, Bk, *see* Panshill
Boiwic, Ht, 82
Boniface, St., 34
Boreham Wood, Ht, 72, 147

165